"A Serpentine Gesture"

RECENCIES SERIES: RESEARCH AND RECOVERY IN TWENTIETH-CENTURY AMERICAN POETICS

MATTHEW HOFER, SERIES EDITOR

This series stands at the intersection of critical investigation, historical documentation, and the preservation of cultural heritage. The series exists to illuminate the innovative poetics achievements of the recent past that remain relevant to the present. In addition to publishing monographs and edited volumes, it is also a venue for previously unpublished manuscripts, expanded reprints, and collections of major essays, letters, and interviews.

Also available in the Recencies Series:

Evaluations of US Poetry since 1950, Volume 2: Mind, Nation, and Power edited by Robert von Hallberg and Robert Faggen

Evaluations of US Poetry since 1950, Volume 1: Language, Form, and Music edited by Robert von Hallberg and Robert Faggen

Expanding Authorship: Transformations in American Poetry since 1950 by Peter Middleton

Modernist Poetry and the Limitations of Materialist Theory: The Importance of Constructivist Values by Charles Altieri

Momentous Inconclusions: The Life and Work of Larry Eigner edited by Jennifer Bartlett and George Hart

Yours Presently: The Selected Letters of John Wieners edited by Michael Seth Stewart

LEGEND: The Complete Facsimile in Context by Bruce Andrews, Charles Bernstein, Ray DiPalma, Steve McCaffery and Ron Silliman

Bruce Andrews and Charles Bernstein's L=A=N=G=U=A=G=E: The Complete Facsimile edited by Matthew Hofer and Michael Golston

Circling the Canon, Volume II: The Selected Book Reviews of Marjorie Perloff, 1995–2017 by Marjorie Perloff

Circling the Canon, Volume I: The Selected Book Reviews of Marjorie Perloff, 1969–1994 by Marjorie Perloff

For additional titles in the Recencies Series, please visit unmpress.com.

"A Serpentine Gesture"

John Ashbery's Poetry and Phenomenology

ELISABETH W. JOYCE

University of New Mexico Press | Albuquerque

© 2022 by the University of New Mexico Press
All rights reserved. Published 2022
Printed in the United States of America

First paperback printing 2024

ISBN 978-0-8263-6381-7 (cloth)
ISBN 978-0-8263-6729-7 (paper)
ISBN 978-0-8263-6382-4 (PDF)
ISBN 978-0-8263-6730-3 (ePub)

Library of Congress Control Number: 2022932764

Founded in 1889, the University of New Mexico sits on the traditional homelands of the Pueblo of Sandia. The original peoples of New Mexico—Pueblo, Navajo, and Apache—since time immemorial have deep connections to the land and have made significant contributions to the broader community statewide. We honor the land itself and those who remain stewards of this land throughout the generations and also acknowledge our committed relationship to Indigenous peoples. We gratefully recognize our history.

Cover illustration: John Ashbery, *Chutes and Ladders III* (for David Kermani), 2008.
Collage (detail), 18.5 × 18.375 in. © Estate of John Ashbery,
courtesy of the Tibor de Nagy Gallery, New York.
Designed by Felicia Cedillos
Composed in Minion Pro 10.25/14.25

Contents

Acknowledgments / vii

Abbreviations / ix

Introduction / 1

Chapter 1. Ashbery and Phenomenology / 9

Chapter 2. Perception and Experience / 35

Chapter 3. Time, Lyric, and Perception / 64

Chapter 4. Space / 108

Chapter 5. Memory: *"That Stalled Moment"* / 137

Chapter 6. Motility and Motricity / 155

Chapter 7. Order and Meaning:
The Transcendence of the Everyday / 169

Notes / 187

Works Cited / 221

Credits / 231

Index / 235

Acknowledgments

While work of this kind is a solitary venture, it does not succeed without the support of many people. I have received endless assistance from the librarians at Edinboro University, in particular Jack Widner, who always asks me what I am working on and always has something to support that work. I thank, as well, the Houghton Library for granting me permission to work on the John Ashbery papers housed there. I thank, especially, the kind librarians at the Wilson Library of the University of North Carolina who digitized William Le Queux's *Beryl of the Biplane* for my work on Ashbery's poem "Europe." I also thank, for their kindness and assistance, James Maynard and Alison Fraser at the Poetry Collection of the University at Buffalo. I thank Edinboro University for its research grants that permitted my work at the Houghton, the Northeast Modern Language Association for its grant that permitted my work at the Poetry Collection, and the Modernist Studies Association for its grant that supported my training at the Digital Humanities Summer Institute. I also thank Edinboro University for the sabbatical that gave me the time to complete this work and for the travel funds to present preliminary work on this book at conferences.

I have also received great support and generosity from colleagues at other institutions: W. Scott Howard, Steven Evans, Ed Foster, and in particular Burt Kimmelman, who connected me to Vincent Katz and to whom I am very grateful for the kind permission to reproduce in this book images by Alex Katz from his work with Ashbery on *Fragment*.

I thank, as well, the University of New Mexico Press, particularly Matthew Hofer and Elise McHugh, not just for seeing promise in my work but for supporting the Recencies series and the publication of new work on poetics.

I am sorry that John Ashbery did not live to see the completion of this project. I am grateful for his work, which has guided me for this span of years. I thank Jeffrey Lependorf and the Flow Chart Foundation for their lovely support for my work. The great organization of the foundation's Ashbery Resource Center I know is due to David Kermani's extensive effort, and it helped me enormously. I thank David so much for granting me permission to quote from Ashbery's poems, prose, and letters so lavishly, and for including images of Ashbery's collages in this book. As well, I thank the Tibor de Nagy Gallery for providing me with these beautiful images.

However, it is to my family that my greatest gratitude is owed. I thank my parents, Bruce Joyce and Elizabeth Pilot, for providing me with the tools for the accomplishment of this work. Jim, Cyrus, Caroline, and Ursula: you have all helped me so much and so generously, and of course, not just with this work. It is to you that I dedicate this book.

Abbreviations

Works by John Ashbery

CP. *Collected Poems, 1956–1987*
CP II. *Collected Poems, 1991–2000*

Works by Maurice Merleau-Ponty

PP. *Phenomenology of Perception* (Donald Landes translation)
PW. *The Prose of the World*
S. *Signs*
SB. *The Structure of Behavior*
VI. *The Visible and the Invisible*
WP. *The World of Perception*

Introduction

THE ENIGMATIC NATURE of John Ashbery's poetry has led scholars to look for concealed messages in his work, which if found, would open up the work to clearer and more specific interpretation. Ashbery resisted requests for the "key" to his poetry repeatedly, as shown in several letters that he wrote. To R. Joseph Adams, he said: "Incidentally there are no hidden meanings in my poems. Somebody once asked me why there aren't and I answered that it was because somebody might find them out and then they wouldn't be mysterious any more."[1] And to George Bowering, he wrote: "I'm glad that you find my poems rewarding. I'm sorry though that you find them difficult. Although nobody ever believes me when I say this, I myself think they should be easy to read since they refer only to themselves and have no hidden meanings consigned elsewhere, in some Swiss bank account of poetry meanings."[2]

In fact, Ashbery turned away from trying to provide assistance interpreting his poetry, for, as he wrote to Stephen Berg in turning down an invitation to write an essay for Berg's collection *My Business Is Circumference: Poets on Influence and Mastery*: "I have always regretted the few statements I have made about my poetry in the past, they have either been turned against me by critics or accepted as skeleton keys to my work. I would rather speak to readers through my poetry than through a statement which might be true only at the moment I made it."[3] There is, therefore, no "skeleton key" to open the coffer of each of Ashbery's poems. In fact, as he notes in a letter to Charles Altieri, his sources for his poetry are often random and not especially "shaped" for a specific poetic message or point: "By the way, I thought you might be interested to know that the line 'the cut driver pushes them to heaven' came from something a friend said in his sleep and which I happened to overhear. I find it a useful source of 'lines' but of course one can't always rely on it."[4]

I do not, therefore, purport to provide any kind of "skeleton key" with which to access all of Ashbery's poetry across his long career. I do, however, intend to set up a lens through which to approach, if not all of his poetry, much of it. That lens is shaped by the philosophical approach of phenomenology, particularly that of Maurice Merleau-Ponty (1908–1961). For Merleau-Ponty, perception is not simply sensory input but also the process of reaching out of ourselves for sensory information (an instance of transcendence), whereby we recognize ourselves and what is around us, taking that information inside ourselves to map it against what we have previously encountered and what is culturally inculcated in us; and in cases where the mapping does not align (i.e., where we have encountered something new), articulating a shift in this internal repository. It is this articulation that becomes poetry, that recognition that the mapping is not aligning, and the creative and innovative reshaping of the map itself. I argue in this book that what Merleau-Ponty is calling perception, Ashbery is calling experience.

Because of my approach to Ashbery as a poet of experience, I have not, therefore, identified or laid out specific structures of the poems to enable readers of the book to access them in terms of embedded organization. Experience is not structured but is, rather, a series of overlapping events, some much less consequential than others. Because of this lack of structure of experience, works like *Three Poems* are long, rambling prose poems in which, I believe, Ashbery is mulling over experience and hoping that talking enough about it will lead to instants of comprehension, moments of clarity, where meaning becomes apparent, what Merleau-Ponty terms "Being." I do not want to grant these ephemeral instants of understanding within a poem the status of epiphanies; they are perhaps only small revelations. While there are moments in these poems, particularly in poems such as "Clepsydra," when the discourse appears to be laying out a careful argument, I see much of that as ironic veneer intended to call rational argument into question.

Merleau-Ponty grew up for the most part in Paris.[5] At the elite École Normale Supérieure, his classmates included Simone de Beauvoir and Claude Lévi-Strauss, and he overlapped with Jean-Paul Sartre, who was a few years older than him. He went on to have an illustrious career, teaching at Université de Lyons, the Sorbonne, and the Collège de France.[6] Taylor Carman and Mark B. N. Hansen declare that there are four main phenomenologists—Edmund Husserl (1859–1938), Martin Heidegger (1889–1976), Sartre, and

Merleau-Ponty[7]—although some suggest placing Derrida, Wittgenstein, and even Foucault under that tent.

There is no question that Merleau-Ponty was influenced by Husserl and Heidegger; he addresses Husserl's approach head-on in his major work, *Phenomenology of Perception* (1945). As well, he was keenly interested in gestalt psychology, leading most particularly to his *The Structure of Behavior* (1942), as well as in Hegelian and Marxist philosophies. Other figures who were deeply influential include Henri Bergson and Ferdinand de Saussure.[8] At his untimely death, he left unfinished *The Visible and the Invisible* (1964), a work that many philosophers feel would have transformed the field of phenomenology and that, even so, has had a remarkable impact. It was in this final effort that he worked through Heidegger's phenomenology the most extensively, what Stephen Priest terms a "phenomenology of Being," and moving toward a "structural phenomenology" as opposed to the "phenomenology of consciousness" and "existential phenomenology" apparent in *Phenomenology of Perception*.[9]

Each of these allegiances led Merleau-Ponty to distinguish his approach from theirs. He drew on their work, but finally set himself apart from each of them.[10] While Merleau-Ponty was clearly a phenomenologist and of the school of Husserl, for example, he distinguished himself from Husserl through his disagreement with Husserl's transcendental ego and phenomenological reduction. For Husserl, the human ego has a "natural attitude" that a complete knowledge of things is possible; the transcendental ego is the "insight" that knowledge of things can only be gained through phenomena.[11] Merleau-Ponty replaces the concept of the transcendental ego with the body,[12] developing what Carman and Hansen call a "new concept of perception and its embodied relation to the world."[13] When Merleau-Ponty says, therefore, that "we are in and toward the world" (*PP*, lxxviii), he is removing separations between what is us and not us and engaging in a philosophy that believes in, not just the intermingling, but the mutual interacting and interreacting of our bodies with all that surrounds us.

Merleau-Ponty's version of phenomenology is an amalgamation of existentialism and phenomenology.[14] He derives much of his existential thought from Hegel, in particular the notions that existence is contingent (via Hegel's "historical contingency") and that a "sharper awareness of life" derives from a consciousness of death.[15] Merleau-Ponty and Sartre became close colleagues, founding and coediting the magazine *Les Temps Modernes*.[16] Merleau-Ponty withdrew from this position in 1953 and attacked Sartre in an essay in 1955. Some of this rupture was political, but much of it was philosophical. Merleau-Ponty felt, for example, that Sartre's existentialism maintained Cartesian dualism, in particular of subject and object,[17] and that Sartre considered individual freedom more in terms of individual action and less in terms of the intertwining of the world.[18]

Other strong influences on Merleau-Ponty include Heidegger and Saussure. While Merleau-Ponty adheres, particularly toward the end of his shortened life, to Heidegger's notion of Being and Becoming, Heidegger pays little attention to perception, a core component of Merleau-Ponty's thinking,[19] and does not work through the intertwining and intermeshing of experience to Merleau-Ponty's liking. Gestalt psychology provided Merleau-Ponty with the notion that "ordinary perception and behavior are always organized around a *normative* notion of rightness or equilibrium."[20] Structuralism, particularly that of Saussure, helped Merleau-Ponty develop his sense that language is a "social institution" and therefore, a "social space" that we are in and that is also at once within us.[21]

As he was influenced by others, both preceding him and working concurrently with him, Merleau-Ponty influenced philosophers in the mid- and later twentieth century, such as Gilles Deleuze, Jean-François Lyotard, Jacques Lacan,[22] and Pierre Bourdieu.[23]

While Ashbery does not believe that there is a skeleton key to provide access to an understanding of his poetry, he does talk about his poetry a great deal in interviews. In nearly every one of them, he talks about how his poetry is his effort to talk about experience. In so doing, I believe, Ashbery enacts again and again what it is to perceive, to take the input of the senses and to make sense of them, to make them sensible, and to bring them into their cultural and historical context.[24] That is, when a poet writes, according to Merleau-Ponty, that person takes up these sensations and reconsiders articulations that transform them into perception, an (always partial) comprehension of a moment, based on how moments of that kind had been articulated in the past and how this particular moment might be articulated in a new shape moving forward. Merleau-Ponty provides a lens through which to "perceive" Ashbery because of his amalgamation of our repeated patterns of behavior, our processing of sensations, our immersion in the world, and, especially, our renderings of these perceptions into language, this "serpentine gesture."

In my first chapter I explain Merleau-Ponty's approach to phenomenology and what I believe is Ashbery's allegiance to this philosophical approach. Core to his philosophy is the notion of human experience, that human beings are just that: experiences. Human understanding of existence derives directly from individual experience. Tied to these experiences, therefore, are the operation of the senses and the comprehension of the passage of time. Ashbery has been explicit about the connection between his poetry and experience, what it feels like to be alive and to live through the myriad incidents and exposures within an hour, a day, a span of life. In seeing Ashbery's work through the lens of phenomenology, therefore, I believe that his poetry starts to make sense. By this I do not mean that everything he writes is readily comprehensible, but that lines appear just as things happen; life is not plotted after all but is, rather, a haphazard series of experiences that we do not always feel compelled to analyze or decipher and that we never can come to completely comprehend.

In the second chapter I explore more completely how perception functions in phenomenology and demonstrate how it functions in Ashbery's poetry as shown in his volume *Three Poems*. In the process of perceiving and experiencing, people take in information from the senses. In order to do so, they must intentionally project outside of themselves, in the process becoming aware of themselves as if from outside of themselves. These are moments of transcendence, according to Merleau-Ponty, when people must leap to move outside themselves and recognize their individual self. People then must pull this matter from the senses back into themselves and align it with what senses and experiences have occurred in the past. In order to "make sense" of these materials, people must discern patterns within them and articulate those patterns. In cases where the alignment is unstable or cannot be established, this pattern recognition and articulation create new patterns and alignments that become components in newly configured repositories, not just of memory but of cultural and historical contexts. Equally essential in this process is that, as people move outside themselves to discern things and people on the horizon of their senses, these things and other people intermingle and intermesh with each other. The prose poems in *Three Poems* explicitly lay out this approach to experience.

The third chapter is a close examination of how time functions in Ashbery's poetry, particularly in "Clepsydra." A clepsydra is a water clock, and while time is of clear importance in this chapter, the primary focus is on the process of experience as it unravels. This poem is, Ashbery suggests in an interview, an "extended argument,"[25] and this is the approach of this chapter: to lay out how this poem develops an argument on the importance of a transcendental phenomenology. The second half of chapter 3 is on time and the lyric. Time for Merleau-Ponty becomes less about the present as situated between the future and the past, and more a notion of presence, a field that integrates this thickness created by the elements of the past that are always at play in the present moment. I extend this argument in this chapter by talking about how the lyric moment cannot exist in the brief form of its definition but must encapsulate longer time spans (and longer poems) in order to depict this field of presence. This discussion turns to Ashbery's poem *Litany*, which develops this thickness of time with its concurrent "parts."

In becoming "thick," time takes on spatial dimensions. The fourth chapter takes up phenomenological space from two aspects: the emblem book and the collage. For the emblem book, I analyze Ashbery's collaboration with Alex Katz that culminated in *Fragment* and his work with Joe Brainard to create *The Vermont Notebook*. Both of these poems appeared in tandem with illustrations, creating a "spatial and temporal pulp" (*VI*, 114). In addition to these collaborations with visual artists, Ashbery created visual and poetic collages on his own. I argue in chapter 4 that the collage creates space by juxtaposing "readymade" elements with each other or with other verses in the poem/collage. I analyze multiple visual collages created by Ashbery as well as the poem "Europe," which relies extensively on collage technique.

Another feature of phenomenology is reflection, the topic of the fifth chapter. Reflection has two aspects, that of mirroring back an image and that of thinking back upon or remembering. The memory component of reflection links to time in terms of the past in that it forces a turn to the moment when a perception occurred. It is, as Merleau-Ponty says, only ever a partial return, for complete return is never possible. Still, this return is critical for phenomenology, for Merleau-Ponty also argues that reflection permits the phenomenal field to evolve into a transcendental field, as reflection entails "thinking about" what transpired in the past and developing self-consciousness about it. Ashbery's poetry calls on memory frequently, and he has talked about the impact of his childhood and his memories of that time on his poetry. This part of this chapter addresses a few of these examples: "Decoy," "Our Youth," and "A Last World" in particular.

The second aspect of reflection, mirroring, links to the imperfection of sensory perception—the notion that, as with imperfections of memory, nothing perceived is ever perceived accurately but is, rather, distorted. Ashbery's "Self-Portrait in a Convex Mirror" is the focus for this section of chapter 5, as he depicts in this poem the warping in Parmigianino's painting of the same title, the painter's self-portrait as seen in his reflection in a mirror with a convex surface.

In order to perceive, we must be able to move, according to Merleau-Ponty. Motricity, the sixth chapter's focus, is the body's ability to move, and it is essential to phenomenology because perception can only transpire successfully through it. Merleau-Ponty argues that movement makes orientation in space possible, and through that orientation, meaning can blossom. Gesture, movement with purpose, that is an intentionality, initiates the effort to achieve this goal of comprehending human existence. Ashbery's poems "And You Know" and "Variations, Calypso and Fugue on a Theme of Ella Wheeler Wilcox" form the core of this chapter through analyses of forward and backward movement. In my discussion of "And You Know," I contrast movement and stillness in order to argue that while there might be a distinction between physical movement and motionlessness, experience persists through consciousness. For "Variations, Calypso and Fugue on a Theme of Ella Wheeler Wilcox," I argue that in his reliance on cliché, Ashbery is actually launching experience through a series of recursions and circular excursions.

The final chapter addresses the culmination of perception—to find order and meaning in existence. This chapter argues, too, that it is through everyday language that the poet achieves transcendence. The poet needs to move between the visible, where perception occurs, and the invisible, where we find meaning. In looking between these two facets of existence, the poet needs to discern order of some kind, some pattern of experience. In order for comprehension of this experience to develop, it is essential to find a form of expression about it. Sometimes, however, the expression is unsaid because the invisible resists articulation. The result of this passage through perception is transcendence, what Merleau-Ponty calls hyper-reflection, the awareness and questioning of perception, always and essentially enmeshed with recollections of past experience (*VI*, 38). This is what I am calling a transcendence of everyday language; it is through these explorations of everyday experience, of how it feels to simply exist as a human being, that Ashbery endeavors to communicate what experience might come to mean.

Chapter 1

Ashbery and Phenomenology

> In school
> All the thought got combed out:
>
> What was left was like a field.
> Shut your eyes, and you can feel it for miles around.
>
> Now open them on a thin vertical path.
> It might give us—what?—some flowers soon?[1]

IN THE FIRST part of this chapter, I will lay out how Merleau-Ponty's phenomenology operates, with particular attention to the key terms that will reappear in this book with regard to Ashbery's poetry. The second part of this chapter will demonstrate Ashbery's affinities with this philosophical approach. Phenomenology is the study of experience with the understanding that it is through experience that we understand ourselves and our existence, and derive meaning in life. We access experience through the body and its sense organs, which enable us to perceive. Phenomenology, therefore, bridges multiple sectors of philosophy. It is metaphysical because it is concerned with questions of Being, as well as of time and space, and it is therefore ontological because of its focus on Being. It is hermeneutical because this perception is ambiguous, never quite specific or clear enough to avoid endless interpretation. It is existential because it adheres to what is given in experience.

When we perceive, we do not necessarily "make sense" of what we perceive. We simply sense what is around us. It requires intention and a kind of transcendence for us to register the objects of our perception as not us but as entities that have their place in our cultural and historical condition, essentially rendering sensations into senses. Samuel Mallin uses the example of a clearing to explain this operation, which I think is somewhat more useful than the "field" used by Merleau-Ponty and most of his exegetes.[2] As simple perceivers, we are as if in a forest, surrounded by trees. The act of intention toward what surrounds us creates a conceptual clearing in the forest, where we have transformed "trees" into a more orderly and distinguishable set of meaningful objects of perception. Each time we perceive the world around us, we are comparing what we are perceiving with what we have perceived in the past. Most of us simply see the same thing and do not require any adjustments to this "meaning," but some of us, especially artists, including poets, must create new meanings out of distinct differences apparent in these new perceptions. In order to make these new meanings tangible, the creators of these new senses must articulate them.

This is a philosophy of the dialectic in that two contrasting poles usually exist, but their existence is one of coexistence; this is not a philosophy of dualism, such as that held by Cartesians, but rather one of mutual coimmersion. The primary dialectic is that of the subject and the object of perception, although it extends, as Gary Brent Madison lists, to "living being and biological milieu, social subject and his group."[3]

Perception

Perception is the core of phenomenology. As opposed to René Descartes's "I think, therefore I am," phenomenology posits, "I sense, so I sense what is around me and I am sensed in turn." Lawrence Hass argues that "in the perceptual faith: my flesh opens up onto things and other creatures that are not me, but not opposed to me either. . . . [It] is only possible to perceive them because they *are* separate from me—separate and different in space, composition, texture, function, diversity."[4] That is, we perceive through our ability to make distinctions, to distinguish foreground from background and one thing from another. Something that is not me is not in the same place, does not look the same as I do, is perhaps composed of different materials or sounds different.

Perception is the recognition of something that exists, that has presence, and therefore that can be captured and presented by the perceiver. Françoise

Dastur explains: "To perceive is always to sketch a figure against the background of the world, to organize an area of the visible, to open oneself to a 'gestalt.'"[5] This ability to perceive contrasts between the perceived thing and what is not the perceived thing makes it possible for us to comprehend space. Our ability to move and to notice differences between one moment of perception and the next makes it possible for us to comprehend time.

Yet, we cannot perceive perfectly. According to Henry Pietersma, "Merleau-Ponty says that meaning is intrinsic to perceptual things, but he denies that our words and concepts can grasp it. Entities elude our grasp to the extent that our words and concepts can grasp it. The meaning he states to be intrinsic to perceptual things cannot be grasped, even in part, by our words and concepts."[6] Life is the failed effort, therefore, to make complete sense of things. We seek that sense, we take in more perceptions, we rethink those perceptions in terms of what we have previously experienced, and we try, over and over again, to get that "grasp" of things. Hass describes perception, therefore, as a paradox because "[p]erceptual experience is a field of *contact* with things, but it is a contact with things and a world that opens up, eludes, and limits our explorations."[7]

The "situation" (labeled interchangeably as "field" or "clearing") is the context of the moment that we find ourselves in. It is utterly ephemeral, for it shifts perpetually, but we can think of it as that "spot of time" within which we can take measure of our perceptions. Taylor Carman explains: "A field is . . . a kind of space or place: it is where objects and their qualities appear to us, relative to us."[8] There is not simply one clearing at a time, either; multiple clearings exist at all times and are all interrelated and enmeshed with each other.[9]

Important here is the notion of perception as spatial in nature; equally important is the sense of perception as temporal. Henri Maldiney explains that it is not just that we perceive something, but that the something is coming into shape as we perceive it: "The circularity, intrinsic to perception, of auto-movement and of appearing means that the perceiving and the world arise together in the same clearing that creates the present in advance of every given moment."[10] Circularity is crucial for an understanding of phenomenology because it is not just that we perceive; we are perceived in turn. These mutual perceptions intertwine with each other, and this is the nature of perception.

Our perceptions are shaped by our horizons, by the extent of the reach of our senses. The horizontal perceptions are simply what our senses give back to us. Maldiney describes this by saying that "[a]s we are engaged in the world, the world unfolds around us in a sliding continuity of horizons, whose renewal accompanies that of our here, which is thereby transformed."[11] Again, this field of perception is replenished at every instant; our perceptions are not the same from moment to moment. Our comprehension of the present flashes by and transmutes into a newly refreshed perception.[12]

Each clearing, each field, each, as Mallin calls it, "structure," has a horizontal aspect. As our attention shifts to elements that had not been in our prime focus, they do not "attain" sharp focus "but rather a general being," a sense of what is not us that we recognize from our "previous experience of otherness[,] and [these elements] are subsequently confirmed and indirectly presented in *every* field."[13] As Mallin puts it: "One of Merleau-Ponty's most important characterizations of the horizontal entity's generality is that it exists only 'within a certain degree of indeterminacy.' He means by *indeterminacy* that these entities merely circumscribe, or delimit within the world, a possible set of vague alternatives which are themselves ultimately indeterminate."[14] The repetition of indeterminate/indeterminacy, the vagueness, depict experience as impossible to grasp, understand, or gather into one entity.

Our perception operates through our highly refined ability to discern difference between elements in our fields of existence. Merleau-Ponty's primary term for this understanding is *écart*. This term can be translated as simply "difference" but also as gap, distance, interstice, interval, divergence, inequality, and even path.[15] It is in these gaps between things—our selves and not our selves, for instance—that perception transpires. Hass writes that "*écart* is a difference-spacing openness at the heart of perceptual experience which is not opposition."[16] It is important to emphasize that phenomenology utterly rejects the possibility that we understand our existence via oppositional perception. Rather, perception involves the recognition of difference in order to discern what is not us, and these "separations," as Hass terms them, are, in Merleau-Ponty's words, a "cohesion [of] extreme divergences" (*VI*, 84). "It is, in a word," Hass argues, "the very relation of *overlapping*—a folding back through difference."[17] These are, therefore, distinctions between perceived elements, but while it is necessary to sense them through dissimilitudes, these variances pull together through imbrications.

Linked to écart is the notion of reversibility. While écart is the idea of separation and difference, reversibility is openness to the world. Hass describes reversibility as "overlapping, encroachment, cohesion, intertwining, chiasm. . . . *Reversibility* [is the] the folding back relation through divergence that runs through the fabric of experience, . . . the overlapping perceptual relation that folds around *écart*—the 'intertwining' or 'cohesion' of what is radically different."[18] We sense our surroundings, and in order to do so, we sense distinctions; these distinctions form a mesh, an "intrication," as Maldiney calls it, that is reversibility, so that we can make sense of our surroundings in terms of how they are not us.[19]

In order to make the écart/reversibility intermeshing function, transcendence is necessary, and transcendence is the vertical aspect of the horizon.[20] In Merleau-Ponty's phenomenology, there is a paradox between immanence and transcendence.[21] That is, we are embodied individuals and so "inhere in the world," but at once in order to sense that we are, to be conscious of ourselves as entities and to be conscious of other beings and other things, we need to "step outside of ourselves," as it were, to leap the gap (seen here as this vertical "movement") between what is us and what is not us and to be able to see ourselves as if we were not our own selves.[22] This paradox is part of what is at the root of the ambiguity of perception. Madison argues that Merleau-Ponty's "*Phenomenology* . . . says that the subject

> inheres in the world but . . . at the same time he is transcendent to
> the world. And it presents this movement of transcendence, which is
> incarnate existence, as a brute, ambiguous, mysterious fact—as a *miracle*
> without any possible explanation. . . . The subject is in the world precisely
> as a transcendental event. The difficulty comes therefore when one
> attempts to *think* of existence as a transcendental incarnation; and by
> insisting above all on the rootedness of the subject, the *Phenomenology*
> teaches an ambiguity.[23]

Another aspect of transcendence is the inexplicability that the thing that we perceive existed before we perceive it. We can only know existence when we perceive it, and we "perceive" ourselves, but if something existed before we perceive it, then we need this "paradox of immanence and transcendence" to make it possible to understand hitherto unknown existences. As Ted Toadvine puts it, in the "inherently paradoxical nature of the perceived: a reality is perceived only insofar as it is experienced, and it is therefore always 'for me': But the perceived thing, to be real, must also present itself as 'in itself.' That is, as preceding and exceeding my experience of it.... This paradox of immanence and transcendence defines the experience of time, others, nature, the body and ideality."[24] We can have a sense of ourselves, but in order to have a sense of anything else, we need to come to some sense of understanding of what is not us and what exists beyond our time frame of knowing it. This action requires transcendence to move beyond our immanent knowledge.

In addition to the questions raised by the paradoxical nature of existence and our inability to understand it is our limited capacity for sensory input. That is, we cannot take too much in at once, but just like we cannot simply stop our tongue from tasting something, we cannot channel or limit or control perception so that its flow at us is sorted or constrained to a reasonable quantity of elements. This mass of perceived bits forces another kind of transcendence, that too much is provided for us to comprehend. Hass describes this experience by saying that "this transcendence in our basic perceptions ... is experienced as contact with things that are not oneself, but it is also experienced as an *excess*. The perceptual field is a field of excess: it spills out ... beyond and around the specific things one attends to."[25] We can focus on one thing or on multiple things, but we can never attend to all at once. This "excess" self-replenishes at every instant, a constant influx of more than we can handle.

Transcendence is what happens through the experience of reversibility. In being open to the world, we must be able to at once be a part of the world (transcendence) and a part of ourselves (immanence). Duane Davis links transcendence to "*écart*, dehiscence, or non-coincidence.... [T]ranscendence is *lived* reversibility[,] a moment of divergence in the shared existence it partially determines. The reason for this divergence is reversibility. The divergence itself, within the lived context of human praxis, is transcendence."[26] Divergence, the comprehension of oneself as different from others, the comprehension of others and other things as distinct from each other, forces the leap from oneself, this transcendence, in order to be able to "make" this clearing.

In one way or another, all aspects of human experience involve some level of some kind of transcendence. As we are living, conscious entities, we are aware of what is around us, and we have self-awareness. Not merely core to this awareness but essential to it is the articulation of perception. Until we talk about something, we do not really have a clear sense about it. In articulating perception, we are gaining meaning about it. As Madison says, "Beneath constituted speech, which only functions as the vehicle for already discovered thoughts, there is an 'operative' or 'originating' speech which is precisely the coming to light of thoughts in search of themselves. New ideas are born and become fully conscious of themselves only by 'speaking themselves out'; before being expressed they are only vague feelings of dubious value."[27] Thoughts do not take actual shape, therefore, until they are voiced.

Not only do thoughts not take shape until they are expressed, but thoughts require articulation for their organization, unification, and even meaning. Articulation does not simply organize thoughts, however; it is essential for the individual to gain a sense of existence. Mallin argues:

> [B]ecause we have a number of diverse and partial primordial contacts with a single world, Existence has a thrown drive to articulate itself in such a way that it gains a unified grasp of itself. Only because we have more than one original opening (for example, of the senses) is there a need for articulation, which is the attempt, through explication, to unify the givenness of all functions and regions. Furthermore, because the self is not imprisoned in the inherence of any one sense, it can attain a distance that allows it to explicate any sense from the point of view of another; this provides the ultimate possibility of self-consciousness and reflection. The finitude or intrinsic incompleteness of Being, which requires it to "separate" and "coil over" in order to grasp itself, is expressed by, and manifested in, the nature of subjectivity itself.[28]

This "thrown drive" is the uncontrollable impetus to express the experience of existence. Because we have this ongoing and forceful flow of sensation of multiple types (sight, hearing, smell, etc.), we need articulation to bring these sensations together into perception. As well, also due to the multiple organs of sense, it is possible to "triangulate" sensations to "articulate" and establish spatial recognition and orientation, and recognition of positioning of others in that perceptual space. Because of this positioning and recognition of others, it is possible for the individual to self-perceive, to discern his or her own self as opposed to the others. And finally, because it is impossible to organize sensations into perfectly meaningful constructs, these snippets of understanding interweave and pull back onto themselves; this is what makes subjectivity.

While sensations are not articulated, there is no meaning. Language, therefore, becomes the interface, what Madison refers to as a "mediation," between silence and its coming into fruition as meaning.[29] This is a moment of transcendence, when the form of nascent thought becomes crystallized in the shape of language.[30] In so doing, too, "speech, written discourse, and gesture" are instances of the transcendence of articulation because they require stepping out of ourselves.[31] An articulated thought is one that has left its owner and resides in the space external to the body. And articulation is transcendence, too, because it takes up a sensation and re-creates it, reshapes it, into the new form of language, what Renaud Barbaras refers to as "*re-presentation.*"[32]

In shaping meaning, articulations are inserting sensation into perception that forms culture. Over time, these articulations form a "sedimentation" to which we turn when we experience sensation.[33] That is, in articulation, sensation transforms into culture. Bernhard Waldenfels says that "[e]xpression itself takes on the form of a transitional phenomenon. *The transition takes place as expression.* . . . [N]ature is transformed into culture."[34] Therefore, our cogito, our sense of our existence, Madison argues, "is a cultural work and acquisition which we possess as an intimate thought of our own only because at one time in the past it was found and expressed in words."[35] Because of this sedimentation over time, our understanding of existence is culturally and historically based; a construct, as Hass puts it, of "[l]anguage that is sedimented by culture."[36] What this means is that everything that we think or speak comes out of that tradition of writing and speaking, and is embedded within the culture of our own making over time.[37]

Creativity, to Merleau-Ponty, therefore comes out of articulation. Perception, as earlier described, works because of the ability to differentiate oneself from another, foreground from background, and so on; to see, in short, how things differ from each other. Creativity derives from the process whereby we take in sensations and compare them to what has been sedimented, what other constructs have been recognized and articulated. There are times when what we experience matches, at least reasonably well, with what is embedded already. In those cases, we simply perceive. However, there are instances when there is no match between our experience and previously sedimented materials. At this point, there is an interaction between this new perception and the established sedimentation, creating new expression.

Hass says that Merleau-Ponty "places the creative, contingent, expressive acts of individuals amid the field of already acquired language. This means that change and transformation burst up from within the 'system' and flow back into it. Bubbling, shifting morphology."[38] This is, therefore, another paradox in the phenomenological construct of Being. "This paradox," Waldenfels argues, "originates in an inner tension of the expressive event, an event that is neither homogeneous nor reducible to its components. The paradox comes together, for Merleau-Ponty, in *creative expression*."[39] It cannot either be pure creation or pure repetition but must be an amalgamation of both. Madison refers to this process as the "recuperative (archeological) and creative (teleological) nature of expression."[40]

This process is the work of the artist, to take up new situations and articulate them. Mallin argues

> The painter is able to transmit authentic situations.... When he is confronted with a totally new situation that is as highly delimited as the artistic, [the painter's] sedimented structures show themselves to be insufficient for mastering its precise requirements. In order to conquer this authentic vision, he must specify and reorganize his sedimented structures in an originating way and acquire the new structure that the artifact demands. The same logic applies to the literary arts, or more commonly, to authentic speech.[41]

Clear here are several issues. The artist has the courage to examine existing sedimented structures, and not be content to accept them as they are but rather to reconsider and reconfigure these structures into new, more appropriate structures for this given context, to create new expression for new sediments.

The problem exists with these new structures that the audience for art might not be able to comprehend these new articulations.[42] Mallin says, however, that an audience is feasible:

> A listener [can comprehend] authentic speech because he shares

sedimented structures with the speaker, who must use the same means to express himself. The incompatibilities and tensions in the given structures will guide the listener toward this new sense but, again, only if he makes a creative effort himself. Until the authentic phrase can be sedimented as a proper cognitive structure and thus become re-expressible in many ways, it remains imprisoned in its original mode of expression. Such is the case with creative literature, and particularly poetry, which uses our linguistic capacities to creatively express other regions rather than cognitively sublimating them or producing a thematic version of them.[43]

Formal sedimentation does not take place instantaneously. Until it does take place, the artist's articulations are very hard to follow. However, since at root the artist and audience "share sedimented structures," if the audience also recognizes that a new articulation must occur to respond to new perception, and if they are willing to, as Mallin says, "make a creative effort," they can come to some comprehension of the artistic expression. Important to note here, too, is the sense that artistic language is less likely to become formally sedimented, and so it is less likely to become a structure that can be easily rearticulated. Mallin, and by extension here Merleau-Ponty, believe that because poetry in particular pulls out new articulations so readily, its articulations are hard to repeat.

Poetic language is transcendental in nature, for it is instrumental in transforming the silence of sensation into language, and therefore into consciousness and meaning.[44] Poetic language must also rethink how accurate sedimented constructs are in representing perception, questioning and refining them, aligning them to the greatest degree possible with sensory materials. Robert Switzer says that "[i]n his last work, Merleau-Ponty calls for an originary return into language, a poetic recasting of words 'against the grain,' using their established significations to undercut themselves, as it were, 'to express beyond themselves, our mute contact with the things, when they are not yet things said' [VI, 38]. Language is not a closed system but rather, like art, 'lives only from silence.'"[45] This phrase, "words 'against the grain,'" suggests this rethinking of sediments and the effort, not to simply accept what lies within them, but to reconsider them, to look into those silent sensations and transport them into articulations.

Merleau-Ponty talks at length about painting, particularly Cézanne's work, in order to explain how art mediates between sensation and meaning. Madison, and by extension Merleau-Ponty, relate painting to poetry; Madison writes: "The language of painting . . . is therefore not 'prose,' the exact reproduction of a world already sufficient unto itself, but *poetry*, the evocation and taking up of a world in the process of being born. Painting 'must be poetry; that is, it must completely awaken and recall our sheer power of expressing beyond things already said or seen.'"[46] Poetry, therefore, "evokes" the act of perception, that coming into Being and consciousness, that effort to say what is not perceivable.

In the course of this effort, the poet is trying to accomplish several things. One is to "make sense" of the world, to attempt to access the order in perception (or, perhaps as well, to exert the force necessary to shape order). Madison says that "in his work the painter—like the poet and the thinker—consolidates and advances a wild logos which is a primordial articulation or dehiscence."[47] This logos is "wild" in its replication of perception; that is, it is not simply recounting sedimented perceptions but "looking" anew at the horizontal and vertical horizons. It is a "primordial" articulation because, again, the articulation is based on direct perception.

This approach becomes the effort of the poet (and other artists and philosophers): to organize sensations into these fields of experience. As Hass puts it: "Carnal contact, coherent things in an open context, radical otherness: . . . these are all experiences that emerge for one's living body; they are all experiences we have of the world's transcendence. . . . Living experience offers up transcendent things . . . amid a surrounding, over-spilling environment, and . . . the living body [has] capacities [to] shape them into *Gestalt* organizations."[48]

In addition to this organizational impetus, the poet is endeavoring to find some kind of truth, be it in the form of accuracy of expression or the rendering of experience as providing some kind of order. Mallin argues that poetry can come close to the truth: "[P]oetry and emotive utterances that successfully communicate an emotion, mood, way of life, and so forth, can be experiences as cognitively evident and thus can be constitutive of the truth to some degree."[49] This truth is simply, according to Madison, the effort to transmit experience in the form of language: "The writer is he who not only lives as other men do but who again thematizes this life in order to *express* it, to reflect it in a work and thereby to transform it into its truth."[50] "Whether they recognize it or not," he says, [artists] are still looking for the truth, only another kind of truth, a truth which would not be that of resemblance."[51]

The poet is, as well, creating through language a clear link between meaning and expression. Madison remarks on this link in terms of poetry because it is so impossible to say exactly what a poem means, to "translate" its language into words that replicate it exactly. He says: "This dialectic or mutual dependence between meaning and expression, thought and speech, is no doubt most apparent in poetry. A poem cannot be summed up; it does not exist apart from the play of words which constitute it, and, when one translates a poem into another language, one does not seek to reproduce its words or ideas but to recreate the same system of correspondences."[52] The poem IS the expression of meaning. These two features, expression and meaning, cannot be disentangled from one another.

The poet is rendering lived experience into the language of the poem. "What destines a man to be a writer," as Madison argues, quoting Merleau-Ponty,

> is the conviction that "the sensible is, like life, a treasury ever full of things to say" [VI, 252]); it is the feeling that the world and experience contain within themselves a "scattered," "buried" [S, 55], "captive," or "hidden" [VI, 36] meaning, a meaning which is *to-be-said*, [the] conviction that lived experience is eminently expressible, that life is full of things to be said, and that the task of the writer is to exploit this bed of lived and almost forgotten experiences by extracting from it what wanted to be said and by transforming it into an enduring work, into its truth.[53]

This quotation is the core of this book on John Ashbery's poetry. Ashbery was driven, as he said repeatedly, to use lived experience for the crucible of his poetry. Madison uses the term "exploit" for how the poet turned to this "bed," this sedimented schist of memory, and although mining can be exploitative, I prefer the notion of mining. To the poet, experience becomes the lode of perception, awaiting panning for treasures, elements poised for translation into language, and not just any language but poetic language, which, as Madison suggests, is "enduring" and as close to truth as possible.[54]

The poet faces multiple issues in this effort to come to the truth, however. The first of these is excess, related to the aspect of transcendence where we receive a preponderance of sensory impulses, too many for us to manage or perceive. Linked to this question of excess is the notion of time, that since it continually shifts, the articulation is always belated and cannot encapsulate what has just happened in the condition of new sensory inputs at every moment. Waldenfels explains that "[t]he event of expression not only precedes itself, it also remains behind itself; what comes to expression is sketched in the moment of expression itself as an 'excess' of what is intended in relation to the said and of the said over what is intended, as a 'determinate void that is filled with words.'"[55] This description is a series of excesses, in fact, with what was planned to say overwhelming what is said and what is said overwhelming what is planned to say. The void is that silence before expression. It is never static but always replenishing and emptying.

The culmination of this activity of perception is Being. It is us and not us; it is other and not other. It is, as Mallin suggests, "indeterminate and ambiguous.... [I]t has an emptiness and 'fissures and gaps' ... that are inherently incompletable."[56] Merleau-Ponty uses terms like "thrust" (VI, 104), "circle," "wave," "coiling over," "closing over upon itself" (VI, 140), "pact," "fold," and "mirror arrangement" (VI, 146) to explain the action of Being.[57] "Being," Mallin argues, "becomes 'consciousness' [VI, 118] in unrolling itself into a multiplicity of presents and is essentially the coming to be of consciousness or 'making visible.' ... Being is an 'undivided thrust' [VI, 104] that seeks to know itself by unfolding itself in time and by spreading itself into multiplicity."[58] "We are ourselves the upsurge of Being," Madison says, "the place where Being qua transcendence becomes conscious of itself."[59]

In perception, there must be what is outside of us. That is, we must be aware of another subject or object. It is in this intentional outward sense that Being comes into being for several reasons, as laid out by Mallin. In becoming aware of another, we become aware, and therefore "visible," to ourselves. In recognizing the other, we understand the field of our situation more clearly; we can discern details in our context through seeing something that is not us. It is through this awareness of and comprehension of something or someone that is not us that we are able to articulate these sensory perceptions, and it is through these articulations that "a socio-cultural world can come into being."[60] These articulations, this "socio-cultural world," these perceptions over time, place Being in history.[61]

Being is, as Madison puts it, is "transcendence in immanence."[62] That is, in recognizing another, what is around us, we recognize ourselves, an act of transcendence. We become conscious. Madison sees this move outside and back into our selves as a "wave," an "upsurge," an "explosion."[63] The ongoing and ever-shifting surge of Being provides us with logos, the sense of order in the world and an understanding of that order. Mallin explains that "[t]here is nothing more to Being than the flux and the world that we find within ourselves.... Being must give rise to a subject and... it can, and in fact must, consist of a plurality of clearings that result in a highly articulated and stable natural world."[64] Madison argues that "[t]he upsurge of the articulation, the configuration sensing-sensible, is the coming to articulation of Being itself; it is Being *articulating itself, transforming itself into logos*.... Being explodes and makes its advent as logos, articulation, configuration, meaning, when, in the midst of the visible or the sensible, vision or sensation springs forth—or, rather, this springing forth, this dehiscence of the sensible, is the *very definition of Being*."[65] Being is not just ourselves separated by what is around us, however; it is ourselves as enmeshed in our surroundings. Madison explains: "Being, the fabric of which things are the articulations or modulation, is not *in front of* the subject but surrounds him and... traverses him.... Being encompasses the object *and* the subject; it is their common inner framework and their single source."[66]

In Being, we are oriented in space. Merleau-Ponty says: "We cannot dissociate being from orientated being" (*PP*, 264). This inability to dissociate comes from the moment of perception when we distinguish one thing from another and foreground from background. An essential component of perception is distance, too; setting up a structure in space. "To appear," Renaud Barbaras says, "means to appear at a distance";[67] that is, if we perceive, and we do, we must perceive what is not us, that is, what is separate from our bodies, and so not in the same place, "at a distance," however small. Barbaras says that "it is not because we are embodied consciousnesses that the perceived world is distant; it is rather because perceived being implies an essential distance that our experience is partly obscured, that is, embodied.... Transcendence or ontological distance is *the form of sensible presence*: to appear means to appear at a distance."[68] And yet this distance, because it can only be spanned through transcendence, is never and always "unfolded": "[T]he sensible is essentially distant, for transcendence is the very form of its presence qua sensible. But, for that reason, the transcendence of the sensible thing is not a spatial distance . . .; it is a length that is not unfolded yet, a depth irreducible to another spatial dimension."[69]

Perception also involves time, and it is a time that is also transcendent, for past and present are, as Waldenfels says, "entangled with one another."[70] The present is "never to be fully present," and a present is "not exactly the same time as the apprehended present."[71] That is, it is impossible to grasp the present, "exceeding any immediate consciousness of it," and once we have gained some understanding of it, it has migrated to the past, so these two presents, the time and the understood moment, are never the same.[72]

Mallin relates this temporality to an *ekstase*, a term referring to being "outside of oneself" with time.[73] It comes out of Being's coming into itself through both its urge to expression and its inability to completely come into being, and this process links to what Mallin refers to as the "inexhaustibility of every present," which interpenetrates with the future and finds in the past "those previously acquired structures which are used in every present and already determine the outline of any future."[74]

A state of ambiguity exists in this flux of Being. Merleau-Ponty says that "what we live or think always has several meanings."[75] Waldenfels explains this ambiguity: "For Merleau-Ponty, a 'good ambiguity' lies in the phenomenon of expression, 'that is, a spontaneity which accomplishes the seemingly impossible, to take separated elements into consideration, and bring together a multitude of monads into a single web of past and future, nature and culture.'"[76] While ambiguity is inescapable, articulations that pull together oscillating pulses of perceptions into a woven fabric of existence leverage enigmatic and paradoxical clearings for greater clarity.

Merleau-Ponty died suddenly at the age of fifty-three. He left unfinished a major work that turned to concepts of the flesh; not the body, exactly, but, as he termed it, "the formative medium of the object and the subject" (*VI*, 147). Essential in this thinking is that object and subject merge, interconnect, interact, and entwine.[77]

This work pays close attention to what is "visible"; that is, to what is perceived. The sensory materials from the eyes are part of vision; perception takes these sensory elements and transforms them into the visible. "The vision of the painter, like the thought of the thinker," Madison says, "expresses and gives an added impetus to the genesis of the visible, which, itself, is an advent (explosion) of Being. This is why [Merleau-Ponty] says that language is the house of

Being [VI, 214], the inscription of Being [VI, 197], that 'it is being that speaks within us and not we who speak of being' [VI, 194]."[78] Articulation takes vision and transports it into the visible, bringing the subject into Being.

Additionally essential in the visible is that our perception is not just based on what distinguishes one thing from another, their differences from each other, but on the distinction between what is absent and present, what is perceptible and imperceptible. Priest says, for example, that "both the body and any other physical being exhibit the 'constitutive paradox' because they are composed of what is absent and what is present to perception; what is phenomenal and what is objective.... The paradox consists in something's being present as the thing it is partly consisting in its partly being absent.... One is both disclosed to oneself and hidden from oneself."[79] It is never possible to make what is perceived fully present or fully visible. As Merleau-Ponty put it: "[C]arnal being, as a being of depths, of several leaves or several faces, a being in latency, and a presentation of a certain absence, is a prototype of Being" (VI, 136).

What is not present or visible becomes a crucial part of perception. Hass explains that for Merleau-Ponty, "below the abstract level of representation, language is a marvelous conjunction of a socio-cultural structure sustained by carnal life, but a structure which can be transformed and transcended by embodied acts of expression. In a phrase, carnal life and non-material linguistic structures are in a relationship of *reversibility*. They are an intertwining of the visible and the invisible" (see fig. 1).[80] Every time we articulate, we shift the sociocultural structure. Expression is the transcendent link and transmission between the body and what it senses. Nonmaterial linguistic structures are both those that exist outside the body and those that do not derive directly from sensory input (from inherent sediments, for example). These nonmaterial linguistic structures and the physical body are in perpetual looping concrescence.

John Ashbery and Experience

The story of Ashbery's life has been told many times, by Ashbery himself in the multitude of interviews of him, and by most of the critics who have attended to his work.[81] Briefly, he grew up near Rochester, New York, and attended Deerfield Academy in Massachusetts before going to Harvard

The Invisible

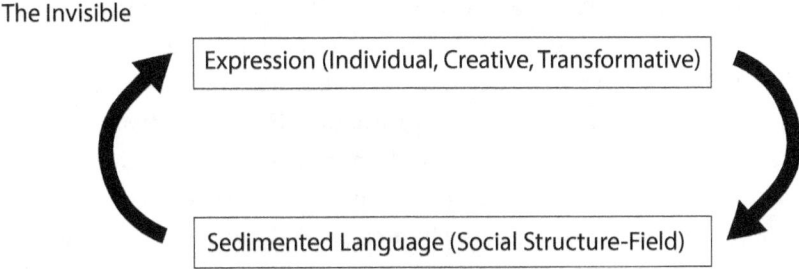

Figure 1.1 "The Invisible," modified from Lawrence Hass, Merleau-Ponty's Philosophy, 191, 195.

University. His classmates in college included Kenneth Koch, Frank O'Hara, Robert Bly, Robert Creeley, and the novelist John Hawkes.[82] At Harvard he read Proust,[83] took a course on symbolism,[84] and studied with F. O. Matthiessen.[85] He wrote his undergraduate thesis on Auden.[86]

Ashbery went to France on a Fulbright scholarship in 1955 and studied in Montpellier before he transferred to Paris to study at the Sorbonne.[87] He renewed his Fulbright for a year and taught in Rennes.[88] He met Pierre Martory, his early main relationship, in 1956.[89] On his return to New York, he began studies in French at Columbia University and taught French at New York University in the Bronx.[90] Koch had had a Fulbright in France the year before Ashbery's, and he brought books back to New York with him by Raymond Roussel that he showed to Ashbery.[91] Ashbery was so struck by this work that when he was back in New York, he started a dissertation on Roussel, so he returned to France in 1958 to conduct research on Roussel's work, finding primary materials before Roussel's popularity grew.[92] In 1963, while Ashbery was still in France, Foucault published his book on Roussel, *Raymond Roussel* (published in English in 1986 as *Death in the Labyrinth*, for which Ashbery provided an afterword). In his interview with Michael Silverblatt, Ashbery talks about his time in France as "crucial development years of [his] work."[93] Ashbery remained in France without returning to America until 1963, when he was able to return for visits in the summers. He returned to New York finally in 1965.[94]

In his interview with Brett Lauer, Ashbery lists his poetic influences as

Auden's earlier poetry, Wallace Stevens, William Carlos Williams to some degree, Marianne Moore, F. T. Prince, and Giorgio de Chirico's *Hebdomeros*.[95] Andrew Epstein describes, as well, Ashbery and O'Hara as "swept up in the distinctive intellectual culture of the Abstract Expressionist painters, which featured a heady mix of influences including surrealism, existentialism, Emersonian self-reliance, the American pragmatism of James and Dewey, and the related 'process' philosophy of Alfred North Whitehead."[96] However, it is important to remember that while Ashbery might have had training by F. O. Matthiessen on the philosophical approaches of Emerson and the Jameses, he had only spent one year in New York before returning there for good in 1965. That is, while Epstein (following his source, George Cotkin) writes about the "[domination of the] literary culture" of existentialism in America, for example, Ashbery was not in the thick of it.[97] He was certainly aware of it but did not embrace it, as suggested in Silverblatt's interview of him in which he described reading Raymond Queneau as a "palliative for existential fiction."[98]

There is no question that Ashbery was aware of the visual arts. While he was on his extended stay in France, as well as on his return to New York, he supported himself by writing art criticism, starting out with writing for the Paris *Herald Tribune* and then writing at various times for other publications, such as *ARTnews*.[99] At this time, post–World War II New York had taken over as the cultural capital of the world, leaving Paris somewhat less avant-garde and certainly less edgy. David Bergman comments that Ashbery was less exposed to the abstract expressionists than his peer, Frank O'Hara, and that he was instead more focused on surrealists such as de Chirico.[100] Ashbery remarks on his appreciation for de Chirico's *Hebdomeros* in several interviews,[101] and he translated de Chirico and Gaston Bachelard from the French.[102] Even so, Ashbery said that he found surrealist poetry "very dull" and that he did not think that his own "poetry [was] influenced by French poetry, in particular, Surreal poetry."[103]

Rather than surrealism, it appears that Ashbery was attracted to cubism. Ashbery explained to Lauer that "[t]here *was* a period in the early fifties when [he] was intrigued by [the painter Fernand] Léger."[104] He describes in this interview that he was particularly interested in Léger's focus on "ordinary objects." As with the great interest in existentialism in the aftermath of the Second World War, there was, as Epstein describes it, a "thirst for everyday life [that exploded] in the post-1945 period . . . a turn toward the mundane, the small, and the everyday."[105] Ashbery links his interest in the "small" and "mundane" in talking about the influence of Wallace Stevens on him as shown in Ashbery's poem "Le livre est sur la table" (*CP*, 38). Ashbery describes "An Ordinary Evening in New Haven" as a "meditative verse in which the feelings in the room and the events of everyday life enter and become almost fossilized in the poem."[106]

In his 1989 piece "Poetic Space," Ashbery declares that "[p]oetry is a kind of phenomenology," so he clearly knew of this philosophical approach.[107] Unclear is whether Ashbery read phenomenologists or knew about their work beyond certain vague clues. He certainly would have known of Merleau-Ponty, if in no other way than of the news of his untimely death, for as he tells Charles Bernstein, he read a lot of newspapers while he was in France, remarking on a commonly reproduced photograph of himself and Martory in which a newspaper is visible under his arm.[108] Other poets, such as Charles Olson and Robert Duncan, were reading Merleau-Ponty in particular.[109] In his interview of Ashbery, Richard Jackson mentions Derrida, Foucault, and Lacan, and Ashbery responds: "While I am not very familiar with these authors, you may have a point in mentioning them," suggesting that they might be relevant to his work.[110] And finally, Ashbery quotes Fairfield Porter quoting Ludwig Wittgenstein in his essay on Porter's painting.[111] In accord with how Epstein puts it, it is less important to me whether Ashbery read any phenomenology, that by Merleau-Ponty in particular, than that phenomenology is, I believe, a very good lens through which to approach Ashbery's poetry.[112]

In Merleau-Ponty's approach to perception, several things are important. The first and most fundamental thing is that when we perceive, it is an intentional act in which our attention is directed toward something. Even with this intentional direction, what we happen to light on is determined by what is around us. There is a contingent aspect of perception. Ashbery said about the poet James Schuyler that "nature is merely what is adjacent, what one looks out at all the time, whether it be trees, people, vehicles or odd happenings that one happens to witness."[113] As Epstein argues, it is because of this random aspect of perception that formal innovations arise: "new and innovative forms and procedures that might arrest the attention and help it come to life—that might give shape to the information and perception that attention yields. . . . [U]se of fragmentation and collage . . . use of . . . found language . . . mixing of media and blurring of genres."[114] In the phenomenological process, when sedimented materials do not suit the moment, the artist must turn to innovation of expression to bring those materials into alignment with the shifted context of the new moment.

Ashbery talks repeatedly about how his poetry is an expression of his experience. This approach is apparent in his gathering of materials for his work; as he tells Tom Smith in an interview, he "[l]isten[s] a great deal to what people are saying" around him, a "mélange of different voices . . . segments of people's thoughts and [his] own thoughts."[115] His poetry is also a reflection of the experience of experience, that just as experience is not a smooth series of logically connected and systematically ordered events of different types, it happens randomly and discontinuously. "My poetry is disjunct," Ashbery tells Michael Hulse, "but then so is life."[116]

Beyond simply being a recounting of experiences, however, Ashbery sees poetry as an expression of inward sensibility. As he notes to Janet Bloom and Robert Losada: "We are somehow all aspects of a consciousness giving rise to a poem."[117] In fact, not only are we these consciousnesses that emit poetic expression in the process of perception, poetry, Ashbery says, is "a kind of meniscus of how experience comes to me."[118] Poetry becomes, therefore, a lens between experience and the self, what Merleau-Ponty sees as that transcendental leap from the self to what is sensed and back toward the self in a form of expression—in this case, poetry.[119]

This is not a question of just experience in general, though. Ashbery is focused on the flickering momentary snippets of experience as well. He says in Jackson's interview of him that he has "been influenced by the music of John Cage in which there are long periods of silence and where the noises of the environment will be picked up and perhaps replayed at some point. I think he's trying to draw attention to the fact that every moment has a validity; it's a valuable unit of time, and the things that might be happening at any time have a value and even a beauty."[120] I would say that this is Ashbery's unit across most of his poetry: the moment. He realizes, however, that even making the moment the focus of his attention in the transformation of experience into poetry is an enormous task. He says at one point that "[w]e can't possibly absorb every aspect of any experience."[121]

Perception also requires a point of focus and a horizon. As Ashbery writes in *Three Poems*, "there is always something fading out or just coming into focus" (*CP*, 298). In accord with the shifts and limits of the horizon, Ashbery writes in "Grand Galop," "The road just seems to vanish / And not that far in the distance, either. The horizon must have been moved up" (*CP*, 442).[122]

In order to perceive, we need this spatial orientation, according to Merleau-Ponty, but we must also be able to pull out of ourselves and at once recognize what is not us and come to an awareness of our own selves. This understanding of the merging of our interiors and exteriors permeates Ashbery's poetry. He writes, "How does it feel to be outside and inside at the same time, / The delicious feeling of the air contradicting and secretly abetting / The interior's warmth?" in "The Bungalows" (*CP*, 224); "Thus your world is an inside one / Ironically fashioned out of external phenomena / Having no rhyme or reason, and yet neither / An existence independent of foreboding and sly grief" in *Fragment* (*CP*, 231–32); and "We carry both inside and outside around with us as we move purposefully toward an operation that is going to change us on every level" in *The System* (*CP*, 301).[123]

Because of this focus on experience and its flux, Ashbery also focuses on time. This is not simply a question of time passing or the human experience of getting older (and therefore dying), but rather a sense of time as always moving, as that continual pressure of the future pressing into the present and of the past sucking the present away. This also is not a simple stream of time but takes on a different character in our perception of it. Jackson asks Ashbery about his conception of time: "In 'Soonest Mended,' you talk about time as an emulsion. . . . Your sense of time seems to be something that 'keeps percolating possibilities' . . . as you say in 'Prophet Bird.' The moment becomes evasive, always separating into parts, yet held in the emulsive suspension of the poem." Ashbery responds:

> When we experience a moment, we feel perhaps a kind of emptiness, but when we look back at it, there will be different aspects and the moment will separate itself into these aspects. We won't be sure what the dominant aspect was, and I guess that results in my sense of a permanent unraveling. This best describes how I experience life, as a unity constantly separating. It's difficult to get that into poetry, though. It takes time to write something when it is situated in a period of say, half an hour. This form is really the base on which the poem is built; it's a conveyor belt and

time gets arbitrarily snipped off at the end of the poem. Temporality is built into the poem.[124]

Part of what makes any moment so complicated is the notion that it is not a single entity but rather an amalgamation of many features. While poetry wants to make it possible to express "the totality of consciousness as it gets by in the flux of the mind-world," it is generally not possible to grasp the entire moment.[125] Left for us is the best that poetry can do, as Ashbery describes in his review of Gertrude Stein's *Stanzas on Meditation*, to "[give] one the feeling of time passing, of things happening."[126] This effort is urgent, as he says in *The System*: "But you must try to seize the truth of this: whatever was, is, and must be" (*CP*, 303). This notion of time is somewhat cubist in nature, the sense that our perspectives flow around and try to encompass the moment's perception of our surroundings. In a late poem, "Are You Ticklish?," Ashbery writes about "the wraparound flux we intuit // as time."[127] It is this idea of the flux of experience as it "wraps around" us that links Ashbery so closely to the phenomenology of Merleau-Ponty.

Expression is the process through which what is sensed and reflected upon becomes sensation. Ashbery says in his interview with Jackson, "As to the bringing together of words and worlds, I don't think we can separate them in poetry. The physical and meaningful aspects of language always reverberate with one another in a way that leads to further language.... Isn't it interesting, by the way, that this urge to depict an object from every possible angle [like the cubists] is doomed to failure, yet the work resulting from the failure, is what makes it so fascinating to people?"[128] Ashbery raises multiple issues here: one is the "bringing together of words and worlds." This phrase describes sensing (the world around us) and combining that sensing with words (expressions of those senses in order to transform them into perception). A second issue is the inability to separate word from world. From a phenomenological standpoint, we are a part of the world around us, and while we can distinguish what is not us from what is us, there is too much commingling to pull ourselves apart from what is external to us. And finally, the reverberation leading to "further language" indicates that in expression and reexpression, there is a perpetual shift, so that further expression is necessary but never the same. Expression, as well, leads to an understanding, what perception potentially provides. Ashbery shows his awareness of this when he tells Lauer that "expression and comprehension go hand in hand."[129]

This process is how Ashbery arrives at his classic statement about poetry being the "experience of experience."[130] We experience the world—that is, we sense it; we must then, in order to make sense of it, recognize ourselves as sensing it, thereby transforming sensation into perception. In the process of this transformation, we are also checking through sedimented perceptions of the past to either accept what we are currently sensing as something that we recognize or to reshape what we are currently sensing into a new layer to become a part of the sedimentations. This is not an exact transcription of Merleau-Ponty, nor does Ashbery cite phenomenologists, but when Laurence Lieberman describes Ashbery's process, it is as if he were channeling them. Lieberman says: "The self ... is filtered through memory, wherein it is demonstrated to have undergone metamorphosis into a repository which receives and selects and assimilates—as by osmosis—the voices of other lives that touch our sensorium."[131] As Ashbery said, "the process and the thought reflect back and forth on each other."[132] There is a continual reverberation between what is sensed and what is considered about that sensation.

Ashbery's poetry is not, I believe, transcendental in the same way as Romantic poetry or Emersonian approaches, or with the sublimity of such art forms as the paintings created by the Hudson River school. This is not a poetry that will lift us soaring into the skies, transported by beauty and awe. Ashbery himself, as Epstein says, is "wary of the poetry of epiphany," quoting Ashbery's 1966 review of a book by Philip Booth: "Rare is the grain of sand in which he can't spot the world; seagulls, dories, and schools of herring are likewise windows on eternity, until we begin to suspect that he is in direct, hot-line communication with it."[133] David Fite says that "[p]oetry may be 'grace,' as our mild-mannered poet comes to assert in his recent long poem, 'Litany,' but it is a grace that neither seeks nor delivers that chimerical Romantic transcendence which remains the preoccupation of many of our best poets and critics alike today. Writing cannot 'transcend life,' Ashbery tells us in 'Litany,' precisely because 'it is both / Too remote and too near.'"[134] However, as Ashbery says in this poem, "It *is* it," meaning that writing *is* life (*CP*, 609), and this sets up the link between experience and expression.[135]

Nor, however, I would suggest, is Ashbery's poetry an example of Sianne Ngai's notion of "stuplimity," as proposed by Stephen Ross, "the experience of aesthetic sublimity through boredom."[136] It is true that Ashbery recognizes this approach, as he writes in the fifth section of "French Poems" ("This banality which in the last analysis is our / Most precious possession"; *CP*, 201), but I do not believe that "sublimity through boredom" is his intention.[137] There are moments when listening to a performance of *Litany*, during which two voices read different passages of the poem concurrently, when the sounds of the voices merge to erase the ability of the ear to distinguish one voice from another, one set of words from the other set, so that the poem becomes sound art. As opposed to a judgment that this type of work is boring, I believe that it is more about meditation and the ability of the poetry to drive us to just listen and feel in order to perceive.

Ashbery's poetry is, therefore, transcendent through the phenomenological sense of that term, that we are trying to make sense of things via our perceptions of them, we are trying to organize these perceptions, and we are trying to transform these perceptions into expressions, thereby both making sense of them and organizing them. Ashbery, in talking about just having read Borges, describes the "imminence of a revelation not yet produced."[138] It is as if, therefore, the only transcendence possible is the possibility of transcendence. Yet, it is through new ways of thinking or expressing that it might come about. In his interview of Ashbery, Jackson says: "What seems important is the process of generating possible revelations in language. Language ... precedes existence in a certain way. There is no 'bottom line' for there are always more words, the imminence of new words." In agreeing, Ashbery responds: "In other words, we're never allowed to relax or rest. We're constantly coping with a situation that's in a state of flux. . . . [T]here is not a one-to-one correspondence [between what a Tarot card represents and what it means] but a looking ahead to what the next situation is going to be, a process, a flux."[139]

This "constant coping" with every shifting and reconfiguring "situation," situations of the kind addressed by Merleau-Ponty, the context of the moment, leads to poetry, to the poet's effort to express sense, to transform what is sensed to what is perceived. In "Tapestry," Ashbery lays out the entire perceptual process:

The seeing taken in with what is seen
In an explosion of sudden awareness of its formal splendor
The eyesight, seen as inner

> Registers over the impact of itself
> Receiving phenomena, and in so doing
> Draws an outline, or a blueprint,
> Of what was just there . . . (*CP*, 674)[140]

In this poem, Ashbery distinguishes, first, between the sensory input from sight and the perception of vision. As well, in spite of the reluctance to consider his work transcendental, there is certainly a moment, within that "explosion," that suggests that arriving at an understanding of a moment, of its meaning and order, is not just a flickering of an instant but a blast that floods the viewer and leaves just as quickly.

The main tropes for perception that Merleau-Ponty relies on are the field (or clearing) and the flesh, but he also refers frequently to folding in, to weaving and meshes and to the circular and perpetual flow of time and constant recycling between sensations, reflections, and perceptions. I would not claim that all poets of the twentieth century base their work on phenomenology, nor that a phenomenological approach is appropriate to each of them, but it is surprising how many of them use comparable tropes to define their work.[141] Matthew Carbery refers to James Schuyler's "restless surface," Rachel Blau DuPlessis's "drafts" and "folds," Robert Kelly's "loom," and Ashbery's "rivers" and "flows."[142] Ross declares that Ashbery is "converting riverine tropes of flow, flux, liquidity, meandering, and undulation into poetic matter and manner" and relies on the "master trope of the 'field.'"[143] Ashbery confirms this trope of the field in his interview with Louis Osti when he says: "The poetry is just what it says. It sets up an imaginary field and moves around in it."[144]

There is also a clear connection to the circular trope that I just laid out. Annette Gilson links Ashbery's focus on "circumference" in "Clepsydra," a figure that David Dick argues "suggests a transcendent poetic whole," and Richard Howard refers to Ashbery's work as a "poetics of continuity and encirclement."[145] Ashbery himself says that people are "constantly travelling in circles. This happens not only to explorers but to writers, to everybody. It's something I keep addressing myself to. I sort of see it as a series of overlapping circles and spirals. We're constantly taking two steps forward and one step backward."[146]

Ashbery's poetry has, of course, received a great deal of critical attention.

Some of these critical works are very comprehensive, such as John Shoptaw's *On the Outside Looking Out: John Ashbery's Poetry*, David Herd's *John Ashbery and American Poetry*, and John Emil Vincent's *John Ashbery and You: His Later Books*, among others. The first volume of Karin Roffman's biography, *The Songs We Know Best: John Ashbery's Early Life*, has provided Ashbery criticism with a very comprehensive portrait of influences shaping him up to his departure for France in 1955.

The three works most pertinent to this study of Ashbery's poetry and phenomenology are Stephen Ross's *Invisible Terrain: John Ashbery and the Aesthetics of Nature*, Matthew Carbery's *Phenomenology and the Late Twentieth-Century American Long Poem*, and Andrew Epstein's *Beautiful Enemies: Friendship and Postwar American Poetry*. Epstein's focus is on pragmatism, and thus also on experience: "Pragmatism posits that truth is created in the course of experience . . . and is a process more than an entity . . . [o]riented toward doing, action, practice and immediate experience rather than abstraction and theory."[147] Carbery notes the link between phenomenology and pragmatism: "It is . . . important to recognize that American poetry concerned with questions of perception, lived experience and being-with-others has . . . been discussed in relation to Pragmatism."[148] Carbery himself applies the theoretical perspective of phenomenology to long American poems but does not include Ashbery's poetry in his study, providing support for the connection between American poetry of the later twentieth century and phenomenology but leaving room for this particular focus on Ashbery's work.[149] Ross's very masterful work on Ashbery focuses, like this one, largely on Ashbery's earlier work, but takes the approach that Ashbery's intention is to transform art into nature. Although he admits that "[t]here is very little of what we might call nature content in Ashbery's poems," he argues that Ashbery develops a kind of "natural ekphrasis—poetry that translates nature to text as if it were already art."[150]

Chapter 2

Perception and Experience

PHENOMENOLOGY IS A philosophy of perception. When Maurice Merleau-Ponty uses the term "perception," he is not simply talking about input from the body's senses. We direct ourselves outside of ourselves, take in sensory information, pull it back into ourselves, register it with our internal repository of past experience, and either accept it as similar to the past or reconfigure ways of talking about it to adjust that repository to accommodate new situations. I argue in this chapter, as well as generally in this book, that Ashbery is making these moves in his poetry, and that this approach is particularly evident in his volume of prose poetry, *Three Poems*. I also argue in this chapter, as well as throughout the book, that when Ashbery talks about experience, he is essentially talking about perception as Merleau-Ponty considers it.

Perception is not a passive operation. In saying that "every perception is perception of something" (*PP*, 73) and "all consciousness is consciousness of something" (*PP*, 5), Merleau-Ponty is talking about the split between the perceiver and the perceived, the one bearing consciousness and the object of that consciousness. In the move outside of the perceiver toward the perceived, there must be intention, an exertion toward the object of perception. As well, in order for a perceiver to become conscious of something, there must be the transformation of the perception into the recognition of what is outside the perceiver. When Merleau-Ponty says that "consciousness is a network of significative intentions" (*SB*, 173), he suggests that perceptions are in fact intentions, whether or not they are articulable, and that it is this "network" that creates what is understood and experienced as consciousness.

Consciousness must be conscious of something, he argues, and this necessity enforces the intentionality of perception: "But it cannot be said that consciousness *has* this power; rather, it *is* this power itself. From the moment there is consciousness, and in order for consciousness to exist, there must be something of which it is conscious, an intentional object, and it can only bear upon this object insofar as it 'irrealizes' itself and throws itself into the object, insofar as it is entirely within this reference to ... something, and insofar as it is a pure act of signification. If a being is consciousness, it must be nothing other than a fabric of intentions" (*PP*, 123). Merleau-Ponty calls these objects of consciousness "an open ensemble of things toward which we project ourselves" (*PP*, 407).[1] Simply put, this approach is why I believe that it makes so much sense to use Merleau-Ponty's philosophy in a study of John Ashbery's poetry. In considering his poetry as this "open ensemble of things toward which we project ourselves," it becomes possible to allow his constellation of perceptions to array themselves for us.

Sensory matter is not discrete; nor is the perception that rises out of it. Perception is, rather, a "field of experience" within which sensory input amasses within the horizon of sense limits (*VI*, 110). It is impossible, therefore, to depict perception as if it were a sequential process. It is instead multiple, overlapping, and concurrent happenings that are interdependent and intermeshing. "To perceive," Merleau-Ponty argues,

> is not to experience a multitude of impressions that bring along with them some memories capable of completing them, it is to see an immanent sense bursting forth from a constellation of givens without which no call to memory is possible. To remember is not to bring back before the gaze of consciousness a self-subsistent picture of the past, it is to plunge into the horizon of the past and gradually to unfold tightly packed perspectives until the experiences that it summarizes are as if lived anew in their own temporal place. To perceive is not to remember. (*PP*, 23)

Interesting in this quotation is the parallel structure that sets up three times what perception and memory are NOT. In order to perceive, we must remember, but perception is not memory. Rather, perception is only possible through recourse to memory. In order to remember, we must turn directly to the past and reconstitute stored perceptions. Doing so does not make those experiences recur, because that is impossible. It does, however, re-create the experiences in the distinctly different context of the present moment. Once we do that, it is as if past and present perception merge into this "immanent sense" of the present.

Charles Bernstein links phenomenology to contemporary poetry in his essay collection *A Poetics*. "'[A]rtifice,'" he says, "is the contraction of 'realism,' with / its insistence on presenting an unmediated / (immediate) experience of facts, either of the 'external' world of nature or the 'internal' world of the mind; for example, naturalistic / representation or phenomenological consciousness / mapping. Facts in poetry are primarily / factitious."[2] The relationship with phenomenology is apparent here in Bernstein's concern with experience and representation. These "facts" are, I believe, what he takes as acts of perception. While he later talks in *A Poetics* about reading as opposed to writing and poetry in specific, it is a reading that is equally intentional and directed toward grasping meaning. "[T]he economy of reading suggested / here is . . . a 'general economy' of meanings as 'nonutilizable' flow, / discharge, exchange, waste."[3] Although this "flow" is "nonutilizable," it suggests a surge of energy coming out of experience. The flow of perception is simply a passing through, an immersion, in the flux of experience.

Ashbery calls out to this "flow" of experience in multiple instances in his poetry, such as in "French Poems."[4] Here, he lays out intention—"The sources of these things being very distant / It is appropriate to find them" (*CP*, 199)—but even more, he worries about the vast amount of sensory influx:

> Now, in associating oneself too strictly with the trajectories of things
> One loses that sublime hope made of the light that sprinkles the trees.
> For each progress is negation, of movement and in particular of number.
> This number having lost its indescribable fineness,
> Everything must be perceived as infinite quantities of things.
> . . .
> at the center of which
> We live our lives, made up of a quantity of isolated instants
> So as to be lost at the heart of the multitude of things. (*CP*, 201)

While it appears for an instant that the "negation . . . of number" refers to a diminishing quantity, it is apparent that in "this number having lost its indescribable fineness," it has expanded exponentially into this "infinite quantit[y] of things," too numerous to account for or to consider in granular form. While we know, therefore, the poem suggests, that our lives are composed of this "quantity of isolated instants," there are so many of them that they merge into a flow of experience, this "multitude of things."

Key to the operation of perception and its development into representation is the concept of experience, a notion that includes within it this flow of perceptions, a flow occurring over spans of time, multiple types and instances of perceptions merging together into the passage of a life. Merleau-Ponty argues, in fact, that "we are experiences, that is, thoughts that feel behind themselves the weight of the space, the time, the very Being they think, and which therefore do not hold under their gaze a serial space and time nor the pure idea of series, but have about themselves a time and a space that exist by piling up, by proliferation, by encroachment, by promiscuity—a perpetual pregnancy, perpetual parturition, generativity and generality" (*VI*, 115).

We are, therefore, merged with our surroundings through perception and experience, and these instances merge in turn with each other into what Merleau-Ponty refers to as a "single, polythetic act" (*PP*, 73). This merging of ourselves with the world he describes as "the system of experience [that] is lived by me from a certain point of view; I am not the spectator of it, I am a part of it, and it is my inherence in a point of view that at once makes possible the finitude of my perception and its opening to the total world as the horizon of all perception.... The perception of the world is nothing but an expansion of my field of presence, it does not transcend the essential structures of this field, and the body always remains an agent in and never becomes an object of this field" (*PP*, 317). Perception is finite in that it is bounded by the horizon set by the limits of sense capabilities. This horizon bounds the field of perception within which we are actively perceiving. This is our "world" of experience.

In several interviews, Ashbery admits to this focus on experience in his poetry. What is essential here is that he does not simply relate specific things that happened to him but instead uses experience as a whole to drive what happens in the poetry. In his interview with Peter Stitt, for instance, Ashbery says: "I don't want to bore people with experiences of mine that are simply versions of what everybody goes through. For me, poetry starts after that point. I write with experiences in mind, but I don't write about them, I write out of them.... This is the way that life appears to me, the way that experience happens. I can concentrate on the things in this room and our talking together, but what the context is is mysterious to me."[5]

It is evident that Ashbery was concerned about and trying to make sense of the contingency of experience. In his interview with Janet Bloom and Robert Losada, he talked about both contingency and sense-making: "Every moment is surrounded by a lot of things in life that don't add up to anything that makes much sense and these are a part of a situation that I feel like I am trying to deal with when I'm writing. . . . I guess what I am doing is merely starting out with the disparate circumstances that . . . are with us at every moment."[6] And in discussing his longer poems, Ashbery says, "They are in a way diaries or logbooks of a continuing experience or at any rate of an experience that continues to provide new reflections and therefore it gets to be much closer to a whole reality than the shorter ones do."[7] Experience is, therefore, an array of perceptions, the conglomeration of which takes us closer to comprehension of the experience of consciousness.

In explaining perception, Merleau-Ponty says: "We do not begin by knowing the perspectival appearances of the thing: it is not mediated by our senses, our sensations, or our perspectives; we go straight to the thing, and only secondarily do we notice the limits of our knowledge and of ourselves as knowing" (*PP*, 338). First, therefore, we access what is around us. It is only after we have directed perception intentionally outward that we reach awareness of that perception and try to make sense of it. It is in that sense-making that we enter into that chiasm and those intransigent unknowings.[8] As Merleau-Ponty describes it, "The world, in the full sense of the word, is not an object, it is wrapped in objective determinations, but also has fissures and lacunae through which subjectivities become lodged in it or, rather, which are subjectivities themselves" (*PP*, 349). There is, therefore, the individual, and there is the world. Perception is how the individual accesses the world. There is a chasm between them but also a chiasm, the intersections where they meet in the act of perception. Perception becomes a kind of merging between the world and the individual. This is where the poetry takes place.

In his art criticism, too, Ashbery emphasizes experience as the primary motivator for art-making of any genre. In his 1970 review in *ARTnews* of the collages of Anne Ryan, for instance, Ashbery argues: "These late works have the order in disorder that can come only with spontaneous emotional thinking. What could be tumultuous is on the contrary sensed as the result of a lucid intelligence dealing with experience in abstract terms. Everything meshes, flexes, seethes in a controlled way to produce the effect of ideation as it begins in the mind. . . . One forgets the materials and enters into the works as moments of living."[9] "Order in disorder," "a lucid intelligence dealing with experience," "meshes, flexes, seethes": these are elements of phenomenological thinking. The artist takes up this "ensemble" of contingent elements of experience and endeavors to bring order to them. The meshwork is the "network of significative intentions" and the intertwining of perception and consciousness. The "flexing" and "seething" suggest the perpetual shifting of time and perception, less eruptive than Merleau-Ponty, perhaps, but nonetheless quite roiling.

What comes out of this flux of perception, this field of experience, is a sense of Being, of the consciousness of existence. It comes to encompass us in our immersion in perception. "Being," Merleau-Ponty says in *The Visible and the Invisible*, is "no longer being *before* me, but surrounding me and in a sense traversing me, and my vision of Being not forming itself from elsewhere, but from the midst of Being" (*VI*, 114). As Merleau-Ponty writes, "One turns toward that Being that doubles our thoughts along their whole extension, since they are thoughts of something and since they themselves are not nothing—a Being therefore that is meaning, and meaning of meaning. Not only that meaning that is attached to words and belongs to the order of statements and of things said, to a circumscribed region of the world, to a certain type of Being—but universal meaning, which would be capable of sustaining logical operations and language and the unfolding of the world as well" (*VI*, 107). This is the goal of poetry: to achieve meaning out of the experience of perception.

In his essay about Elizabeth Bishop's poetry, Ashbery lays out how the poet, in particular, takes up a focus on experience in order to come to some sense of meaning. He talks about Bishop's work as "our coming to know ourselves as the necessarily inaccurate transcriber of the life that is always on the point of coming into being [which involves] [t]his continually renewed sense of discovering the strangeness, the unreality of our reality at the very moment of becoming conscious of it *as* reality. . . . [T]he universe is constantly expanding into vast generalizations that seem on the point of taking fire with meaning and contracting into tiny particulars whose enormous specific gravity bombards us with meaning from another unexpected angle."[10] In this essay, Ashbery also talks about the neutral openness to experience of phenomenological perception: "A sleeping ear—that is as good a metaphor as any for the delicate but imperfect instrument the poet has to use in order to construe the bewilderingly proliferating data of the universe that is continually surging up around him, threatening to submerge him at the moment he in turn threatens to pierce it through with a ray of interpretation. . . . The poet's act—the looking so intense that it becomes something like death or ecstasy, both at once perhaps."[11] Also apparent and embedded in these statements are Merleau-Ponty's approach to phenomenology: open perception, a field of experience, and intentionality.[12]

Several poems by Ashbery explicitly state the objective of gaining Being and thereby meaning. In "Clouds," for example, while "The external look / Of the nearby world had become confused with the cobwebs inside . . . [,] No noise was to underline the notion of its being. // Thus the thing grew heavy with the mere curve of being, / As a fruit ripens through the long summer before falling / Out of the idea of existence into the fact of being received" (*CP*, 221–22).[13] This repetition of being, with the elusive pronoun reference, appears to lead back to a light in the forest, what I would argue is the discernment of meaning in the field of experience and certainly what life means in a state of mortality. In "The Bungalows," he wrote, "Each detail was startlingly clear, as though seen through a magnifying glass, / Or would have been to an ideal observer, namely yourself— / For only you could watch yourself so patiently from afar . . . / Sometimes disappearing into valleys, but always *on the way*, / For it all builds up into something, meaningless or meaningful" (*CP*, 225). By "[building] up into something," while that "something" might end up being merely "meaningless," the effort remains to attain that glimpse of the "meaningful."

This glimpse is the ephemeral inkling of meaning, often only apparent in faint traces. Bernstein talks at length in the essay "Artifice and Absorption" about how writing is visible (in the "mark" on the page), but also how reading these marks makes them disappear in the transformation of the marks into meaning. Thus, he says, "The 'mark' is the visible sign of writing. / But reading, insofar as it consumes & / absorbs the mark, erases it—the words disappear / (the transparency effect) & are replaced by / that which they depict, their 'meaning.'" Important here, however, is what he calls "antiabsorptive" writing, a type of poetic language that resists this disappearance of these marks: "Thus," he says, "absorption is the 'aura of listening' destroyed / in this writing: Antiabsorptive / writing recuperates the mark by making it opaque, / that is, by maintaining its visibility / & undermining its meaning, where 'meaning' is / understood in the narrower, utilitarian sense / of a restricted economy."[14] In preventing the visible marks of writing from becoming invisible, meaning is less available.

These traces bear their marks in Ashbery's "French Poems," with its "Invisible marblings" (*CP*, 199) and this "certain lightness" (*CP*, 200). The first poem in this series refers to "contacts" twice, the ephemera of sensations that are lost "in the mass / Of the mist" but that have "'seals'" "affixed" to them, the remaining remnants of these contacts. "It is probably on one of the inside pages / That the history of his timidity will be written," says the poem (*CP*, 201), in indicating the slight marks of past existence that linger.

Merleau-Ponty uses a weaving analogy to explain what the poet is doing, that there are chiasms between articulations and silences, and that silences are those moments when perception cannot rise to the surface sufficiently to permit these articulations, these expressions of experience. These chiasms create a fabric woven of language and silence, and the poet works, as he says, "on the wrong side of his material" to pick out the silences and bring them to expression, that is, to tap into those perceptions lost to consciousness. In *Signs*, Merleau-Ponty says:

> Like the weaver, the writer works on the wrong side of his material....
> Or to put the matter another way, we must uncover the threads of silence
> that speech is mixed together with. In already acquired expressions
> there is a direct meaning which corresponds point for point to figures,
> forms, and established words. Apparently there are no gaps or expressive
> silences here. But the meaning of expressions which are in the process
> of being accomplished cannot be of this sort; it is a lateral or oblique
> meaning which runs between words. It is another way of shaking the
> linguistic or narrative apparatus in order to tear a new sound from it. (*S*,
> 44–46)

Here, Merleau-Ponty is describing the function of articulation. These "already acquired expressions" were created and established at previous times to match the articulation with the particular perception, and they are stored internally. However, not all experience matches a previous encounter, and so it must "tear a new sound" to articulate it more closely. This act is inspired, I argue, by "this hope (which doesn't exist) . . . Precisely a form of suspended birth, / Of that *invisible light* which spatters the silence / Of our everyday festivities" (*CP*, 200). Light becomes in "French Poems" the inspiration to provoke articulation, to break that "[spattered] . . . silence."[15]

Bernstein suggests a weaving metaphor as well, with absorption and impermeability as the "warp & woof of poetic composition," and in doing so he calls on Merleau-Ponty directly: "The *intersection* / of absorption & impermeability is precisely / *flesh*, / as Merleau-Ponty uses this term to designate the intersection of the visible / & the invisible . . . [A]bsorption & impermeability / are the warp & woof of poetic composition— / an intertwining or chiasm whose locus / is the flesh of the word. Yet writing re- / verses the dynamic Merleau-Ponty out- / lines for the visible & the invisible: / for it is the invisible of writing / that is imagined to be absorbed / while the visible of writing usually goes unheard / or is silenced."[16] Here are multiple strands requiring teasing out. There is a clear push and pull, he argues, between absorption, in which the words on the page disappear to permit the eruption of meaning, and impermeability, in which the words resist disappearance and that resistance blocks meaning or access to the poem. It is where these counterpulls intersect that chiasms form; this is the weaving of the fabric of poetry and experience, the intersection between the visible, what is accessible to perception, and the invisible, what perception cannot access and what cannot achieve articulation.

There is failure in perception, therefore, and it is multiple, for in the moment we try to get the perception exact and the moment that we simply become perception in this exactness, "Being," Merleau-Ponty argues, "is extinguished":

> The visible things about us rest in themselves, and their natural being is so full that it seems to envelop their perceived being, as if our perception of them were formed within them. But if I express this experience by saying that the things are in their place and that we fuse with them, I immediately make the experience itself impossible: for in the measure that the thing is approached, I cease to be; in the measure that I am, there is no thing, but only a double of it in my "camera obscura." The

moment my perception is to become pure perception, thing, Being, it is extinguished. (*VI*, 122)

This is a paradox in perception, that the moment we address experience by articulating that we are perceiving and recognizing what is outside of us, we "cease to be." We lose that distinction between ourselves and others through the act of perception, and so fail to perceive.

Poetry, however, is one approach to fill these gaps, these perceptual flaws, and to articulate what meaning is gained from the consciousness of perception and its imperfections.[17] In *Signs*, Merleau-Ponty argues that "[s]ince perception itself is never complete, since our perspectives give us a world to express and think about which envelops and exceeds those perspectives ... [,] why should the expression of the world be subjected to the prose of the *senses* or of the concept? It must be poetry; that is, it must completely awaken and recall our sheer power of expressing beyond things already said or seen" (*S*, 52). Literature, and I would argue poetry in particular, is essential in our consciousness of perception, what Merleau-Ponty calls in his working notes in *The Visible and the Invisible*, an "*inscription* of Being" (*VI*, 197). And language and its link to experience becomes what poetry is about.

How the poet enacts this is by allowing full access to unexplored phenomena nested within, and by focusing inward, to fracture connections with the outside, what Merleau-Ponty calls the "natural world." It is in these fractures that the poet finds a place for poetry. In so doing, the poet not only gets at a closer perceptual comprehension of the world but merges with it, as Merleau-Ponty says: "The poet ... replaces the usual way of referring to things, which presents them as 'well known,' with a mode of expression that describes the essential structure of the thing and accordingly forces us to enter into that thing.... In the poem, as in the perceived object, form cannot be separated from content; what is being presented cannot be separated from the way in which it presents itself to the gaze" (*WP*, 100–101).[18]

The poem is, in fact, the closest that language gets to inarticulate utterances, and because of its position in communication, it comes more directly out of the body and is more closely connected to experience and to the consciousness of that experience, which is Being. Merleau-Ponty explains that "poetry ... is essentially a modulation of existence. The poem is indistinguishable from the cry because the cry employs our body such as nature gave it to us, that is, as poor in expressive means, whereas the poem employs language, and even a specialized language, such that the existential modulation, rather than dissolving in the very instant that it is expressed, finds in the poetic apparatus the means to make itself eternal" (*PP*, 152). Poetry, Merleau-Ponty argues, is able to capture experience, to articulate experience as it transpires.[19]

This theory is the underlying approach to this book, that John Ashbery is taking up those strands of experience as they come to him from the past and reflection and the present and presences in a field of immersion. He, as Jonathan Morse argues in "Typical John," "sublimates all that is nonverbal of his life onto the page, becoming . . . himself a true poem."[20]

Three Poems and Perception

Ashbery's volume of prose poems, *Three Poems*, came out in 1972,[21] and while these poems turn to a range of topics and issues, *The New Spirit*, *The Recital*, and *The System* also lay out his clear affinities with phenomenology to the point where some of this discussion will appear repetitive because I am treating the poems separately.[22] All three poems take up issues in phenomenology and so overlap quite a bit. I have chosen not to combine these poems as if one unit in order to avoid this repetition, not only because I prefer to respect the poems as separate entities but also to emphasize that Ashbery is talking about these questions of aesthetics over and over again in his work.

The Recital is the shortest of the three poems, yet even so, it lays out the process of perception and emphasizes the importance of articulation in coming to an understanding of that perception. One long quotation sets up much of this approach in the poem:

> [E]ven these simple, tangible experiences were themselves subject to description and enumeration, or else they too became fleeting and transient as the song of a bird that is uttered only once and disappears into the backlog of vague memories where it becomes as a dried, pressed flower, a wistful parody of itself. Meanwhile all our energies are being absorbed by the task of trying to revive those memories, make them real, as if to live again were the only reality; and the overwhelming variety

of the situations we have to deal with begins to submerge our efforts. It becomes plain that we cannot interpret everything, we must be selective, and so the tale we are telling begins little by little to leave reality behind. It is no longer so much our description of the way things happen to us as our private song, sung in the wilderness, nor can we leave off singing, for that would be to retreat to the death of childhood, to the mere acceptance and dull living of all that is thrust upon us, a living death in a word; we must register our appraisal of the moving world that is around us, but our song is leading us on now, farther and farther into that wilderness and away from the shrouded but familiar forms that were its first inspiration. (*CP*, 319)

Here is evidence of time's quick passage, bringing along with it these brief moments of sensory perception. As ephemeral as they are, they are "tangible," and so caught up in our processing of existence. In saying that these instances are "subject to description and enumeration, or else they too [become] fleeting and transient," the poet is arguing that it is in articulation, in bringing experience into language about it, that the brief moments are captured. If not articulated, these "fleeting" sensory inputs are stored in a repository of memory that is "vague" and "a wistful parody of itself." Articulation, therefore, does not simply capture but renders experience, and tries to render it as it really is.

While the senses are collecting input, in order to understand them, to transform them into perception, we must turn to our memories, "to revive them" in order to match them with what we are experiencing, but also to shape our experience through this intermingling of what we experience with what we remember. The poem worries here that this articulation cannot be comprehensive, for the flood of senses mixed with the mass of memory is far too great to encompass: "we cannot interpret everything, we must be selective." The poem emphasizes here the imperative of articulation, that we must articulate in order to avoid a "retreat to the death of childhood, to the mere acceptance and dull living of all that is thrust upon us, a living death in a word." However, it says, in doing so, we move further from the instant of sensation, "farther and farther into that wilderness."

While the goal is to "synthesize" elements of experience, to understand them and bring them together in some kind of coherent order ("The point was the synthesis of very simple elements in a new and strong, as opposed to old and weak, relation to one another" [*CP*, 325]), the poem holds a very bleak prediction throughout, that it is never possible to attain order in that wilderness or gain meaning from existence:

> Any reckoning of the sum total of the things we are is of course doomed to failure from the start, that is if it intends to present a true, wholly objective picture from which both artifice and artfulness are banished: no art can exist without at least traces of these, and there was never any question but that this rendering was to be made in strict conformity with the rules of art—only in this way could it approximate most closely the thing it was intended to reflect and illuminate and which was its inspiration, by achieving the rounded feeling almost of the forms of flesh and the light of nature, and being thus equipped for the maximum number of contingencies which, in its capacity as an aid and tool for understanding, it must know how to deal with. (*CP*, 322)

Articulation for a poet arrives in the form of the poem, and that is the focus in this section of *The Recital*. The transformation of experience, the phenomena that we sense, cannot possibly be comprehensive or accurate.[23]

However, the poem argues, this effort is inescapable, never completely fulfilling, and ongoing, for it says, "It seems as though every day is arranged this way. The movement is the majestic plodding one of a boat crossing a harbor, certain of its goal and upheld by its own dignity on the waves, a symbol of patient, fruitful activity, but the voyage always ends in a new key, although at the appointed place; a note has been added that destroys the whole fabric and the sense of the old as it was intended. The day ends in the darkness of sleep" (*CP*, 324). The metaphor of the boat, moving with intention through the "waves" of experience, sets up the notion of movement persistent in perception. As well, this "new key" suggests the transformation enacted by the day's passage and the making sense of it. Because this "new key" is not perfect, in a mixed metaphor, it disrupts the "fabric" of the comprehension of existence as well as the settled notion of the past. This failure, this jarring mismatch, ends the day (experience) in "the darkness of sleep," that meaningless state of existence.

Even so, over time, this "fabric" of existence gets modified and refined:[24]

"Then it became apparent that certain new elements had been incorporated, though perhaps not enough of them to change matters very much. Finally... something like a different light began to dawn, to make itself felt: . . . these tremors slowly took on the solidity, the robustness of an object. And by that time everything else had gone away, or retreated so far into the sidelines that one was no longer conscious of those ephemera that had once seemed the very structure, the beams and girders defining the limits of the ambiguous situation one had come to know and even to tolerate, if not to love" (*CP*, 325). The "ephemera," those brief instances of experience, start the process of perception, but once these "elements" are synthesized, that is, brought inside from one's exterior and integrated with past elements, it is as if the elements that formed the armature for the perception disappear in the overall comprehension of experience.

The New Spirit and *The System* are much more complicated and extended meditations on existence. In addition to its turn toward phenomenology that I will address here, *The New Spirit* talks at length about how each individual changes in the course of embarking on an intimate relationship with another person.[25] Added to this discourse are elements of the tarot and astrology, an established influence for modernist poets. Even so, phenomenological perception persists as a salient strand of the poem.

As explained earlier in this book, Ashbery is deeply concerned with experience. When he uses this term, I believe, he is using it to describe senses before they have been processed into perception and the attempt to derive meaning from them. This sensory input appears in the "valley hundreds of miles in length and full of orchards and all sorts of benevolent irregularities of landscape. . . . This casual, poorly seen new environment" (*CP*, 250–51), "the hunter's moon," and "those lacquer blobs and rivers of daylight, shaken out of a canister—so unmanageable, so indigestible . . ." (*CP*, 250). This input is arbitrary and unsorted, random bits of what our senses register.

In order to comprehend these inputs, we must do something with them, as the poem argues, where "the eyes [are] directing out, living into their material and in that way somehow making more substance than before" (*CP*, 251). A primary focus for this poem is directing the eyes out, but rather than to the arbitrariness of objects around us, toward other people. "I am the spectator," the poem says, and "you what is apprehended, and as such we both have our own satisfying reality, even each to the other, though in the end it falls apart, falls to the ground and sinks in" (*CP*, 255). In an interesting repetition from a couple of pages earlier, the poem says, "In you I fall apart, and outwardly am a single fragment, a puzzle to itself. But we must learn to live in others, no matter how abortive or unfriendly their cold, piecemeal renderings of us: they create us" (*CP*, 253). The first quotation refers to the element of failure in perception, gone into at length in this poem, as I will discuss shortly. In the second one, and very tellingly, the "falling apart" happens in the perception of the other. "We must learn to live in others," the poem argues, because perception transpires through the intermingling of us with what is around us, including, in particular, other persons. We "fall apart" in them because this intermersion requires a commingling of ourselves with others, and so a dispersal.

The poem asks whether this intermingling between ourselves and others builds into something beyond this simple perceptual sharing: "Do these things between people partake of themselves, or are they a subtler kind of translucent matter carrying each to a compromise distance painfully outside the rings of authority?" (*CP*, 251). It responds that in perceiving the other, something is gained beyond elementary sense perception and sensations of nonhuman situations: "For we never knew, never knew what joined us together. Perhaps only a congealing of closeness, deserving of no special notice. But then the eyes directing out, living into their material and in that way somehow making more substance than before" (*CP*, 251). This "living into their material" of the sensing eyes, this incorporation of the self with the other, "[makes] more substance than before," as if to suggest that more than one individual in co-perception is closer to a comprehension of meaning than one alone. In saying, "Your body could formulate these things, projecting them into me, as though I had thought of them" (*CP*, 253), the poem proposes even further that, just as our perceptions direct outside of us, the other individual(s)' perception of us directs into us and becomes a part of our interior conception of meaning, "as though I had thought of them."

The poem describes quite clearly how perception works, that we open ourselves to what is around us, a random mix of things: "I am to include everything: the furniture of this room, everyday expressions, as well as my rarest thoughts and dreams, so that you may never become aware of the scattered nature of it, and meanwhile you *are* it all, and my efforts are really directed toward keeping myself attached, however dimly, to it as it rolls from view, like a river which is never really there because of moving on someplace. And so the denser moments of awareness are yours, not the firm outline I believe to be mine and which is probably a hoax as well" (*CP*, 254). The individual projects outward in an intentional fashion, taking in these disordered bits of experience and ordering them as a part of this excursion into the other. This effort is ongoing through the flux of time and perpetual inflow of experience ("like a river"). These "denser moments of awareness" derive from the intersection, that crossing, of the two intentional perceptive forces.

As with most of the poems in this book, time is an ever-present and ever-shifting component of perception in *The New Spirit*, what it refers to as the "saw-toothed anomalies of time" (*CP*, 251). Time is not a consistent, even, smooth quantity. It is, rather, an ongoing sense of buffeting, in which each moment differs from the rest to a varying degree. The poem describes how this irregular experience of time feels in saying that people "might break open the one physical act they know and reveal the kernel like a picture that is taking place before them in order to proceed definitely into the future, sweeping aside all ifs and buts at the stately pace of a caravan disappearing into an undivided somewhere, all its secrets locked, swaying with the progressive movement toward and away from. But what is needed is some act other than pressing a button and having it all happen, some way of living into the layers as they occur and not losing momentum in order to strike" (*CP*, 265). This "kernel" is the core of what experience might mean, but in layering his metaphors again, Ashbery links it to depiction, that the closest one can get to this essence is through the intermediary of re-creating it in image or language. "Living into the layers" suggests the process by which we pull our sensory inputs back into ourselves and map them to the "layers" of memory or established cultural understandings, "a present time draped backward over the past" (*CP*, 265).

Essential to Merleau-Ponty's thinking is that senses evolve into perception in the effort to discern meaning and order in them. We must, he says, look in order to see. Sight becomes, in this thinking, according to the poem, vision; not just the physical sight of things, but a deeper understanding of them.

> One gets the narrowness into one's seeing, which also seems an inducement to moving forward into what one has already caught a

glimpse of and which quickly becomes vision, in the visionary sense, except that in place of the panorama that used to be our customary setting and which we never made much use of, a limited but infinitely free space has established itself, useful as everyday life but transfigured so that its signs of wear no longer appear as a reproach but as indications of how beautiful a thing must have been to have been so much prized, and its noble aspect which must have been irksome before has now become interesting, you are fascinated and keep on studying it. (*CP*, 263)

While "visionary" suggests access to the future, here it indicates that even in the mundane experiences of everyday life, this "transfiguration" of the smallest of details by the act of perception leads to, not just a greater understanding of existence, but an exceptional appreciation of it, "[infecting] the mind's suburbs . . . with the new spirit":

[I]n some cases [perception] will take the form of clumsy removal of the barriers [to comprehension] by force—a slow but probably useful process; in others, getting used to inhabiting the ruins [of the past] and artfully adapting them to present needs; in still others, standing up in the space certain that it is the right one, and feeling the sense of its proportions leave your mind like rays, striking out to the antipodes and polishing them, perfecting them through use. One can then go about one's business unencumbered by nostalgia but still feeling the habit of this place where one has accomplished things before; it will change and you will go on thinking about it to your mutual satisfaction and joy. The fact that you did all this—cleared away all the debris so that the created vacuum would expel you forward into an exact set of conditions replying to exact demands—fertilizes each instant as it is born, increases and dies, spontaneously generating the light that flushes through the silver-outlined mask of your face—baleful silver and black, the enchanter's colors—so that the lines gradually become invisible and disappear in the total modest radiance that builds up on its surface and finally blends with the ordinary daylight outside. (*CP*, 264)

Light is a core metaphor in this quotation from the poem. It appears twice here in the form of rays. Rays of light emanate less than provide a direct and targeted spotlight. They are optimistic in that they appear when the light from the sun is partially blocked, permitted only shoots of brightness to stream out from the edges of clouds. They also have religious connotations, as in the seven rays of light embodying multiple significances across multiple religions. Even the halo marking saints and angels is a disk of light rays.

In representing the act of perception as light streaming out into a field-like "space," Ashbery follows Merleau-Ponty's model exactly. Each time we sense something, in this case, each time we use our sight to access our surroundings, we check on past experiences of that sight ("feeling the habit of this place where one has accomplished things before") and adjust the current perception to accord with the current situation ("it will change"). By finding order in these senses ("clearing away the debris"), new senses flow in. This cycle "spontaneously [generates] the light" of understanding that dissipates quickly, leaving only this "total modest radiance that builds up on [the] surface" and then fades away behind the "mask of your face," that emblem of your existence.

Given that this poem is called *The New Spirit*, it should not be a surprise that it calls out, as with the rays of light, to the breath of the spirit. This sense of the word is clear in the poem when it says, "the concave being, enfolding like air or spirit, does not dissolve when breathed upon but comes apart neatly, like a watch, and the parts may be stocked or stored, their potential does not leak away through inactivity but remains bright and firm, so that in a sense it is just as much *there* as if it were put back together again and even more so: with everything sorted and labeled you can keep an eye on it a lot better than if it were again free to assume protean shapes and senses, the genie once more let out of the bottle, and who can say where all these vacant premises should end?" (*CP*, 258). Overlaying tropes of air, watch, and genie work to shift the material aspect from immaterial, to intricate workings, to dispersed and irregular elements. Core here is the notion that perception works not just to "sort" and order but to retain that sorted order; losing the order leaves no understanding.

Reference to the breath in the poem is also essential for its connection to language.[26] Comprehension, access to meaning, according to Merleau-Ponty, is not possible without articulation, and the poem supports this insistence, while linking articulation to breath: "But the act is still proposed, before us, / it needs pronouncing. To formulate oneself around this hollow, empty sphere.... To be your breath as it is taken in and shoved out. Then, quietly, it would be as objects placed along the top of a wall: a battery jar, a rusted pulley, shapeless wooden boxes, an open can of axle grease, two lengths of pipe.... We see this moment from outside as within. There is no need to offer proof. It's funny.... The cold, external factors are inside us at last, growing in us for our improvement, asking nothing, not even a commemorative thought" (*CP*, 248). This quotation is a near-exact rendering of perception as conceived by Merleau-Ponty. "Pronouncing" perception, rendering it into language, must occur.[27] But then the poem steps backward into what is going to become the fodder for articulation: the random array formed through the intersection of the breathing body and what it sees outside of itself. By saying that "this moment" is sensible "from outside as within," the poem lays out how perception works, that we direct ourselves outside us, take in sensory elements, and pull them inside to work with them by ordering them and mapping them to what we hold in our perception repository.

The poem emphasizes the importance of phenomena, those exterior and sense-provoking objects, actions, people, and so on. These are "everyday phenomena" (*CP*, 259), "commonplace events" (*CP*, 266), and, while "brilliant," also "modest" (*CP*, 261). This act of perception "includes your outside view, openness, your penetrability and force to penetrate through outside agents that are merely the logical extensions of your inner decision to act and to bring this action to bear on the constellation of everyday phenomena" (*CP*, 259). The individual's "penetrability" and ability "to penetrate" enact the operations of perception, to reach out and to be reached into in turn.

Yet, these phenomena are "baffling" (*CP*, 266), and the poem urges the quest-like effort to find some kind of truth:

And you know at last the condition of weightlessness and everything it implies: for the future, the present and most of all for the past into which you now slip helplessly, no longer prevented by the grid of everyday language, remaining in suspension in that greenish aquarium light which is your new element, compelled to re-enact the same scene in the old park, with snow on the ground and the waiting look on the faces of the nearest buildings, some distance away. All this in the interests of getting at the truth. (*CP*, 267)

This quotation presents many of the components already laid out in the act of perception: this enmeshment in time, "most of all . . . the past," this reconsideration of "the grid of everyday language," the compulsion to dig into reflections at the same moment as taking in external sensory signals (both objects—buildings—and people—personifications of the buildings), and this drive to "[get] at the truth."

This urge for the truth is also apparent in a poem embedded within the prose poem of *The New Spirit*: "So this meaning came to arise . . . With a place for each member of the family / And . . . For every thought and feeling that had passed or would come to pass . . . Simultaneously it was penetrable / And was being saturated by the direction of the journey we must take . . . / And so the meaning is brought down / To be with us together, never the same again. We have passed through" (*CP*, 268). "[Passing] through" is the transcendence core to Merleau-Ponty's theory, that in order to perceive, we must move out of ourselves and essentially into what is not us, thereby recognizing our own selves, and coming back into ourselves and reconfiguring what was outside us to come to an understanding of it.

As stated previously, I do not suggest that Ashbery is a transcendental poet out of the Emersonian tradition, but he is certainly a transcendental of the quotidian, those instants of comprehension, those moments of clarity. Countervailing pressures at once support and recognize potentials for transcendence and recognize the low probability of achieving them. While we are "intentionally cut off from the forces of renewal, [we are] obliged to spend a certain penitential time of drawing in and not utilizing those intuitions that gave wings, inspirations to fly abruptly out of the windows of the house to the stars" (*CP*, 258); that is, while we have to think at times, we are aware of the potential of "intuitions" to give us flight. This tension is evident in the poem where it says, "yet individuality was not lost for all that, but persisted in the definition of the urge to proceed higher and further as well as in the counter-urge to amalgamate into the broadest and widest kind of uniform continuum" (*CP*, 278). Pressure here appears in the persistent drive to merge into one mass of humanity, but there is equal compulsion to retain idiosyncrasy through transcendence. In saying "it is to be transcended" (*CP*, 248), the passive voice enacts the same contradictory impulse: to achieve truth through transcendence but at once to void agency and diminish potential for this accomplishment.

While elements of phenomenology are quite apparent in both *The Recital* and *The New Spirit*, it is in *The System* where Ashbery really lays out his affinities with this philosophical approach.[28] This extended discourse, with its prolonged paragraphs and a fairly casual, almost conversational style, addresses the function of the senses, time, and articulation in the hope to come to an understanding of existence. This poem purports to a logic that I believe it also undermines. That is, it speaks directly about how to consider existence, reflects on several possible approaches, and describes the shortcomings of each at length. It talks, therefore, about "twin notions of growth" (*CP*, 293), "life-as-ritual" (*CP*, 293), and being "latent or dormant" (*CP*, 294), as well as about two forms of happiness, "the frontal and the latent" (*CP*, 293).

In an unambiguous statement, the poem lays out three possible methods for achieving a "moment of knowing" (*CP*, 291): using "sensory data," "right reason," or a "knowing combination of both" (*CP*, 291). It dismisses the third option out of hand, as it "seems the least like a winner." The second one it finds "problematic." It determines, therefore, that "only the first [option] has some slim chance of succeeding through sheer perversity" (*CP*, 291), suggesting that "intellectual understanding" (*CP*, 209) and logical consideration are the best paths toward achieving meaning in existence.

I argue, however, that close analysis of the text of this poem demonstrates Ashbery's allegiance to the first option, not the combination of sensory data with right reason, but an integration of the two, in which we pull what we see outside us into ourselves and map it to what we have seen in the past. Perception, the understanding of existence, rises out of our articulation of that mapping; more often than not a remapping, too, as each new situation that we see is never quite like those that we have seen in the past. When the poem complains that the "philosophy broke down" (*CP*, 304), it is, I believe, shifting toward this perspective, one more aligned with Merleau-Ponty's and representative of Ashbery's approach as a whole.

Perception, if it has a starting place (as a cyclical, overlapping, ongoing process), begins with the senses: "We are to read this in outward things" (*CP*, 310). *The System* proposes explicitly that the senses make it possible to pull in experience in order to synthesize it:

> [It] is our senses that are of some use to us in distinguishing verity from falsehood. For they never would have been able to capture the

emanations from that special point of life if they were not meant to do something with them, weave them into the pattern of the days that come after, sunlit or plunged in shadow as they may be, but each with the identifying scarlet thread that runs through the whole warp and woof of the design, sometimes almost disappearing in its dark accretions, but at others emerging as the full inspiration of the plan of the whole, grandly organizing its repeated vibrations and imposing its stamp on these until the meaning of it all suddenly flashes out of the shimmering pools of scarlet like a vast and diaphanous though indestructible framework. (*CP*, 297)

The poem lays out very specifically that we take up sensory inputs and organize them. In using this weaving metaphor (taken up later in my discussion on this poem), the poem explains how sensory material is stored and then becomes a part of future experience. That is, we take in information from the senses, these "emanations," and have them at hand, so that in later experience we tap back into them, intermingling previous experiences with those that we are currently undergoing. These become "woven" into each other, as it were, but not to the point where all of the "threads" of these experiences merge into one another; some of them remain distinct. The intermeshing of current and past sensory moments finally at times provides access to comprehension of existence, this "meaning of it all."

Access to sensory input is limited by the horizon, of which Merleau-Ponty speaks. There is only so far that we can see at any one moment, only so much or from so far away that we can hear. "There is always something fading out or just coming into focus," says the poem,

and this whatever-it-is is always projecting itself on us, escalating its troops, prying open the shut gates of our sensibility and pouring in to augment its forces that have begun to take over our naked consciousness and driving away those shreds of another consciousness (although not, perhaps, forever—nothing is permanent—but perhaps until our last days when their forces shall again mass on the borders of our field of perception to remind us of that other old existence which we are now called to rejoin) so that for a moment, between the fleeing and the pursuing armies there is almost a moment of peace, of purity in which what we are meant to perceive could almost take shape in the empty air. (*CP*, 298)

The horizon represents the "borders of our field of perception," a phrase that might have derived directly from Merleau-Ponty's conception of it.

In order to take in sensory information, we must move, to distinguish what is us from what is not us, what is external from what is internal:

> [T]he eye and the mind focused on a nonexistent center, a fixed point, when the common sense of even an idiot would be enough to make him realize that nothing has stopped, that we and everything around us are moving forward continually, and that we are being modified constantly by the speed at which we travel and the regions through which we pass. (CP, 295)[29]

This movement is not just physical movement, but one of time. The future is the unexpected, the unknown, the unanticipated, and the past is quite useful in terms of gaining meaning about existence, but it is the present that is so hard to manage. It is the part of existence that is disordered and unprocessed.

> [S]omething in the nature of daily being or happening ... quickly gets folded over into ancient history. ... [E]ach thing is coming up in its time and receding into the past. ... [O]nce it has entered the past's sacred precincts ... bending under the weight of an all-powerful nostalgia, its every contour is at last revealed for what it was, but this can be known only in the past. It isn't wrong to look at things in this way—how else could we live in the present knowing it was the present except in the context of the important things that have already happened? No, one must treasure each moment of the past. ... These windows on the past enable us to see enough to stay on an even keel in the razor's-edge present which is really a no-time, continually straying over the border into the positive past and the negative future whose movements alone define it. Unfortunately we have to live in it. We are appalled at this. Because its no-time, no-space dimensions offer us no signposts, nothing to be guided by. In this dimensionless area a single step can be leagues or inches; the flame of a match can seem like an explosion on the sun or it can make no dent in the matte-grey, uniform night. (CP, 315)[30]

Essential to note here is the understanding that we can only come to terms with the present in light of the past, "in the context of the important things that have already happened." It is our internal maintenance of the past and our adherence to it that anchors the present, this uncomfortable "no-time" that repeats in the anxiety about it.[31] Also of note in this quotation is the conception of the passage of time, as if lifted from Merleau-Ponty, as though emulating conditions of differing pressures, such that a high-pressure area pushes into a low-pressure one; here, the "negative" future is pulled into the "positive" past, flowing over and through the "no-time" of the present.

Memory, according to Merleau-Ponty, involves traces of past experience. This approach to memory appears repeatedly in this poem, as in "we might correctly consider ourselves shut off from the main source, never to be in a position to contemplate its rightness again, yet despite this able to consider its traces in the memory as a supreme good" (*CP*, 297); and "we can if we are quick enough seize the meaning of that assurance, before returning to the business at hand—just, I say, as we begin each day in this state of threatened blankness which is wiped away so soon, but which leaves certain illegible traces, like chalk dust on a blackboard after it has been erased" (*CP*, 299). The "main source" for memory is experience. We are "cut off" from it after it has happened, and we are left with only its residue. Each moment that we experience, each day, passes away from us, but deposits these "illegible traces," this "dust" of recollection.

In order to make sense of these accumulations of the past, it is essential to articulate them and their relationship to present experiences. The poem discusses the importance of articulation at length but also what happens if there is no articulation, if there is silence.

"Life became a pregnant silence," the poem says, "but it was understood that the silence was to lead nowhere" (*CP*, 287), "your present silence" (*CP*, 317). However, because a part of perception is inherent in the recognition of the person sensing, "the silence continues to focus" (*CP*, 309) on that person and provides the stage for articulation: "And who is to say whether or not this silence isn't the very one you requested so as to be able to speak?" (*CP*, 308). "I'm just a mute observer," the poem proclaims. "[It] isn't my fault that I can really notice how everything around me is waiting just for me to get up and say the word, whatever that is" (*CP*, 309).

Articulation activates perception by completing the process of directing outside oneself, gathering sensory input, bringing it back inside oneself, mapping it to that repository of the "dust" of the past, and rejiggering everything in the case of the need to realign the mapping. Articulation creates that new way of seeing, as the poem says: "It needs a new voice to tell it, otherwise it will seem just another awkward pause in a conversation largely made up of similar ones, and will never be able to realize its potential as a catalyst, turning you both in on yourself and outward to that crystalline gaze that has been the backing of your days and nights for so long now" (*CP*, 311–12). This "voice," this articulation, "needs" to be "new" in order to reshape perception for the perpetually shifting context within which it finds itself.

A second quotation says much the same thing. I include it in order to reinforce the argument that Ashbery is relying on principles very much in alignment with Merleau-Ponty's version of phenomenology:

> [W]e were surrounded by old things, such as need not be questioned but which distill the meek information that is within them like a perfume on the air, to be used and disposed of; and also by certain new things which wear their newness like a quality, perhaps as an endorsement of the present, in all events as a vote of confidence in the currency of the just-created as a common language. (*CP*, 287)

Some things that we sense do not require a shift in perception; others do. In "[wearing] their newness like a quality, perhaps as an endorsement of the present," those things we sense within our horizon that do not match exactly the things of the past that we have perceived, shift the present into a novel context and force a reshaping of a newly reconfigured way of talking about them that becomes this "common language," how we communicate and how we conceive of our culture.

Enacting this process requires that we move outward to sense and then inward to analyze: "what matters is us and not what time makes of us, or rather it is what we make of ourselves that matters. What is this? Just the absorption of ourselves seen from the outside, when it is really what is going on inside us" (*CP*, 300); "this doesn't matter once we have accepted it and taken it inside us to be the interior walls of our chamber" (*CP*, 301).

The act of perception entails two overlapping and mutually constituting goals: order and becoming. Becoming is that moment of understanding, of ascertaining the meaning of existence, and of accessing some kind of truth of that existence. Order is the recognition of and/or shaping of at least somewhat regular patterning out of the randomness of experience. Both of these goals permeate this poem; each requires devotion and intention.

The becoming is always ephemeral, as in "the draconian requirements of a conscience eternally mobilized against itself, feeding on itself in order to re-create itself in a shape that the next instant would destroy" (*CP*, 286)—this constant effort to forge the "shape" that would permit access to understanding, while "mastering the many pauses and the abrupt, sharp accretions of regular being in the clotted sphere of today's activities" (*CP*, 280). This "regular being," a normal everyday existence, in this "clotted sphere," a congealed mess of what happens, is penetrated by the "abrupt, sharp accretions," gusts of perception that lead to this "monodrama of becoming" (*CP*, 288), because "even this limited understanding can lead to a conception of beauty" (*CP*, 290).

Contributing to and a part of becoming is making order. Because of the intentional aspect of perception, we are the ones who create the organization and in so doing, create ourselves. None of these activities happen solely within each of us but are the result of a constant intertwining of what is inside and what is outside. "It is what we make of ourselves that matters ... the absorption of ourselves seen from the outside, when it is really what is going on inside us" (*CP*, 300). In addition to the fabric and woven trope above, Ashbery uses entanglement ("you returned to investigate the more tangled way, and for a time its intricacies seemed to promise a more complex and therefore more practical goal for you"; *CP*, 306), mesh ("unseen mesh that draws around everything"; *CP*, 311), and web ("as you continue gazing embarrassedly into the eyes of the beloved ... [y]ou become aware of an invisible web that connects those eyes to you, and both of you to the atmosphere of this room which is leading up to you after the vagaries of the space outside"; *CP*, 310), to explain the intertwinings of ourselves with our surroundings.[32]

The poem describes the effort to create order, as we try to lay out a clear path in the "labyrinth" of experience:

> What is required is the ability to enter into the complexities of the situation as though it really weren't new at all, which it isn't, as one takes the first few steps into a labyrinth. Here one abruptly finds one's intuition

tailored to the needs of the new demanding syndrome; each test is passed flawlessly, as though in a dream, and the complex climate that is formed by the vacillating wills and energies of the many who surround you becomes as easy as pie for you. You take on all comers but you do not advertise your presence. Right now it is important to slip as quickly as possible into the Gordian contours of the dank, barren morass (or so it seems at present) without uttering so much as a syllable; to live in that labyrinth that seems to be directing your steps but in reality it is you who are creating its pattern, embarked on a new, fantastically difficult tactic whose success is nevertheless guaranteed. You know this. (*CP*, 304–5)

Crucial here is the final part of this quotation, that it might appear that the "morass" of the labyrinth might be in control, but the individual is in fact the force behind the "[creation of] its pattern," that those who are willing to make new "languages," whether visual artists or poets or philosophers, are in fact creating new patterns in response to new contexts and situations.

This ordering requires reflection of two kinds: of thinking carefully about something and bouncing back, in slightly distorted representation, what has been perceived. The poem includes, therefore, reference to a "reflective intellect" (*CP*, 283), but also to the "mild shoals of possibilities that lay strewn about as far as the eye could see . . . as [if] gazing into a mirror reflecting the innermost depths of the soul" (*CP*, 285), "bent on self-discovery in the guise of an attractive partner who is *the* heaven-sent one, the convex one" (*CP*, 283).

However, as hard as we might try to find and/or create order, as hard as we might try to either match current situations with what has come before or to create new ways of articulating situations that do not match with previous ones, the poem suggests that while we must make this effort, our efforts can never quite succeed, and hardly any of us will even glimpse moments of comprehension:[33]

> Indeed this is truly what we were brought into creation for, if not to experience it, at least to have the knowledge of it as an ideal toward which the whole universe tends and which therefore confers a shape on the random movements outside us—these are all straining in the same direction, toward the same goal, though it is certain that few if any of those we see now will attain it. (*CP*, 294)

Part of the problem posed in the closing sections of the poem is that in deciding that any experience is worth recording, however mundane and individual, the amount of stored essences of the past becomes overwhelming, and the individual loses power over it.

> The rejected chapters have taken over. For a long time it was as though only the most patient scholar or the recording angel himself would ever interest himself in them. Now it seems as though that angel had begun to dominate the whole story: he who was supposed only to copy it all down has joined forces with the misshapen, misfit pieces that were never meant to go into it but at best to stay on the sidelines so as to point up how everything else belonged together, and the resulting mountain of data threatens us; one can almost hear the beginning of the lyric crash in which everything will be lost and pulverized, changed back into atoms ready to resume new combinations and shapes again. (*CP*, 316)

These "misshapen, misfit pieces that were never meant to go into it," these ordinary, ephemeral, and prosaic elements of daily life are normally not included in any books, particularly historical ones. Here, however, they are not just included; they are essential components, but they are too much to handle. In this "lyric crash," the order that had been established will devolve back into the amalgamation of memory and perception.

Yet, in the midst of this pessimism, a belief that success is possible endures. While not many among us will achieve it, we recognize its existence, "this sudden opening up, this inundation" (*CP*, 293), this "sudden tremendous moment of intuition that comes only once in a lifetime" (*CP*, 289). It is "a lightning existence that has come into our own" (*CP*, 280) that is capable of "lifting life into the truth of real pain for a few moments" (*CP*, 281).

While these are instances of exceptional insight, generally speaking, this effort to gain understanding of existence is a daily, quiet, thoughtful experience:

> And you turn away from the window almost with a sense of relief, to bury yourself again in the task of sorting out the jumbled scrap basket of your recent days, without any hope of completing it or even caring whether it gets done or not. But you find that you are unable to pick

up the threads where you left off; the details of things shift and their edges swim before your tired eyes; it is impossible to make even the rudimentary sense of them that you once could. You see that you cannot do without it, that singular isolated moment that has now already slipped so far into the past that it seems a mere spark. You cannot do without it and you cannot have it. At this point a drowsiness overtakes you as of total fatigue and indifference; in this unnatural, dreamy state the objects you have been contemplating take on a life of their own, in and for themselves. It seems to you that you are eavesdropping and can understand their private language. They are not talking about you at all, but are telling each other curious private stories about things you can only half comprehend, and other things that have a meaning only for themselves and are beyond any kind of understanding. And these in turn would know other sets of objects, limited to their own perceptions and at the limit of the scope of visibility of those that discuss them and dream about them. (*CP*, 302)

Here again is the full process of perception, in which the individual is outwardly directed and looks to gain that "sensory data." This person takes that data inside, in the case of this quotation, both literally and figuratively, and works on creating order, this "sorting out the jumbled scrap basket of . . . recent days." The mass of experience just from a few days is too hard to gather up into an organized whole. Instead, even in the desire to capture one "isolated moment" of note, all becomes a "jumble" of disorganized memory. It is as if, here, these massed instances of experience interact and intermingle in ways to create new meanings and even intersect and reconfigure in combinations with others, suggesting that perception is a shifting, mutable, elusive proposition.

Chapter 3

Time, Lyric, and Perception

To Peter Gizzi, for sending me down this path.

THIS CHAPTER EXPLAINS how time functions in phenomenological thinking, particularly as concerns Ashbery's poem "Clepsydra," a poem clearly focused on time due to its title as a water clock, but a poem that also enacts the phenomenological approach to time, to its passage and to how it operates in perception. This chapter also turns to a discussion of the lyric, considering it in its contemporary form as a longer dwelling on the instant of time, that is, the present, and on experience. Maurice Merleau-Ponty talks about the "thickness" of the present; in order to consider its thickness, this chapter concludes with an analysis of Ashbery's "simultaneous" poem, *Litany*.

"Clepsydra"

"Clepsydra," written in 1965 and one of the last poems that Ashbery wrote during his sojourn in France, represents his effort to lay out a phenomenological agenda for his poetry and serves, in essence, as a manifesto for his poetics, along with, I would argue, *Litany* and *The System*.[1] It therefore might, as John Shoptaw argues, follow the course of an argument based on a love relationship that terminates, but it takes a parallel trajectory in laying out what Shoptaw concedes is a "philosopher's system."[2] While pursuing a phenomenological argument, however, since a clepsydra is a water clock, this chapter is also about time, and the function of time in phenomenology. Even more, however, this poem is about the effort on the part of the poet, and by extension on the part of humans, to perceive, to find meaning out of ordering experience, and to articulate that meaning. Yet, and most tellingly, this effort is never quite successful. For, as the poem says, "Each moment / Of utterance is the true one; likewise none are true, / Only is the bounding from air to air, a serpentine / Gesture which hides the truth behind a congruent / Message, [and] is, in fact, / Tearing it from limb to limb this very moment" (lines 18–23).[3] An articulation might on its surface appear to be just and accurate, but time moves through, experience shifts accordingly, and any apparent truth is simply undermined by this "serpentine gesture," this act of perception that cannot be matched by an adequate formulation.

Gesture is core to Merleau-Ponty's approach to phenomenology.[4] Inherent in it is the body, that a gesture is in itself the movement of the body or of some part of it expressly to convey some kind of meaning: hello, come here, over there, stop!, I surrender, and so on. A gesture can as well be an emphasis of an utterance, as those who "talk" with their hands as much as with their mouths. A gesture can also be an act with symbolic import, such as burning a flag or giving a flower bouquet. It implies within it movement that "speaks" without words.

Merleau-Ponty says, though, that gesture is not simply a physical movement, but what ability has been accorded the human body to communicate and to transcend its physical core. "The sense of the gesture," he says, "is not contained in the gesture as a physical or physiological phenomenon. The sense of the word is not contained in the word as a sound. Rather, it is the definition of the human body to appropriate, in an indefinite series of discontinuous acts, meaningful cores that transcend and transfigure its natural powers. This act of transcendence is initially found in the acquisition of a behavior, and then in the silent communication of the gesture: the body opens itself to a new behavior and renders that behavior intelligible to external observers through the same power" (*PP*, 199). Essential here is the notion of the audience, those "external observers." When he says that "the sense of the gestures is not given but rather understood, which is to say taken up by an act of the spectator" (*PP*, 190), he argues, rather, that the gesture means nothing until it is not just received by the audience but reacted to by the audience. That is, a gesture only has meaning when what it indicates, such as "please sit down," is followed by someone taking a seat—a person seeing the gesture, understanding its direction, and physically responding to it.

Because of this interrelationship between the physical gestural act and the corresponding response that actually gives meaning to it, the gesture itself becomes a part of experience. Merleau-Ponty says: "The sense of the gesture thus 'understood' is not behind the gesture, it merges with the structure of the world that the gesture sketches out and that I take up for myself" (*PP*, 192). "I take up" the gesture because it is a part of the full experience of perception; that is, it is one component of the array of perceptions.

What is important here is the approach to language in terms of gesture, that language is just another gesture, something done with the body to convey meaning. "Speech is a gesture," Merleau-Ponty argues, "and its signification is a world" (*PP*, 190). He goes on to talk about poetic language as a type of linguistic gesture: "If we consider only the conceptual and final sense of words, it is true that the verbal form . . . seems arbitrary. This would no longer hold if we took the emotional sense of the word into account, what we have above called its gestural sense, which is essential in poetry, for example. We would then find that words, vowels, and phonemes are so many ways of singing the world, and that they are destined to represent objects, not through an objective resemblance . . . but because they are extracted from them, and literally express their emotional essence" (*PP*, 193). Poetic language, from this standpoint, does not simply convey literal meaning but what is embedded and transported within it, a critical emotional component. The poetic gesture is, therefore, a nearly nonlinguistic gesture that tells its audience to feel some kind or kinds of emotions.[5]

This notion of emotion as an integral fusion within poetic language might be why the poem refers to it as "serpentine," too—that the gesture producing it is tangled and at once entangled, hard to comprehend as yet another perception contributing to experience, imbricated with emotion, a response to what is perceived.

The poem "Clepsydra" becomes a gesture expressing the meaning of perception and experience in the form of an articulation, but it is an articulation that expresses the consciousness of the inadequacy of itself, not just of the moment but of the fact of its instantaneous obsolescence through the perpetual "drip" of time. This poem, as well, in this sweep of experience, pursues and develops elements of phenomenology. I will not pretend that Ashbery had phenomenology in mind as he wrote this poem, but more often than not it is almost as if he had a manual of its principles in front of him as he wrote. This chapter will, therefore, lay out many of these principles as they appear in the poem. It will not, however, conduct a line-by-line analysis of the poem through this lens. Ashbery said himself that his poetry resists paraphrase;[6] treading down the path of this poem as it lays out its "drips" of experience does not lead to a coherent reading. It is essential to note, however, the paradox of this poem and of Ashbery's poetry in general: his urge is for order, to find and/or make order out of experience, but the poetry reflects the impossibility of achieving that order in anything more than an entirely momentary manner.

Part of this impossibility is due to the condition that perceptions available at any particular moment are enfolded perceptions, previously encountered intentions, that flow up into the moment, the field of the present, to merge present and past without call to memory per se. Ashbery says that in poetry in general, "[t]here are no themes or subjects in the usual sense except the very broad one of an individual consciousness confronting or confronted by a world of external phenomena. The work is a very complex but, I hope, clear and concrete transcript of the impressions left by these phenomena on that consciousness. The outlook is Romantic. . . . Characteristic devices are ellipses, frequent changes of tone, voice (that is, the narrator's voice), point of view, to give an impression of flux."[7] This description of the "individual consciousness confronting or confronted by a world of external phenomena" is clearly phenomenological at root, the notion that perception shapes consciousness and that poetry comes out of that experience.

Ashbery's poetry is therefore about what he is experiencing as he experiences all of it, that "flux" of impressions.[8] The resulting poetry is, as Richard Kostelanetz describes it, "definitely indefinite," for, he says, "it is meant to reflect the difficulty of living, the ever-changing, minute adjustments that go on around us and which we respond to from moment to moment—the difficulty of living in passing time, which is both difficult and automatic, since we all somehow manage it."[9] This "definitely indefinite" "flux" is indeterminate by its very nature.

In Kostelanetz's article on him that appeared in the *New York Times Magazine* in 1976, Ashbery establishes that he sees "Clepsydra" not just in terms of time but in terms of phenomenology, of how consciousness arrives, and of how it links to transient experience. Kostelanetz writes, for example: "In 'Clepsydra,' one of his last Parisian poems, he remembers 'feeling for the first time a strong unity in a particular poem. After my analytic period, I wanted to get into a synthetic period. I wanted to write a new kind of poetry after my dismembering of language. Wouldn't it be nice, I said to myself, to do a long poem that would be a long extended argument, but would have the beauty of a single word? "Clepsydra" is really a meditation on how time feels as it is passing. The title means a water clock as used in ancient Greece and China. There are a lot of images of water in that poem. It's all of a piece, like a stream.'"[10] The stream metaphor links the idea of the water clock and its connection with time to the length of that argument, the "flow" of words over the course of the poem and throughout experience.

This water theme is most apparent at a core moment of the poem, when a fountain emerges, but it is not visible to the eye: "An invisible fountain continually destroys and refreshes the previsions" (89). Time becomes here a constant and ever-replenishing circulation of future "previsions" into the present and through to the past, while perception, as well, circulates perpetually between the internal and the external, the present and the past. Perception derives, therefore, from dialectical experience that avoids, and in fact, rejects, Cartesianism, through the intermersion of interior and exterior, past and present, sense and perception.

Phenomenology is clearly based on this dialectic.[11] Samuel Mallin describes, for instance, the "dialectic between the two sides of a situation. In order to understand or experience one side, one must take the other into consideration."[12] And while phenomenology is based on a dialectic, it rejects dualism. The two sides of experience fold into each other, intertwining. This is why Merleau-Ponty uses analogies like fabric, mesh, and weaving.[13]

Merleau-Ponty describes this intermersion as not simply being our body or our sensory capabilities reaching out to whatever or whoever is not our body, but, as shown in chapter 1, as "a sort of dehiscence [that] opens my body in two, and because between my body looked at and my body looking, my body touched and my body touching, there is overlapping or encroachment.... [W]e must say that things pass into us as well as we into the things" (*VI*, 123). In this "intercorporeal being" (*VI*, 143) that we are, he argues, "we situate ourselves in ourselves *and* in the things, in ourselves *and* in the other, at the point where, by a sort of *chiasm*, we become the others and we become world" (*VI*, 160, emphasis in the original).

The poem is based on a series of dialectics, too, that it pulls together and merges, using circular or flowing tropes. These dialectics (or, in a structuralist turn, oppositions) include the visible and invisible and the light and dark.

Water, as a critical component of the water clock and the invisible fountain, becomes one of the elements to form the meshing of perception. Other essential elements of perception and phenomenology that recur in this poem include time, the horizon, and the effort to articulate meaning.

At the time of his death in 1961 at the age of fifty-three, Merleau-Ponty left unfinished what many philosophers agree would have been a work representing a serious shift in his philosophical approach and in philosophy in general. It was far enough along to be gathered together, along with relevant notes and letters, into the volume titled *The Visible and the Invisible*. There is a clear link in his thinking between the invisible of the inner world of the individual and the visible, perceptible, world of the body, what is apparent to the senses, what has potential for meaning-making in the field of presence; and it is in this link that we make that meaning, that we come to an understanding of experience. In *The Visible and the Invisible*, for example, Merleau-Ponty argues: "[M]y body, which is one of the visibles, sees itself also and thereby makes itself the natural light opening its own interior to the visible, in order for the visible there to become my own landscape, realizing . . . the miraculous promotion of Being to 'consciousness'" (*VI*, 118). However, even if that link between interior and exterior fields is established, what comes out of them—meaning, order, understanding—is not visible. "Meaning is *invisible*," Merleau-Ponty says, "but the invisible is not the contradiction of the visible: the visible itself has an invisible inner framework (*membrure*), and the in-visible is the secret counterpart of the visible, it appears only within it. . . . [O]ne cannot see it there and every effort to *see it there* makes it disappear, but it is *in the line* of the visible, it is its virtual focus, it is inscribed with it (in filigree)" (*VI*, 215, emphasis in the original). Here again, while he relies on the dialectic of the visible and the invisible to set up his conception of how senses evolve into perception, he at once undermines the binary by suggesting that the "membrane" between them is so close to being visible that it is nearly tangible.

Set up within this dialectic is a continual reverberation between the visible and the invisible, a membrane crossing, and it is through this intermersion that Merleau-Ponty is able to pull language into the realms of both the visible and the invisible:

[S]o also, if my words have a meaning, . . . it is because that organization [of the "systematic organization" of language], like the look, refers back to itself: the operative Word is the obscure region whence comes the instituted light, as the muted reflection of the body upon itself is what we call natural light. As there is a reversibility of the seeing and the visible, and as at the point where the two metamorphoses cross what we call perception is born, so also there is a reversibility of the speech and what it signifies; the signification is what comes to seal, to close, to gather up the multiplicity of the physical, physiological, linguistic means of elocution, to contract them into one sole act, as the vision comes to complete the aesthesiological body. And, as the visible takes hold of the look which has unveiled it and which forms a part of it, the signification rebounds upon its own means, it annexes to itself the speech that becomes an object of science, it antedates itself by a retrograde movement which is never completely belied—because already, in opening up the horizon of the nameable and of the sayable, the speech acknowledged that it has its place in that horizon; because no locutor speaks without making himself in advance allocutary, *be it only for himself*; because with one sole gesture he closes the circuit of his relation to himself and that of his relation to the others and, with the same stroke, also sets himself up as *delocutary*, speech of which one speaks: he offers himself and offers every word to a universal Word. (*VI*, 154, emphasis in the original)

This quotation is long and complex and bears close analysis. Merleau-Ponty is arguing that language operates through much the same process as perception and that, in fact, like perception, it enables, if not order itself, the ability to conceive of order as a possibility. Essential to note here is how Merleau-Ponty equates speech and its intentions with sense and perception, that there is a continual "reversibility" between speech and what it is trying to articulate. Here, too, Merleau-Ponty does not simply draw parallels between articulation and perception but aligns them as two knitted human functions, both with "horizons" of access, both requiring "gestures" for completion. Through articulation, he suggests, we "close the circuit," a circular metaphor of this persistent reverberation between what has been said and saying it anew, this continual interior-exterior passage between what is inside of us and what surrounds us.

It is because of this perpetual and insistent reciprocation that

Merleau-Ponty refers to poetry as "essentially a modulation of existence" (*PP*, 152). Language, particularly that of poets and philosophers, he argues, "[effects] the mediation between [the] as yet unspeaking intention and words. . . . Organized signs have their immanent meaning, which does not arise from the 'I think' but from the 'I am able to'" (*S*, 88). Poetic language becomes, therefore, a gesture of meaning, one that is recognizable but never exactly the same, one instance to the next.

Ashbery recognizes this shifting in articulation in "Clepsydra," as shown, for example, in the earlier quoted passage, this "Gesture which hides the truth behind a congruent / Message, [and] is, in fact, / Tearing it from limb to limb this very moment" (21–23), for "each moment / Of utterance is the true one; likewise none are true" (19). By truth I suggest that he is referring to accuracy of articulation. One might be close to accuracy at the instant of composition, but even at the moment of articulation, existence has shifted and warped the match between sense and meaning through articulation. As well, truth is not attainable, for it is never possible to penetrate that membrane between the visible and the invisible to achieve a perfect union between interior and exterior existences, as interrelated as they are. "Expression," Merleau-Ponty says, "is never total" (*S*, 89); it can never completely encapsulate experience. It is "stammering," as "Clepsydra" says (203).

"Clepsydra" goes so far as to reach back to the beginning of language. Once language was established, it became possible for individuals to face a situation, check back on its previous existence, and make the choice of running with what they had in that past formation or conjuring a new form of expression. However, there was a time when a repository of situations did not exist. "Clepsydra" approaches this in the following manner:

> But there was no statement
> At the beginning. There was only a breathless waste,
> A dumb cry shaping everything in projected
> After-effects orphaned by playing the part intended for them,
> Though one must not forget that the nature of this
> Emptiness, these previsions,
> Was that it could only happen here, on this page held
> Too close to be legible, sprouting erasures, except that they
> Ended everything in the transparent sphere of what was

> Intended only a moment ago, spiraling further out, its
> Gesture finally dissolving in the weather. (94–103)

In a situation where no articulation is possible, no meaning is possible, either. The poem links the quality of inarticulation with the artform of poetry, a type of writing that cannot always be deciphered; in this indecipherability, words "sprout erasures" and dissolve themselves as they appear on the page. In this state of inarticulation, perceptions—sense projected intentionally outward—cannot culminate in meaning or in meaningful expression. The "gesture" of articulation "dissolves" like the "erasures" of the text.

Gestures in a time beyond the commencement of linguistic structures are less "transparent," if not less ephemeral, for the poem describes "A moment that gave not only itself, but / Also the means of keeping it, of not turning to dust / Or gestures somewhere up ahead / But of becoming complicated like the torrent / In new dark passages, tears and laughter which / Are a sign of life, of distant life in this case" (125–30). This moment becomes a part of the repository of existence, one that is "complicated" in the constant state of new experience, both present and previsioned.

In the earlier quoted long passage from *The Visible and the Invisible*, Merleau-Ponty says, "in opening up the horizon of the nameable and of the sayable, the speech acknowledged that it has its place in that horizon" (*VI*, 154). When Merleau-Ponty talks about horizons, he is referring to the extent of the span of our senses. We can only see so far, or hear so far, or smell so far, and so on. The circle of the horizon has within it our experiences, including our articulations. The horizontal horizon is this span of senses; the vertical one is our act of garnering meaning out of those senses via our repository of the past. "In regaining the 'vertical' world or existence," Merleau-Ponty says,

> we learn about a dimension in which ideas also obtain their true solidity. They are the secret axes or (as Stendhal said) the "pilings" of our spoken words. Ideas are the centers of our gravitation, this very definite void which the vault of language is built around, and which has actual existence only in the weight and counterweight of stones. But are the visible things of the visible world constructed any differently? They are always behind what I see of them, as horizons, and what we call

visibility is this very transcendence. No thing, no side of a thing, shows itself except by actively hiding the others, denouncing them in the act of concealing them. To see is a matter of principle to see further than one sees, to reach a latent existence. The invisible is the outline and the depth of the visible. (S, 20)

We cannot see the elements existing within the span of the vertical horizon, therefore. Our ability to perceive them comes out of the transcendence beyond the visible toward meaning.

Part of what is under consideration in "Clepsydra" are horizons. Because of its opening question, "Hasn't the sky?," the poem calls immediately to the span of the sky, to where its limits might be and to where the horizons curtail it. Through the course of the poem, the horizon and its bounds resurface and reinforce the extent and compass of perception. Another clear reference to horizon in the poem is the landscape, what is visible to the eye, literally "shaped land" or a representation of the condition of the land. In addition to an early reference to "landscape" (6), the poem turns later to the detached quality of the landscape: "in an empty yet personal / Landscape, which has the further advantage of being / What surrounds without insisting" (110). This stretch of land "surrounds" us in a neutral, nonintentional manner.

The horizon, however, has clearly demarcated boundaries, set by that "circumference now alight / With ex-possibilities become present fact" (248–49). The phrase "now alight" indicates that the vision is of the present and that it now has illumination. The horizon can shift its breadth according to the time of day, therefore, with greater visibility "possible in the widening angle of / The day" (153–54). This metaphorical shaping of the day is not accidental, for with the angle comes a geometric organization of the space delineated by the horizon, matched with the later "acute / Angles of the rooms" (240–41), an interior space, but one that also curbs visibility.

Scale can also shift over time, rendering some things more or less visible than they were a moment ago. The poem describes the loss of sight as "It had reduced that other world, / The round one of the telescope, to a kind of very fine powder or dust / So small that space could not remember it" (141–43). The "it" referred to here is the "contract" (138), the "formal agreement" (135), that we make with each other and with ourselves to take sensory elements and understand them more or less in accord. "[It] was / Like," the poem says, "standing at the edge of a harbor early on a summer morning / With the discreet shadows cast by the water all around / And a feeling, again, of emptiness, but of richness in the way / The whole thing is organized, on what a miraculous scale, / Really what is meant by a human level, with the figures of giants / Not too much bigger than the men who have come to petition them" (118–24). Scale here is how the "giants" come to appear as close to the same size as these men, revealing its inconsistency and, at once, its radius out to the horizon of the sea.

There is a double effort here between the linear geometry of vanishing perspective and the spherical concerns involving π. Perspective is apparent in "lines contracting into a plane" (42), "although each tapered / Into the distant surrounding night" (70–71), and "the way / A telescope protects its view of distant mountains / And all they include" (107). Each of these instances, but particularly the latter one, explores the extent of visibility and, therefore, horizon. Even with its ability to take visibility much further, the telescope only allows us to see so far. The sphere presents itself not just in the sky of the primary force of the poem, this "transparent sphere" (102), but in the movement of the stars: "As though [the stars'] round time were only the reverse / Of some more concealable, vengeful purpose to become known / Once its result had more or less established the horizon" (78–81). This "round time" is therefore setting up the span of the horizon.

Steven Strogatz talks about π in an article in the *New Yorker* as "[putting] infinity within reach" and providing the "order inherent in a perfect circle."[14] He also describes as embodied in π the "tension between order and randomness," and to some degree, this is the concern of phenomenology, that sensory input is random in nature. We might put together a series of inputs, so that when we hear a rustle in the leaves overhead, we know that an acorn is about to slam into our head, but we do not know exactly when we will hear a truck drive by or when the odor of its exhaust will reach our nose. We compile these instances and try to make sense of them, but there is always a force at work to dismantle this perfect spherical order.

At root, therefore, perception is incomplete. When Merleau-Ponty says that it is intentional, these intentions are not always wholehearted. The poem talks about "inten[tions]" (102), but they are only "half-meant, half-perceived" (12), and they are never adequate, for "the little / That was present, the miserable totality / Mustered at any given moment" (55–57) does not achieve a totality that is not miserable and that can last more than an instant. It is "as though a smallest / Distant impulse had rendered the whole surface ultra-sensitive" (163–64) so that senses can register sensible information, but an "impulse" is not a focused intention; it is, rather, an urge that is closer to a whim.

Time is crucial to the function of perception, while at once being its nemesis in perpetually undoing what perception has been gained. Interestingly, even though the primary metaphor for this poem is the time clock, it is not as essential in terms of time passing as it is in terms of how the passage of time makes meaning impossible to grasp, as shown in the quotation at the start of this chapter. Elements of perception surface over time but become components of the agglomeration of perceptions, for these "pieces / Are seen as parts of a spectrum, independent / Yet symbolic of their staggered times of arrival" (28–30). This time is "furthered" (64) and "divide[d]" (65), not in contradistinction to the flow of a stream or of the fountain in the poem, but considered as well as the separate droplets of the water clock: "He was out of it of course for having lain happily awake / On the tepid fringes of that field or whatever / Whose center was beginning to churn darkly, but even more for having / The progression of minutes by accepting them, as one accepts drops of rain / As they form a shower" (210–14). This field, this situation, could have come out of Merleau-Ponty's work, with the notion of time passing and shifting the field of perception, but not too quickly, just individual drops at a time.

People find themselves struggling, however, because they are "darting from / Untruth to willed moment, scarcely called into being / Before it swells" (16). "Dart" suggests that the urge for truth forces compulsive shifting away from inadequate meaning to an intentional focus on another instant.[15] The pronoun "it" in this quotation, what is growing, is ostensibly the reply to the question that opens the poem, but I would also suggest that the reply to a question is a coming to meaning, "scarcely called into being" and made meaningful before expanding into other possible articulations.

The opening question creates the possibility of an explicit other in the poem, but this reply confirms it. Perception not only focuses on objects that are exterior to our bodies; a major focus is other people. Just as we interact with what is available to our senses outside of us to the point of confluence, we experience conjoining with other people. "When I speak or understand," Merleau-Ponty argues,

I experience that presence of others in myself or of myself in others which is the stumbling-block of the theory of intersubjectivity, I experience that presence of what is represented which is the stumbling-block of the theory of time, and I finally understand what is meant by Husserl's enigmatic statement, "Transcendental subjectivity is intersubjectivity." To the extent that what I say has meaning, I am a different "other" for myself when I am speaking; and to the extent that I understand, I no longer know who is speaking and who is listening. (S, 97)

In coming to meaning, in articulating perception, there is such complete convergence between interior and exterior, self and other, that who is doing the perception becomes elusive to the point where, he suggests, it is as if we become two entities that perceive: one that is our body and interiority and the other that is our awareness of ourselves as if from outside us.

Important to phenomenology, too, is the notion of interchange between people, largely carried out through expression, as described by Merleau-Ponty:

There is, in particular, one cultural object that will play an essential role in the perception of others: language. In the experience of dialogue, a common ground is constituted between me and another; my thought and his form a single fabric, my words and those of my interlocutor are called forth by the state of the discussion and are inserted into a shared operation of which neither of us is the creator. Here there is a being-shared-by-two, and the other person is no longer for me a simple behavior in my transcendental field, nor for that matter am I a simple behavior in his. We are, for each other, collaborators in perfect reciprocity: our perspectives slip into each other, we coexist through a single world. (*PP*, 370)

Interaction becomes, therefore, a creation of an interchanging space, where the interlocutors merge with each other to form a new approach to perspective. The poem alters its point of view to lay out explicitly that there is a plural point of view and a dialogue, largely in the form of question and answer, started by the opening line of the poem. "We hear so much," the poem lays out, "Of its further action that at last it seems that / It is we, our taking it into account rather, that are / The reply that prompted the question" (42–45). The pronoun "it," here, refers to the light, which I will explore later in this chapter. The point of essence at this moment is that the "you" of the opening of the poem has resolved into a plural pronoun, and because it is the first-person plural, it indicates more than one person doing something together. In this case, this mutual activity involves "taking it into account," which is a description of using the senses to consider the declining light and using those senses and their awareness of this change to come to a consideration of the meaning of this moment.

As the narrator is "preparing to continue the dialogue into / Those mysterious and near regions that are / Precisely the time of its being furthered" (62–64), the poem emphasizes the function of the dialogue developed in the poem through the commencing question and the corresponding responses that recur throughout. It is through dialogue, a manifestation of the interconnectedness between the perceiver and the perceived, that it is possible for their roles to merge and interchange. This interaction is not simply a meeting of persons, but a conjoining, a crossing.

At this moment in the poem, too, there is an assessment and reassessment of perception, that rather than simply flowing to us, we consider each one as we access it, but at that time we also think about what perceptions might have risen to us in the past. Merleau-Ponty refers to this back-and-forth as "cross-checking": "The supposed conditions of perception become anterior to perception itself only when, rather than describing the perceptual phenomenon as a primary opening up to an object, we presuppose around it a milieu in which all of the developments and all of the cross-checking that will be performed by analytical perception are already inscribed, and in which all of the norms of actual perception will be justified—a realm of truth, a *world*. By presupposing this realm, we strip perception of its essential function, which is to establish or to inaugurate knowledge, and we view perception through the lens of its results" (*PP*, 17). Perception becomes, then, not simply a response of the senses to an external phenomenon, but a continual assessment of them; we can only perceive from the perspective of that assessment.

This "cross-checking" is apparent in the poem, not just in assessing what perceptions have previously been stored and enculturated but in moving between interior and exterior being. The poem says, therefore, "But the condition / Of those moments of timeless elasticity and blindness / Was being joined secretly so / That their paths would cross again and be separated / Only to join again in a final assumption rising like a shout" (81–85). The chiasm established here is that of joining and pulling apart in perception. We essentially leave ourselves in order to "see" ourselves as if from outside of us. It is at those instances when we step out of time and access what we cannot see in order to attain meaning. Meaning is not a visible entity.

The poem also demonstrates perception as the act of achieving our own selves through the other, through what and/or who is not us. "In this way any direction taken was the right one," it says, "Leading first to you, and through you to / Myself that is beyond you and which is the same thing as space" (201–2). We arrive at our own selves by moving out of ourselves and toward the other. This movement serves to permit us to see our own selves as if they were not us. In moving outward and looking back, we establish space, as the poem says, a spatial orientation away and back toward our interior beings.

What we hope to achieve from this passage out and away from ourselves and back toward our own persons is a sense of who we might be and how we might look in the sense of being perceptible and visible; that is, what we might gain in meaning of existence and our own persons. The poem closes by saying:

> What is meant is that this distant
> Image of you, the way you really are, is the test
> Of how you see yourself, and regardless of whether or not
> You hesitate, it may be assumed that you have won, that this
> Wooden and external representation
> Returns the full echo of what you meant
> With nothing left over, from that circumference now alight
> With ex-possibilities become present fact, and you
> Must wear them like clothing, moving in the shadow of
> Your single and twin existence . . . (242–51)

Here it is clear that we cannot grasp our own selves as they really are. We only grasp this "wooden and external representation." It is not an accurate depiction, but only an "echo." It is not who we really are, but just a surface layer, and, like clothing, a concealing and arbitrary presentation of our identities.

Contrasted with the "timeless elasticity and blindness" (82) is the water clock, after which the poem is named. It recurs every so often in the poem in the form of breath ("the very breath so / Honorably offered, and accepted in the same spirit" [113–14]) and drops gathering in rainfall ("Whose center was beginning to churn darkly, but even more for having / The progression of minutes by accepting them, as one accepts drops of rain / As they form a shower" [210–14]). I would like to argue, however, that the extended metaphor of the water clock in the poem is essential in how it makes time material, just as the language of the poem becomes material in articulating experience. The water clock makes time tangible in bringing all senses to bear: the sound of each drop of water, the physical and therefore visible presence of each drop, the percussive feel as each drop hits a surface, the smell of dampness and the minerals dissolved in the water, perhaps, too, the smell of the water containers and whatever mossy lives the water supports.[16] The overlay of the persistent and regularly paced dripping on the stream of thought and experience sets up the poem as a phenomenological experiment.

The colon, a persistent force in the poem, is one method through which Ashbery renders language into material form.[17] There are nine colons in the poem (lines 8, 23, 26, 35, 105, 156, 158, 179, 205). The colon is most often used, in the current day, to set up a list in a sentence, but it bears historical links to poetry, as it was the term for parts of a "rhythmical period united under a principal ictus," or metrical stress.[18] However, the term derives from the Greek word for limb and also means "to bend, crooked."[19] The colon is often used in philosophy to set up propositions or precede an explanation or example, and while the poetry aspect underlies Ashbery's prosodic 10–14 syllable lines, it is the philosophical approach that takes precedence in this poem. Rather than providing clear examples, however, the post-colon sections of the poem are largely bent away from strict logic. In this poem, Ashbery purports to pursue the strict logic of the philosophical argument, partially signaled by the colons, but he takes a crooked path through it. That is, the colon prepares us for an equal measure on either end of it, a proposition balanced with an explanation, but our expectations for balance are not met. The two halves of the sentence do not map to each other; nor does the second half explain or provide an example for the first.[20] The colon, therefore, purports to clarify or emphasize, but instead, in this poem, it obfuscates meaning.

In relying on colons so extensively in this poem, Ashbery also creates the potential for access to human existence, though. In his discussion of Martin Heidegger's approach to the colon, David Farrell Krell argues:

> Heidegger distinguishes between the colon that merely introduces an assertion, opening up to some sort of statement, and the colon that *gathers up* all that is to be said. In this second, essential instance, Heidegger says of the colon that "the tone of the concluding verse gathers itself in the word 'renunciation,' that is to say, in the word whose colon finally gathers up the ultimate revelation of 'Das Wort.'" Further, Heidegger expressly concedes that the colon, as a mark of punctuation, is a characteristic of *writing* rather than of speech: the colon marks the inevitable *writing* of the saying of renunciation. Finally, the colon gathers nothing less than the essence of language into the language of essence.[21]

Ashbery's focus in this poem is on "[gathering] up all that is to be said" and, by use of the colon, on accessing the "revelation" of this transformation of the "essence of language into the language of essence," as Krzysztof Ziarek calls it, from the "being of language" to the "language of being."[22] The colon makes it possible, through the written codes, to move through to questions of being as opposed to simple description. In this transformation from existence through language to how to express existence, therefore, Ashbery inverts the normal setup-explanation/example of the colon progression, launching the poem in the direction of essence through the placement of the conceptual expression after the colon.[23] "[T]he windows no longer speak / Of time," the poem says, "but are themselves, transparent guardians you invented for what there was to hide" (233–35). Windows become here the visible essence of language. They are barriers to accurate linguistic representation; in articulating, the poet comes close to accurate depiction and can almost see it, but can never quite attain it.[24] Like these windows, as Jasmine Kitses argues, "[a]s an inconspicuous mark of directness and clear speaking, the colon [points] to transparency, promising it—yet its spacing . . . reminds us of the stain language itself leaves behind."[25] "I see myself in this totality," says the poem, "and meanwhile / I am only a transparent diagram" (190–91), as if to say that the act of perception takes us close to a true and complete view of ourselves, but what is, like the windows, only transparent and only a schematic as opposed to a depiction of the real thing.

If accurate depiction is impossible to achieve, so is access to order and thereby to meaning. Merleau-Ponty says that "[the world] of the healthy, civilized, adult human being strives for ... coherence. Yet the crucial point here is that he does not *attain* this coherence: it remains an idea, or limit, which he never actually manages to reach.... He is invited to look at himself without indulgence, to rediscover within himself the whole host of fantasies, dreams, patterns of magical behavior and obscure phenomena which remain all-powerful in shaping both his private and public life and his relationships with other people. These leave his knowledge of the natural world riddled with gaps, which is how poetry creeps in" (*WP*, 73).

The poem states the desire for meaning and order, this coherence, but recognizes the impossibility of the achievement of that goal, or rather, perhaps, that in that effort, what we end up with is a mess, "the welter / Of a future of disunion just to abolish confusion" (66–67). The tone of the poem creates a general sense of hopelessness about the entire endeavor. This is a world in which there is "no luck" (32), "sadness" (104), and "defeat" (79). The effort to attain this goal leaves us spent: the "last word is exhausted" (49), as in consumed but also as in completely worn out; and "this / Existence saps your own" (237–38) as if to say at once that Being is enervating and that Being as experienced through moving outside ourselves and intermingling with that exterior world diminishes what we are. All that is left is both deeply unhappy and meager—"the little / That was present, the miserable totality" (56)—and just not the truth: "[N]one are true" (19), the poem says, and our perception, in spite of itself, "hides the truth" (21). What we are left with is instead some kind of "dream" (46–48) or "mirage" (12, 55), as suggested above by Merleau-Ponty. We never, the poem says, "[get] any closer to the basic / Principle operating behind it than to the distracted / Entity of a mirage" (10–12).

Still, even though it demonstrates extended and repeated anguish about this effort to attain the goal of the comprehension of existence, the poem maintains hope in that effort, a hope that encourages the narrator to pursue this goal in the face of sure failure. Expression of this optimism appears most strongly toward the end of the poem:

There should be an invariable balance of
Contentment to hold everything in place, ministering

> To stunted memories, helping them stand alone
> And return to the world, without ever looking back at
> What they might have become, even though in doing so they
> Might just once have been the truth that, invisible,
> Still surrounds us like the air and is the dividing force
> Between our slightest steps and the notes taken on them.
> It is because everything is relative
> That we shall never see in that sphere of pure wisdom and
> Entertainment much more than groping shadows of an incomplete
> Former existence so close it burns like the mouth that
> Closes down over all your effort like the moment
> Of death, but stays, raging and burning the design of
> Its intentions into the house of your brain, until
> You wake up alone, the certainty that it
> Wasn't a dream your only clue to why the walls
> Are turning on you and why the windows no longer speak
> Of time but are themselves transparent guardians you
> Invented for what there was to hide. (216–35)

In saying, "there should be," the poem indicates that there might not be this "invisible balance of / Contentment to hold everything in place," but yet it emphasizes that we need to reconcile ourselves to those "stunted memories" and not worry too much whether at any point or another we might have had access to the truth. As well, this section states clearly the belief that this truth exists, that we cannot grasp it, but that it is worth the repeated yet Sisyphean effort to attain it, this "sphere of pure wisdom and / Entertainment" that we glimpse but cannot hang onto.

The "raging and burning" demonstrate the intensity of this drive to achieve this truth, as do other features in the poem, in particular a quiet emphasis on mapping, on the intentional organization of a disorganized space. "The past is yours," the poem says, "to keep invisible if you wish / But also to make absurd elaborations with / And in this way prolong your dance of non-discovery / In brittle, useless architecture that is nevertheless / The map of your desires" (168–72). Even though the individual might avoid self-discovery, in having a past replete with memory, no matter the circumvention of facing the truth, these elements from the past create this "map" of "desires," a form of organization that lays them all out in some kind of order. The poet turns to a blessing of a sort, in "may your years / Be the throes of what is even now exhausting itself / In one last effort to outwit us; it could only be a map / Of the world" (176–78). Essentially, "if only / You desire to arrange it this way" (174), it might take all that we have, but it is possible to create and access this "map / Of the world," a full-scale representation and delineation of the mess that is existence.[26]

Merleau-Ponty says that "[t]he unity of the object is established upon the presentiment of an imminent order that will, suddenly, respond to questions that are merely latent in the landscape" (*PP*, 18). The poem's opening question, "Hasn't the sky?," explicitly acts on exactly this principle. It seeks this "order" by mapping existence onto the landscape. As stated earlier, the sky also establishes the parameters for the horizon of perception. As well, it lays out a dialectic in the poem between light and dark, as a metaphor for the visible and the invisible, also inherent in "Clepsydra." Light is apparent in the sky (1, 24, 204), sunlight (2, 50, 54), day (154), the "recurring whiteness" (32), and in "the light of the stars / That drenched every instant of being" (76–77). In the "peculiar light of someone's / Purpose" (239–40), while light bears its luminescence reference, it also refers to a particular context, "peculiar" here in both senses of odd and particular.

Contrasting with light in this poem is a persistent turn to darkness and to the invisible. There is a direct shift from dark to light, for instance, in "keep its root in darkness until your / Maturity when your hair will actually be the branches / Of a tree with the light pouring through them" (195–97). Also, in its link to the sky, part of the "lightness" of the poem derives from "air" (8) and other transparent, so invisible, yet palpable essences of perception. The only thing that is true, says the poem, "is the bounding from air to air" (20). The "diagram" of existence is "transparent" (191), and "the windows . . . are themselves transparent guardians" (234–35).

The poem becomes, then, a litany of nonpresence, as the visible fades into imperceptibility. This "dissolving" (103), these "erasures" (100), meet "surprise at your absence" (60) and "the truth that, invisible, / Still surrounds us like the air and is the dividing force / Between our slightest steps and the notes taken on them" (221–23), and become "the invisible look of the distant / Ether" (188–89). Sound is lost here, too, in this "dumb cry" (95) that is "breathless" (94).

Supporting this emphasis on invisibility in the poem are various references to darkness and other situations impeding vision. Inferences with visibility include "steam" (5), "air hides the sky" (22), "dust" (34, 126, 142), and "upper shadows" (39). Just as the day expands and grows brighter in the concern for light in the poem, the day wanes, bringing with it less light and lower visibility, apparent in "the light / Has already gone from there too" (40–41), "the distant surrounding night" (71), "as darkness comes on" (110), "the light sinks into itself, becomes dark and heavy / Like a surface stained with ink" (155–56), "the toe of approaching night" (173), and "faces of evening" (253). Here, there is an "exclusion from the light of the stars" (76) and a "blindness" (72, 82).

This "blindness," in fact, this inability to perceive, makes it likely "that / Neither would ever see his way clear again" (71–74). These efforts to "see," according to the poem, are "half-meant, half-perceived" (12). "Half-meant" suggests intention; "half-perceived" suggests perception. Merleau-Ponty talks about how we perceive, these half-perceived instances and these half-meant ones, half-meant as in half-intended and half-considered. As shown previously, looking is an act of the visual sense; seeing is the perception gained by processing the sensory input and gaining meaning from it. It is, as he suggests, that "decisive moment of perception: the springing forth of a *true* and *precise* world. When reflection is equally capable of clarifying both its living inherence and its rational intention, it will be assured of having found the center of the phenomenon" (*PP*, 53).

Like the regular drips of the water clock that signal through sound and feel that a moment is passing, the poem turns to particular instances repeatedly. These "moments" (116, 125, 131) look into the past by "[boring] back into the centuries . . . and an old way of looking" (116–17) in acts of reflection. They are also, as potential components of that repository, not completely ephemeral: "A moment that gave not only itself, but / Also the means of keeping it, of not turning to dust / Or gestures somewhere up ahead / But of becoming complicated like the torrent / In new dark passages, tears and laughter which / Are a sign of life, of distant life in this case" (125–30). In so saying, the poem proposes that in "becoming complicated," a moment of perception will "not [turn] to dust / Or gestures" in the future but will instead become an element in the repository of the interior. Finally, too, the poem grants acceptance in the inadequacy of perception to gain complete understanding or meaning, this "calm / Of this true progression hardened into shreds / Of another kind of calm, returning to the conclusion, its premises / Undertaken before any formal agreement had been reached, hence / A writ that was the shadow of the colossal reason behind all this / Like a second, rigid body behind the one you know is yours" (132–37). We know that there is a "second, rigid body" that is the "real" one that we cannot access in this acknowledgment, and while we never stop trying to achieve true perception of it, we tolerate our failure to do so.

This "Thickness" of Time: Lyric, Time, and *Durée*

There are, traditionally, three types of poetry: epic, drama, and lyric,[27] and lyric has traditionally taken all poetry under its tent that does not fit into the categories of epic or drama. Elizabeth Willis distinguishes lyric from these other forms of poetry in its "privileging of sound over meaning; its difference in time signature; [and] its divergence from mimesis."[28] She shares with other critics an unquestioned acceptance of three other features of lyric poetry: it must be short, it must be in the present tense, and it refers to a "moment" of time.[29] Willis, in fact, determines the length of the lyric poem to be "under one hundred lines and usually less than fifty."[30] A large number of poems that are longer than that are categorized as lyric, however, since there is really nowhere else to put them. I recall distinctly having people refer to Susan Howe's poetry as lyric, for instance, when I do not think she has one example in her oeuvre that would come close to Willis's length requirement. Helen Vendler refers to John Ashbery's poetry as "intimate lyric,"[31] and Jonathan Culler, in *Theory of the Lyric*, devotes extensive attention to Ashbery's work in "This Room" and "Paradoxes and Oxymorons," but most of Ashbery's work is much heftier than these examples and much longer than Willis prescribes.

The problem becomes then, for me anyway, a question of what to do about these longer poems that are not necessarily in the present tense and that are clearly neither epic nor drama. One solution would of course be to create a new category, such as the "long poem," an approach addressed by multiple critics, Brian McHale and Lynn Keller among them.[32] I am, frankly, not sure if that is the direction that I would like to take here because I am not sure if length determines what poetry is trying to do (though it is clear that the length of a poem might have an impact on *how* the poem is getting there). So, rather than setting up a new category for poetry, or trying to cram poems into ill-fitting categories, I would like to think about what might be happening in these poems in terms of time, for I see the lyric "moment" as linked to time, but a time that might be too complex for the traditional lyric feature of brevity.[33]

There is an immediate tension when talking about time and any type of language, because language is sequential. While there is some flexibility in word order, too great a deviation from certain word order restrictions can lead to incomprehensibility. In her book on Emily Dickinson's poetry, for instance, Sharon Cameron talks about how poems require sequentiality "to achieve their meanings,"[34] yet at the same time she argues that "the poem is a sequence that conceals its progressions, or synthesizes them so that it appears a completion no process could have prepared for."[35] She does not exactly propose a paradox, that poems are sequential but not sequential, but argues rather that they need to hide this sequence in order, I believe, to reinforce their supposed focus on one concentrated moment, for, as she says, "the moment is to the lyric what sequence is to the story."[36]

However, I do not believe that it is possible to address just one moment, not for traditional lyric and certainly not for longer "lyrics," because of how time works, and specifically how the present functions. Similarly, the requirement that the lyric be written only in the present tense creates undue limitations, because the present is less about the now than about some kind of *durée*, or rather, less about the present than about presence. That is, the present is not a possible state, not only because of its reliance on what has come before it but also because of its inescapably ephemeral quality.

Rather than conceiving of the present as a static stage in the progress between the past and the future, Merleau-Ponty says that perception provides us with a "field of presence" (*PP*, 277). Michael Kelly explains this approach by suggesting: "Present speech casts a light which is not found in any merely 'possible' expression. It is an operation in our linguistic 'field of presence' which ... serves as our model for conceiving of them. Reflection is no longer the passage to a different order which reabsorbs the order of present things; it is first and foremost a more acute awareness of the way in which we are rooted in them."[37] That is, it is not just that we can use the present tense or behave in the present moment, but, and most importantly, we are conscious of this state, of being in the now and of being able to consider how we have gotten there. In his conception of the present as a "field of presence," Merleau-Ponty expands the idea of the moment so that it has spatial properties; in linking time to space, he permits inclusion in the "moment" of a broader range, a wealth even, of elements: our consciousness of what is apparent to our perception at an instant, our sense of our connection to these bits of perceptual information, our recognition of the incompleteness of these perceptions, and our channeling of all of these ephemeralities through the present instant.

Time is, therefore, the concretion of the present with the past, but also with the future, what Cameron refers to as "temporal fusion." She argues that these "fusions are a consequence of the way in which past and future rise up to meet the present on its own ground. Given the desire to frame the present in the stasis of perception, it is easy to see why the lyric confuses present tense with the presence that, distinguished from action or story, will bring them to a halt."[38] However, since, in spite of this desire for an instant in time, neither the present nor perception exist in anything close to a "static" state, there is no "halt," nor a present, but simply a myriad of perceptions that bring forth presence.

Phenomenology resists this notion of "fusion," therefore, in its interest in conceptualizing instants as less melded and more stratified. Because of this approach, Merleau-Ponty sees the instant as never singular but rather as a "series of presents." He conceives of "time, as a thrust and a passage toward a future," and because of that "thrust," it is "time, as a spread-out series of presents[,] [that] is the one affected; the affecting and the affected are identical because the thrust of time is nothing other than the transition from one present to another" (*PP*, 449). Time is, in this consideration, at once the force creating impact and the instance being impacted, creating impact through the shifts between the past, present, and future and being impacted by having to take in these ever-present and flickering elements. "Thrust," a word that he employs reasonably often in this context, is *poussée* in his original French;[39] it suggests force and movement, the movement of a mass of matter, as in a surge.

The impact of this "series of presents" is that the time of the present moment has a "thickness" (*PP*, 232). "If in being inscribed within me each present loses its flesh, if the pure memory into which it is changed is an invisible," Merleau-Ponty says, "then there is indeed a past, but no coinciding with it—I am separated from it by the whole thickness of my present; it is mine only by finding in some way a place in my present, in making itself present anew. As we never have at the same time the thing and the consciousness of the thing, we never have at the same time the past and the consciousness of the past" (*VI*, 122). As the present occurs—as we perceive—it dissolves, and the memory into which it is evolving also dissipates. These layers of perception intercede between our current perceptions, that is, presence, and previous ones. We can retrieve them, but only by reconstituting them. Bernhard Waldenfels explains this conception: "Thickness... means that time is compressed... and that the time layers superpose one another."[40] They "superpose," but yet they remain; the layers might stratify, but they do not dissipate into each other, always retaining some of their essential matter.

This thickness, therefore, is another instance of linking space to time, in giving time a dimension. The spatial dimensionality is, as well, connected to what Merleau-Ponty describes in *The Visible and the Invisible* as a transcendent moment when "the immersion in a Being in transcendence... contains an intentional reference which is not only from the past to the factual, empirical present, but also and inversely from the factual present to a dimensional present... where the past is 'simultaneous' with the present in the narrow sense. This *reciprocal* intentional reference marks the limit of the intentional analytic: the point where it becomes a philosophy of transcendence" (*VI*, 243–44). Intentionality is key in Merleau-Ponty's conception of perception as suggesting a purposeful act of turning toward what is external to our bodies; we focus out while retaining our sense of what is within us. Similarly, presence contains within itself the spatial relationship between the past's connection to the present and the present's connection to the past. It is "the past," he says, that "adheres to the present and not the *consciousness* of the past that adheres to the *consciousness* of the present" (*VI*, 244); that is, the interconnectivity between the present and the past is not related to our perceptions of either of them.

Because of this interconnectivity, it is always possible to discern the present in the past and the past in the present, so that the context of the present, of how it came about, is available, making it possible for "[e]ach moment of time [to give] itself as a witness to all the others. It shows, by taking place, 'how this was bound to happen' and 'how it will have ended'" (*PP*, 71). No "moment," therefore, exists in a vacuum; it must always retain within it reference not just to all other times but to those other times in their entirety.

What should be clear by now is that time is not an instant, some kind of snapshot of a moment in time, but both a meld of multiple presents and pasts with each other and a process of perception. The process is related to what Culler describes in reference to Heidegger and poetry, that "unconcealment of presencing of Being and the happening of Truth."[41] In the world of phenomenology, we come into Being, that is, into a sense of ourselves and our own existence, through our perceptions. Willis connects this complex of perception to lyric poetry: "The work of the modern and contemporary lyric is not to unify or commodify or even represent human experience but to stress language in such a way as to evoke an alternate experience for its readers, not an objective correlative to a universal experience but an engagement in the process of finding out."[42]

However, and ultimately constraining, we can never achieve this truth because we can never attain to an exhaustive presencing or unconcealment. Perception is never complete because we are unable to see all aspects or all sides of any one thing at any one instant in time. Because perception is never complete, gaps exist in both time and space. Phenomenology sets itself within this interspace. Cameron sees this space as multiple: "As the present is neither the past nor the future, as desire is not equivalent to the object of longing, as there is a space predicated between the landscape and the human subject who regards it, between language and what it hopes to word into being, so the same radical inequality is manifested between lyric speech and the voice or voices it represents."[43] Space exists here between times, the ideal and reality, the perceived and the perceiver, and the poem's words and the intentions for those words.

Waldenfels explains that it is the "chiasm of time [that] makes the present reappear with the past, the past with the present."[44] That is, it is as time intersects, where the future transforms into the present and the present evolves into the past, that the present "adheres" to the past, that these time frames do not replace each other but instead coexist. Kelly uses the term "dihescence" for this gap, as a way to emphasize that it is not merely an empty fissure, but that elements move into it and erupt out of it: "Time relates to itself, constitutes itself, in a dihescence—that is, a gaping or opening by divergence of parts, especially as a natural process; time is an auto-consolidating transcendence, which, like a 'fountain jet,' returns to itself in leaving itself."[45] The result of this rupture, according to Werner Wolf, is a "proliferation of gaps of meaning," that the incomplete particles of near-meaning never coalesce into truth or complete substance, never resolve, but simply accumulate.[46]

This endless fracture leads to a situation commonly reflected upon by the postmodernists, that in the desire to gain resolution in a context where it can never be achieved, a delay is created, a time-space gap in hope. In a recognition of this pause, Robert von Hallberg comments on how Mikhail Bakhtin imagined that poetry aims at a delayed response "in the subsequent speech or behavior of the listener," when the poem launches on its trajectory in such a way that no immediate return is possible.[47] It is, as David Morris and Kym Maclaren identify, a "[t]ime characterized by circularity, delay, and porosity."[48]

It is experience, the passing through of these presents, presences, and, ultimately, gaps, that, according to phenomenology, brings us the closest to meaning that is possible. "We are experiences," Merleau-Ponty argues, "thoughts that feel behind themselves the weight of the space, the time, the very Being they think, and which therefore, do not hold under their gaze a serial space and time nor the pure idea of series, but have about themselves a time and a space that exist by piling up, by proliferation, by encroachment, by promiscuity—a perpetual pregnancy, perpetual parturition, generative and generality (*VI*, 115). Merleau-Ponty is positing two main issues here: that space and time are interrelated and interconnected and that, therefore, there is a unity of time and space (that simultaneity), but that there is also at once a multiplicity and a sense of constant change. Merleau-Ponty identifies this "multiplicity of points or of 'heres' [that] can only, in principle, be constituted by an interlocking of experiences in which one of them is perpetually given as an object and that turns itself into the very heart of this space" (*PP*, 104). It is as if experiences are multiple and in flux, the cycling through them being their focus. This is, he says, a "literal simultaneity in space, simultaneity in the figurative sense in time . . . and the intertwining (*entrelacs*) of space and time" (*VI*, 117). Experience is, therefore, according to Merleau-Ponty, a constant movement through time and space: "[T]he 'synthesis' of time is a 'transition synthesis' and the movement of a life that unfolds, and the only way to actualize this life is to live it; time has no place, rather time carries itself along and launches itself forward. Time, as an indivisible thrust and as a transition, alone can make time as a successive multiplicity possible" (*PP*, 447).

What does this mean for the brevity of the lyric? I suggest that, given that the "moment" is now conceived in terms of its multiplicity, changeability, fluidity, and betweenness, a short poem will not be able to come close to the lyric intention. Rather, poems must have the time to present multiple perspectives, multiple perceptions, multiple interlinkings between the past and the present and the launchings into the future, and multiple essays into and out of and through those instances between the past and the present and those "thrusts" toward the future. Poems must create the thickness of presence, with its "interlacing" between time and space and between the past and the present. Rather than simply identifying a short poem by John Ashbery as a perfect example of a lyric, for instance, it is essential to look at all of his poems as lyrics, as lyrics of the truth trying to, as Vendler suggests, depict "[e]xperiential change . . . , one of Ashbery's two great moral subjects (love is the other)."[49]

Because of the sequential nature of language noted above, poets, or anyone using words for communication of any kind, must lay out one idea after another. Perceptions, therefore, follow each other, creating a string of experiences. These impressions are laid out, one over the other, through the course of the poem, creating these layers of presence that are compressed into a "field." In "Night," for example, all senses are activated: smell—"when I've / Smelled the smell of . . ."; sight—"a little / Light falls just on the patch"; sound—"Noise that thought came from his own leg"; touch—"Was grown chilly"; and taste—"There are numerous / Distinct flavors" (*CP*, 53-55).[50] The poem, like experience, becomes this "heap of detritus" (*CP*, 53) including flowers, alligators, fishing rods, more flowers, and prisons, creating "a reservoir / Of truth" (*CP*, 55). Perceptions, as well, are not just momentary snapshots, but are the effort to make sense of the whole by seeing "in the round."

Yet, as shown in "Sunrise in Suburbia," each effort, each "Banging of the shuttle," each "repeated [swipe] of the wind," is distinct from all others, and yet is always "intentional" (*CP*, 209).[51] We are "Never satisfied on the way" as we experience these sensory inputs: "[Our] eyes [register] the recent happenings as they advance through [us]" (*CP*, 209). These instances are, at least, singular, since "There is reasonable assurance in the way it is not seen again" (*CP*, 209). Each day is a new territory of unexperienced instants that we are hard pressed to decipher or make meaning out of: "A blank chart of each day moving into the premise of difficult visibility / And which is nowhere, the urge to nowhere" (*CP*, 209). And yet we have this "urge," this intentional force within us that is always pushing us to make sense of things, of these ongoing and perpetual perceptions, and "[asking] the question of this what is to be" (*CP*, 208).

Time is always shifting in "Sunrise in Suburbia," "a new mode . . . sunning into the past: . . . And back to the safe beginning, because it starts out / Once more, drawn to and fro in a warm current of breathing," the in-and-out flow of air like the here/now and past flow of time (*CP*, 208). This experience is impossible to comprehend: "It is all noticed before it is too late / But its immobility gives no comfort, only chapter headings and folio numbers / And it can go on being divine in itself / Neither treasured nor cast down in anger / For we cannot imagine the truth of it" (*CP*, 210). For the poet, and for those who attempt to articulate these perceptions, who "have translated the foreground of paths [of sensory experience] into quoted spaces," this experience is also idiosyncratic, individual for each of us, and "we [therefore] go separate ways" down our own paths of intentional efforts at sense-making.

Several poems by Ashbery also address the effort to amalgamate multiple perceptions for fuller and more complete "fields of presence," but also how these perceptions need to be adapted for the sequential constraints of language. Ashbery's poem "Definition of Blue," for instance, addresses these concerns explicitly.[52] Early on, the poem talks about perception in terms of "impetuses": "These different impetuses are received from everywhere / And are as instantly snapped back, hitting through the cold atmosphere / In one steady, intense line" (*CP*, 211). "Impetus" bears within in it Merleau-Ponty's notion of intention and the sense of time as a "thrust," a forceful move through myriad instances and perceptions. The passive voice here suggests that the perceiver is simply a stationary, or relatively stationary, recipient of perceptions, something like a satellite dish or an aerial. The "[snapping] back" is akin to the transformation through the act of poetic composition of perceptions into language; the poet must gather together all of these perceptions and align them into a series of words that appears in the form of this "steady, intense line."

As imperfect as this transformation must be, it replaces the perceptions; only the words remain. The poem refers to the metamorphosis of perception into language as "packaging" when it says, "There is no remedy for this 'packaging' which has supplanted the old sensations" (*CP*, 211). If these multiple perceptions are to move us in the direction of the knowledge of our own existence and a sense of meaning out of that existence, we must make do with their imperfections and with the imprecision with which we turn perception into language. "The most that can be said for them further," the poem says, "Is that erosion produces a kind of dust or exaggerated pumice / Which fills space and transforms it, becoming a medium / In which it is possible to recognize oneself" (*CP*, 211). This "field of presence," of multiple perceptions, therefore, is a space of drifting elements that language "transforms" into a "medium" that we can access and comprehend, that we can use in our efforts to come into Being.

The more perceptions we receive and process, the more precise the composite is that forms out of them. The poem refers to the final product as a "portrait" out of time or space, and that is essentially what is occurring in the "field of presence," that time is compressed and space is deferred in order to remove the instant of time or the sense of time passing so that it is possible to experience presence: "Each new diversion adds its accurate touch to the ensemble, and so / A portrait, smooth as glass, is built up out of multiple corrections / And it has no relation to the space or time in which it was lived. / Only its existence is a part of all being, and is therefore, I suppose, to be prized / Beyond chasms of night that fight us / By being hidden and present" (*CP*, 212). Here, the poem suggests the phenomenological approach to perception, that each time new sensory information does not align with what has occurred previously, each "diversion," that is, makes the repository of past and sedimented experience that much more "accurate." This "portrait . . . has no relation to the space or time in which it was lived" because it is stored out of that time. "Its existence is a part of all being" because this portrait provides access to the meaning of existence, and in so doing, to being.

The poem closes by describing unaddressed or perhaps unperceived perceptions as if they float in this field, for while it is a desired goal to "see" everything, it is not possible to achieve complete perception: "And yet it results in a downward motion, or rather a floating one / In which the blue surroundings drift slowly up and past you / To realize themselves some day, while you, in this nether world that could not be better / Waken each morning to the exact value of what you did and said, which remains" (*CP*, 212). The pronoun "it" refers to the portrait in the previous stanza; in looking at the composite of perception, the whole us, we are ever aware of the missed perceptions, of the incompleteness of the portrait. We might possibly "see" these elements in future moments. All we have to go on for sure is an accounting of what we "did and said"; these are tangible acts.

Thickness of the Present

Both *Litany* (*CP*, 553–658) and "To the Same Degree" (*CP*, 114–15) are poems composed in two columns, meant to be read simultaneously.[53] In order for them to be experienced, two people must read them out loud, but *Litany* in particular is a very long poem and takes a long time and a lot of effort to read. The readers need to stay focused on the present of the reading at all times, because even though there are no explicit directions, the way the poem is laid out directs a reading in which the two readers stay in line with each other, perhaps because at some instances, the two pages call out to each other. So, the readers need to pace themselves to stay in accord with each other, and not have one reader get ahead of the other in the reading. This effort precludes thinking about anything but the poem at the moment of reading. In the presentation of the poem, therefore, the readers must think only about the present and the timing; there is little opportunity to consider the poem's intent at any one moment. The readers are both, then, pushed into the present moment so that they can only experience each instant as it passes; at once, though, they are pulled away from the present by how the poem's presentation experience blocks comprehension of the poem. For the audience, those hearing the simultaneous readings, the present is equally thick, for while the synchronous presentations permit "glimpses" of the poem's words, these are only brief, overtaken quickly by the dearticulated overlapping stream of language.

In his interviews with Richard Jackson and Rich Kelley, Ashbery identifies the inspiration for this poem as Elliott Carter's 1975 *Duo for Violin and Piano*: "Litany" may have been inspired—I'm never too sure of these things—by hearing Carter's *Duo* performed by a violinist and pianist who were situated far apart from each other on the stage at Cooper Union in New York. They could almost have been in different worlds, except for the fact that they were obviously listening to and spying on each other, each trying to get the upper hand. It was quite striking when the modest-toned violin sometimes won out over the piano."[54]

The word "litany" derives its meaning from a religious context and a commonplace one. In the religious context, a litany is a "resonant or repetitive chant," or a "prayer" involving "invocations" by the religious leader and "responses" to them by the "congregation." In the secular context, a litany can be a long list or set, but also a prolonged or tedious account. The word comes from Latin and Greek words for supplicant and entreaty.[55] Because of these two distinctly separate source words and because of the overlapping but also separate contexts, the word bears extensive complexity. That is, it is not simply a repetition, but that repetition invokes sonorousness and reverberation. Litany also sets up how the notion of an appeal or petition can be intermeshed with the person conducting that solicitation and holds within it a sense of desperation. Equally at work in these concomitant notions is the list, often a whiny or irritable one, and this list is generally taken as fairly trivial.

There are multiple lists in the poem, in particular of flowers, colors, and things out of nature, and they are not necessarily enumerations of great importance, as the poem says: "Anyway, I am the author. I want to / Talk to you for a while, teach you / About some things of mine, some things / I've put away, more still that I remember . . ." (*CP*, 624). The audience is apparent here, this "you"; the response, however, is lacking. It is clearly, as the poem states, "maybe just / A long list of complaints or someone's / Half-formed notions of what they thought / About something" (*CP*, 609). The inconsequence of these items, the self-deprecation of the list, downplay the poem's importance as if to say that it is simply small items the poet recalled and maybe wanted to complain about.

In the length of the poem, lists evolve into motifs, the wind, in particular, in order to create a sense of constant and irregular movement and how time sweeps through us: the future into the present and the present into the past.[56] "The wind pulls at / The leaves of the calendar," the poem says, "peels them off one by one / In a fitful expression of what time is like / As it goes by, that's like a look / Out of a window, and then the moment has gone away / From the window. The vast quantities of scum / Did not materialize" (*CP*, 636). Here, the wind is an active agent in the shifting of time; here, too, the poet links the passage of time, via the wind, to individual sense perception of brief, ephemeral moments of vision and thought, fled from us equally as quickly. A particular type of wind, the Zephyr, also recurs in the poem (*CP*, 629, 624).[57] The gentleness of the Zephyr and its connotations of breath contrast with a call and response in the poem where "blowing drawings" resonate with tumbleweeds and blowing dust (*CP*, 557–58).

However, at the same time, as part of the not just overlapping but interlinking of the litany, there are multiple elements in the poem with religious or at least spiritual intent. Certainly, in overlaying the two voices, the poem becomes chantlike; the words become sounds and the readers must take on a clear rhythm in coordinating with each other. The poem also refers directly to chants, albeit ones that are stifled: "We called on love for, to lead us / To farther tables and new, surprised, / Suffocated chants just beyond the range / Of simple perception" (*CP*, 638). Here it is evident that litany relates to the act of perception, that these repeated incantations, these articulations, are what we might gain if we were to access meaning. They are, sadly, smothered by our inability to do so.

An essential component of this list/entreaty is its focus on poetry, and on the poet's own concern for what could do versus what it does do. He says in this poem, for example, that "[he wants] to write / Poems that are as inexact as mathematics" (*CP*, 621), seemingly setting up a paradox, but mathematics in its theoretical propositions moves into the Pythagorean "harmony of the spheres" where astronomy and musical conceptions are conjoined. This approach to poetry contains its lists, as in: "And so / I say unto you: beware the right margin / Which is unjustified; the left / Is justified and can take care of itself / But what is in between expands and flaps / The end sometimes past the point / Of conscious inquiry" (*CP*, 615). This is a list with three items: the two margins and what happens between them. The poet sets up the list with a biblical phrasing, placing it into the religious context of litany, but undermines it with the commentary on margins. However, having pulled away from the religious connotations, he pulls back into philosophy, with his conception of what the text of the poem itself is doing: to "expand" is to fill out the space; "flap" involves the movement entailed in perception and the previous wind allusion. In going "past the point / Of conscious inquiry," it is as if the poem takes us beyond what we feel and into a realm of understanding.[58]

How we get to that point, I believe the poem suggests, is through a phenomenological approach to perception. We start with our senses. As the poem argues, it "leads us, each of us, / Back to the fragment of sense which is the place / We started out from" (*CP*, 649). In its recurring turn to circularity, the poem emphasizes this persistent looping back, to "coils / Of remembrance" (*CP*, 555) because "this is where it all / Had to take place, / Around a drum of living, / The motion by which a life / May be known and recognized" (*CP*, 558). In order to perceive, therefore, we must circle around this "drum of living," this site of human experience.[59]

The primary sense for Merleau-Ponty, and, I would argue, for Ashbery, is that of sight. The setting at a particular moment in the poem (*CP*, 612) places the narrator in a square in Europe, probably Italy, due to his use of the word "piazza." Here he equates experience and the passage of time with the act of drawing, in writing: "loss / Of time, that ever, with nervous, accurate fingers / Cross-hatches the shade in the corner / Of the piazza where I stand, and leave / The lighted areas scarcely perforated, almost / Pristine" (*CP*, 612). In this quick movement from the "book [with] shifting characters like desert sand" to the sketch and then to what he perceives, the depiction of the scene, both linguistic and visual, takes precedence over the actual experience. The description of the fingers as "accurate," if "nervous," indicates their ability to re-create the scene. Yet, in this reconception of what he sees, this perception of the scene, inaccuracy is inherent. We need to persist in this effort in spite of this "gap" between what we see and how we depict it, linguistically and visually. Later, the poem says, "this knowledge plants / A seed of eternal endeavor for fear of / Happening just once, and goes on this way, / And yet the originality should not deter / Our vision from the drain / That absorbs, night and day, all our equations" (*CP*, 653). In declaring that these reconceptions carry "originality" with them, the poem identifies the new articulations that remap experience to meaning. Still, these moments of clarity linger for mere instants, as the poem says, "And then / What might have been written down is seen / To have been said, and heard, and silence / Has flowed around the place again and covered it" (*CP*, 615).

In order to gain these instants of understanding, we must sense what is outside of us, to essentially leave our interior selves to access not only what is not us, but what is us.⁶⁰ The poem talks about this shift between the interior and exterior states when it says about landscapes that "we can see into them and come out on the other side. With / People we just see another boring side of ourselves, / One we may not know too well, but on the other / Hand why should we be interested in it?" (*CP*, 626). The query literally asks why it is that we are impelled to see ourselves as if from the outside and to direct ourselves outside ourselves to access those around us. To a large degree, it is also saying that those who seek meaning are compelled to make this shift, that they must make it whether or not it reaps any benefits.

Closely aligned to the shift between the interior and the exterior is movement, also core to Merleau-Ponty's thinking. While there are intermittent explosions and gusts of wind in this poem, most of the movement is almost languorous: "There is only the slow but febrile motion / Of sky and cloud, a toast, a promise, / A new diary, until one gets too close / And becomes oneself part of the meaningless / Rolling and lurching" (*CP*, 602). In the disorganized flux of sensation, there is movement, but it is undirected and lacking in meaning and sometimes simply circular, in a statement that could have come out of a poem by Yeats: "Who can elicit these possible, / Rubbery spirals? Return of all that's new, / Antithesis chirping / To antithesis" (*CP*, 563). However, it is through this spiraling that meaning becomes possible, flowing from inside to outside and back again. And, while the effort to gain intentional movement might not be successful, as in there is "no / Promise of relief in movement" (*CP*, 610), as earlier stated, movement must occur for perception to take place: "this is where it all / Had to take place, / Around a drum of living, / The motion by which a life / May be known and recognized" (*CP*, 558).

Movement is constricted by multiple constraints, the greatest of which is the horizon, as noted by Merleau-Ponty, that extent of our sensory capacities. When the poem addresses "the horizon of the universe," it is to "[Raise] it up into something bald and filled / With unexpressed and inexpressible menace, / No word of which would ever / Attest to the configuration of desires / That had gone into its construction, dark now, / Absent-minded flowers, reticent birds, and much / Else that is scarcely present" (*CP*, 627). This is the unarticulated experience, "unexpressed and inexpressible" and without the words to "attest to the configuration of desires"; and until there is articulation, there is no meaning. When the poem turns to the horizon, "it seems / Almost tame, or not as ripe / As we always imagined it would be" (*CP*, 625), as if to say that it does not hold the promise that we had anticipated. Added to this lack of optimism, ambiguity appears in this quotation from the poem: "But there are times when darkness / Hides this not very real horizon, and it turns / Steadfast for us" (*CP*, 627). The "it" that "turns / Steadfast for us" is probably the horizon, but the overlay with "darkness" leaves the phrase in irresolution. Still, if the horizon is "not very real," it is partly because the dim light impedes our sight. "Steadfast" suggests that this horizon, while limited, is at least something we can count on. In its despair, the poem turns again to the religious aspect of litany in saying, "can God / Let the eroding happen at all, since it is all, / As you say, horizontal, without / Beginning or end, and seamless / At the horizon where it bends / Into a past which has already begun? In / Truth then, if we are particles of anything / They must belong to our conception / Of our destiny, and be as complete as that" (*CP*, 618). Here, the horizon becomes a circular loop, linking the present to the past. Erosion is a concern, for "if we are particles," we could disperse like the poem's motifs of dust in the wind.

Perception occurs in the moment, that fleeting instant of the present. The poem turns repeatedly to this concern, as it provides an equally transitory access to comprehension. "[Now] the now is what matters" (*CP*, 582), the poem asserts, for "There comes a time when the moment / Is full of, knows only itself. / Like a moment when a tree / Is seen to tower above everything else / To know itself, and to know everything else / As well, but only in terms of itself / Without knowing or having a clear concept / Of itself . . . The moment / Not made of itself or any other / Substance we know of, reflecting / Only itself. Then there are two moments . . ." (*CP*, 578). Consciousness of oneself, of one's moment in time, is one of the consequences of taking hold of a moment and coming to terms with it. "Then there are two moments" considers the movement of time, that we can grasp a particular moment in a flash, but it is immediately overtaken by the next moment, sometimes in coexistence and sometimes in replacement.

The poem wrestles repeatedly with time: time passing, how to make sense of time, the perpetual time shift from future into present and then into the past.[61] "But, what is time, anyway?" the poem asks. "I think the things that are in it / Are more like it, though not quite it" (*CP*, 640). This conception of time indicates that regardless of what understanding of it comes out or what any moment contains, it is our experience of what is around us at any second that shapes our sense of time. We do not know what the future will hold, this "unfurled / Question-mark of the shaved future" (*CP*, 568). In using "unfurled" with "question-mark," the poem, as with the colon discussed earlier in this chapter, renders text as a material essence, so that a punctuation mark lays out time as it unrolls into a straight line. Yet, the poem says, "There is no longer time for a line / Or rather there are no lines in the time / Of ripeness that is past, / Yet still pausing on the ridge / Stealing into permanence" (*CP*, 580, 582). Lines are not adequate to "articulate" time, nor can they provide access to the past that is still apparent on the horizon but seeping into the repository of memory. "Around us are signposts," says the poem, "Pointing to the past . . . nothing directs / To the present that is / About to happen" (*CP*, 555). There might not be a line to the past, but we have a sense of how to connect to it; we cannot know what in the future will actually become the present that we experience.

Because of this access to the past, we check in continually, in the "cross-checking" that Merleau-Ponty identifies. We "[sample]" the past, the poem avers, and find that it "is again / The right one, and in testing / For the zillionth time we are / As built into the fixed wall of water / That indicates where the present leaves off / And the past begins, whose transparencies / Admit impressions of traceries of leaves / And shallow birds among memories" (*CP*, 568). We are, therefore, always placing the focus of our perceptual intention on that intersection between the past and the present, in this "time-cusp" (*CP*, 567) that is almost "transparent," so that we can see the water of time flow away from us. Time is a sense of a span of experience, the poem says, in that in it "duration / Only conjugates, the last happening / Is seen as inadequate only after the passing / Of much else varied stuff. / Only in being turned inside out / Can it deny itself so that the meaning / Pierces in any given point . . ." (*CP*, 569). In turning itself "inside out," duration, how long an instant takes to flee by, allows a space of consideration, and thereby allows "meaning" to "pierce" the instant, transforming sensation into perception and the acquisition of understanding of a moment.

What we access in the past is memory, what becomes over time irregular shards of past experiences.[62] A motif in the poem is dust, often blown around by the wind, particles remaining from the past, contributing to the layered repository of memory. The poem talks about memory extensively and specifically links time to memory (*CP*, 640). Memory, however, is imperfect.

> The prettiness urges
> Far into the body, deep
> Into the coffin of reactions, splitting light
> Into two unequal portions. One for me, the other for my things
> Like my memories and the changes I'd
> Want to introduce each time I'd come to a
> Particular one but would turn over instead,
> Disappointed with the other way it'd
> Turn out shoveling no matter what
> Into the boiler to keep that engine going
> And it would all reduce to this or that other
> Blackened memory, always the same, always
> Healthy in spite of it. O who
> Can judge their memories lest they have
> Already been sized up by them? (*CP*, 643, 645)

Here, sensory input, that "prettiness" of the visual, enters the body, that "coffin of reactions," and as if the entering of the body is like light passing through a prism, the sensory input takes two routes, one into the immediate impression and the other into the repository of memory. When we turn to memories, the poem suggests, our current situation will have an impact on them, modifying them with each tap into them. Memory becomes "blackened" by the incessant stream of sense intake, captured here in the form of coal of sense shoveled into the boiler of experience of the engine of life, leaving the burnt ash deposit of memory.

Yet this endless stream of sense that evolves into perception and memory moves too continuously, if not too quickly, for complete attention and processing. "As leaves are seen in mirrors / In libraries / Half-noticed, the sound / Half-remembered and the / Continuing chapter half-sketched— / O were we wrong to notice / To remember so much / When so little else has survived?" (*CP*, 562). "Half-noticed," "Half-remembered," "half-sketched": perception is only partial, the narrator in self-chastisement for not paying closer attention to elusive and whispered glimpses.

These stored memories become traces, according to Merleau-Ponty, lingering but faint remnants of past experiences.[63] Very near the end of the poem is an extended consideration of how it might be possible to understand the human condition of aging, and certainly mortality along with that. This effort to gain meaning from this situation "spurs us on to a higher pitch / Of elocution" (*CP*, 653) in accordance with Merleau-Ponty's emphasis on articulation, that it is only through rendering perception into speech that we might come closer to comprehension. This "elocution" fails, according to the poem, because others not making that effort won't "buy" it, as in refusing to accept it. The result of the effort, however, is that while the poet has touched on "abstract sleek ideas that come only once in / The night to be born and are gone forever," these ideas are only sutures to awkwardly resolve the paradoxes of existence. Still, and most importantly, the stitches "[leave] their trace after [they] have / Been removed," which is to say that their remnants, both what they mean and that they existed, linger. "[Who] is to say," the poem asks, whether "they are / Traces of what really went on and not / Today's palimpsest?" (*CP*, 653). "Today's palimpsest" is the sediment compacted of memory traces, elements of the past, intermingled and disordered, overladen yet permitting momentary and partial views of vestiges of past experiences.

This palimpsest forms, in its "accumulation" (*CP*, 583), a deposit, like the coal lode recurring in this poem. "These [names of things around us] one gets to know," says the poem, "and by then / They have formed tightly compartmented, almost feudal / Societies claiming kinship with the word . . . / And their age flows out of time, is left / Like a bluish deposit on the brown ploughed fields / That surround our century: like the note of a harp" (*CP*, 634, 636). The poem suggests here that language forms a "deposit," creates an order around that "central crater / Which is the word" and which we access "To have it make sense" (*CP*, 634).

A stronger analogy for these repositories of memory and language in the poem connects to fabric, to individual threads and to the woven intermingling of those threads.[64] The poem talks about "a remnant / Of a memory, a gesture time made / To no one in particular, to itself / Or not even to itself, a tic, / A twinge long invisible now / On the low-pressure area / On the weather map" (*CP*, 589) in describing the randomness of minute portions of the past that are left to us, like a "tic" or small "twinge" no longer felt but remaining on some level in the repository of memory. As a part of this gesture of memory, the poem argues, "There is a germ of you that lives like a coal / Amid the hostile indifference of the land / That merely forgets you. Your hand / Is at the heart of its weavings and nestlings. / You are its guarantee" (*CP*, 600). Movement here forms the weaving of past experience into the memory that we can access. In a longer description of this process, the poem says:

> You can stand up to breathe
> And the garment falling around you is history,
> Someone's, anyway, some perfectly accessible,
> Reasonable assessment of the recent past, which
> With its pattern dips into the shadow of the folds
> To re-emerge and be striking on the crest
> Of them somewhere, and thus serves
> Twice over, as plan and decoration,
> A garden plunged in sun seen through a fixed lattice
> Of regrets and doubts, pinned there
> For a variety of good reasons, alive, stupid
> As a sail stunned in a vast haze . . . (*CP*, 620)

Existence in the body is here the simple act of standing up and breathing, but that is just the start of the process of perception. Integral with this moment of Being is the past, that history that is both yours and "someone" else's. The analogy for the memory/past repository is here the folds of fabric, of "the garment falling around you," so that the past is not simply like a deposit of memories in the land but also all over us like clothing—it is part of us; it is us. Memories shift, rising and falling, as the garment moves with us and its folds rearrange, creating different "folds" and different "crests" or ridges of access. The interlay of the second analogy, of the garden, with the garment, complicates the poem but at once clarifies the act of perception. For the goal of perception is organizing the mess of experience, isn't it? These folds of fabric, this fluid and shifting mass of present and the shards of memory, lie out in the orderly garden, in this "fixed lattice," for retrieval and retrospection.

In the introduction of this book, I noted Merleau-Ponty's emphasis on the visible, the transformation of the sense of sight in particular, but any sensation in general, into the perception of external experience. *Litany* turns to this issue repeatedly in the form of the degree to which visibility is possible and its concerns with impediments to visibility, either partial or entire. "Now that the things of autumn / Have been sequestered too in their chain," it says, "The other part[65] of the year become / Visible / And the summer night is like a goldfish bowl / With everything in full view, yet only parts / Are what is actually seen, and these supply / The rest. It's not like cheating / Since it *is* all there, but more like / Helping the truth along a little: / The artifice lets it become itself, / Nestling in truth" (*CP*, 576). If autumn has been "sequestered," the poem should normally turn to winter, but instead it argues that once autumn is gone through (that is, once the present has become the past), it is possible to discern the past preceding that time. Conceiving the night as a "goldfish bowl / With everything in full view" assists with full access to the past, that it is possible to leverage all past information to gain the "truth." This shift from sense to perception is also apparent in "A new alertness changes / Into the look of things / Placed on the railing / Of this terrace: / The beheld with all the potential / Of the visible, acting / To release itself / Into the known / Dust under / The sky" (*CP*, 559). The "beheld" is here the visual image of the thing(s); it bears within it "the potential / Of the visible," the push outward to comprehend the meaning of experience.

The poem provides these moments of clarity, but it often turns instead to the more frequent experience of the partially or occasionally visible. This is "a landscape always seen through black lace" (*CP*, 597); "it merely mocks the idea / Of a whole comprised by all those now mostly invisible / Ideas, ghosts / Of things and reasons for them" (*CP*, 605); and it sees only "Pockmarked flecks of polluted matter / Infrequently visible in the hail of ventilated indifference" (*CP*, 584). The poem also asserts concerns with the utter incapacity for the visible. "These traumas / That sped us on our way," it says, "Are to be linked with the invisible damage / Resulting in the future / From too much direction, / Too many coils / Of remembrance" (*CP*, 555). Memory of difficult or damaging experiences lies within those "coils of remembrance" as if lurking in invisibility but not in nonexistence. This is because, the poem argues, "the heft [of experience is] Now invisible [and] only the fragments / Of the echo are left / Intruding into the color, / How we remember them" (*CP*, 559).

Left to us in our memory are only these "fragments," and not just "fragments" but "fragments of echoes," inaccurate and incomplete essences of the past. It is not just that these instances are not visible to us in lying in the "folds" of our memory repositories; we are sometimes just not able to "see" them: "Even as I am invisible in the eye / Of the storm, we two are blind, /

And blind to the inaudible repercussions, / The strange woody aftertaste" (*CP*, 578). Not only can we not see, as in comprehend, in this "storm" of existence, but we are unable to gain any comprehension of what these experiences might come to mean or what kind of impact they might have. These "repercussions" are also "inaudible" because unarticulated. Part of this inability to "see" is because it is uncomfortable and even scary to do so. In articulating, in creating meaning, we are also risking failure or lack of acceptance of others. In saying "Under / The intimate light of the lantern / One really felt rather than saw / The thin, terrifying edges between things / And their terrible cold breath" (*CP*, 574), the poem is relating perception to time; like the time-cusp described earlier in this chapter, the perception-cusp requires a frightening leap "between things" and beyond them.

Perception is a core issue in this poem, particularly in that it is a process, not a state, and we continually launch ourselves toward it. Experience becomes the passage through time and how we make sense of it: "Living / On the tranquil slope of an inactive volcano / All these days which group themselves / Into decades, consuming / The egg puddings of each one of these days / Is like unto form as subject matter / Perceives it through the cracks in its / Makeshift cell . . ." (*CP*, 646). Here, getting through each day is like eating a dessert, and then the days are "grouped" in retrospection into separate ten-year time spans. The comparison of the grouped days with how content understands form links perception to the intersection of the present with the past. Core to this understanding is how we achieve perception through the movement from our interior to our sensory acquisitions outside us and then back into ourselves for the reflection on our memory repository: "[Time] will not remain / Any more outside of me for all that. / It is the marrow of my thought . . ." (*CP*, 640, 642). Contributing to this layering of trope on trope is the biblical turn in "Is like unto form," creating an atmosphere of accepted yet utterly enigmatic process of perception.

Essential to the urge for perception is the quest for order, to make sense of the disorder of experience.[66] The responsibility for this quest, according to Merleau-Ponty, lies with artists and philosophers. In this poem, Ashbery demonstrates his efforts in ordering, to "rescue [people] / From the desperate, tangled muddle of their / Frustrated, unsatisfactory living" (*CP*, 601, 603). A lengthy section of *Litany* talks about poetry and criticism of poetry, and in it, Ashbery lays out poetry's obligation to its readers: "It behooves /

Our critics to make the poets more aware of / What they're doing, so that poets in turn / Can stand back from their work and be enchanted by it / And in this way make room for the general public / To crowd around and be enchanted by it too, / And then, hopefully, make some sense of their lives, / Bring order back into the disorderly house / Of their drab existences" (*CP*, 601). This is the hope, then, for poetry, to "make some sense" of existence and to "bring order" into people's lives.

The struggle is, therefore, how to articulate this meaning, or at least to articulate the process of trying to gain access to it. The poem struggles with sense of "an object which the mind can never / Control, leading to frosted silence / And cold unregard" (*CP*, 637):

> The dust blows in.
> The disturbance is
> Nonverbal communication:
> Meaningless syllables that
> Have a music of their own,
> The music of sex, or any
> Nameless event, something
> That can be taken as
> Itself. . . .
>
> Especially since it persists
> In dumbness which isn't even
> A negative articulation—persists
> And collapses into itself. (*CP*, 556)

If there is no articulation of experience, there is no realignment of current experience with sedimented cultural memory. It is only articulation that can lead to an ordering or comprehension of experience. It is, the poem argues, "An experience / Unlike any other, leaching / Back into the lore of / The songs and sagas, / The warp of knowledge. / But now it's / Come close / Strict identities form it, / Build it up like sheaves / Of nerves, articulate, / Defiant of itself" (*CP*, 557). There is the warp of knowledge and the weft of lore, and there is also, in another overlapping metaphor, the sheaves of sensory input. All of these together form the perfect conditions for the comprehension of, and articulation of, experience. In one of the few calls and responses in the poem, as a part of the litany, "articulation" repeats on these facing pages, so that both readers at once call attention to its essential role in perception (*CP*, 556, 557).

Arriving at this moment of clarity in the poem is almost like a cartoon: "those flying / Bits of newspaper and plastic bags scarce / Bode better for him who sits and picks at / The secret, when suddenly / The meaning knocks him down, a light bulb / Appears in a balloon above his head" (*CP*, 614). It takes a poet to raise that light bulb of understanding, and it takes the poet to articulate these experiences. "Just one minute of contemporary existence / Has so much to offer," says the poem, "but who / Can evaluate it, formulate / The appropriate apothegm, show us / In a few well-chosen words of wisdom / Exactly what is taking place all about us?" (*CP*, 599). It is the poet, *Litany* suggests, who can do this, who can look around, state concisely (though interestingly, not so concisely in this particular poem) what is out there, and try again and again to articulate human experience.

Chapter 4

Space

> "Joseph Cornell"
> ... collage materiel is highly vulnerable
> better to "let well enough alone" than
> attempt wiping off the blemishes ...
> there's a frame here for it.[1]

THIS CHAPTER FOCUSES on emblem books and collage in order to talk about the spatial qualities of phenomenology, largely as it relates to time. Clearly, the "thickness" of presence, as discussed in the previous chapter, sets up a three-dimensional model of time. Merleau-Ponty links time and space explicitly to each other in his conceptualization of this theory. In *The Visible and the Invisible*, he argues, for instance:

> What makes the weight, the thickness, the flesh of each color, of each sound, of each tactile texture of the present, and of the world is the fact that he who grasps them feels himself emerge from them by a sort of coiling up or redoubling, fundamentally homogeneous with them; he feels that he is the sensible itself coming to itself and that in return the sensible is in his eyes as it were his double or an extension of his own flesh. The space, the time of the things are shreds of himself, of his own spatialization, of his own temporalization, are no longer a multiplicity of individuals synchronically and diachronically distributed, but a relief of the simultaneous and of the successive, a spatial and temporal pulp where the individuals are formed by differentiation. (*VI*, 113–14)

This quotation bears close explication because it is at once quite complicated and such a complete and comprehensive statement of not just phenomenology but the role of space in it. Perception is here in the form of touch, sight, and sound, but it is confounded by having touch become accessible through sound (each sound of each tactile texture) and by having sight bear a physical quality (that flesh, that weight, that thickness). These explicit entanglements of senses with each other and with their embodiment demonstrate their fluidity and lack of finiteness. To Merleau-Ponty, we cannot separate our senses, so that when we see, we might also smell, and in fact, in order to perceive, we must activate more than one sense for comprehension of that perception.

As well, in this perceptual moment, sensation becomes embodied in this "coiling up or redoubling." The moment of sensation is not simply that we access the world outside us through our senses and leave it at that. We pull those activated sensory instances back into ourselves (that coiling, that redoubling), and they become an integral part of us, so that as we cannot distinguish one sense from another, we cannot distinguish sensation from ourselves. It becomes, as he says, "an extension of our own flesh." We cannot split those sensual inputs apart from each other; they merge in our experience of them. This instantaneous movement, as it were, between ourselves and the external world creates not just this "temporalization" but a "spatialization." It is because of this interaction and interweaving that Merleau-Ponty argues not just that that "every sense is spatial" (*PP*, 229), but that "existence is spatial" (*PP*, 307).

Merleau-Ponty's approach to perception is spatial in the sense of its metaphoric conception as a field or clearing, as shown in chapter 1. In order to perceive, one must move outside of the body and into the senses to "see" oneself and the surrounding context of other people and other things. As Merleau-Ponty says, existence "opens to an 'outside'" (*PP*, 307). Perception requires access to the horizontal axis of the senses and the vertical axis between the visible and the invisible. "To perceive," Merleau-Ponty says, "is to believe in a world . . . [to open] to a world" (*PP*, 311). These openings, having openings at all, being amenable to them, but finally, and most importantly, moving through them, create and acknowledge space in the process of perception. The space created by art is particularly inherently spatial, as Merleau-Ponty described in his notes: "The aesthetic world [is] to be described as a space of transcendence, a space of incompossibilities, of explosion, of dihescence, and not as object-immanent space" (*VI*, 216). The aesthetic space is not one, therefore, of simply aesthetic objects, but rather a metaphoric clearing or field within which articulation transpires. It is the artistic production that is the culminating articulation of perception, that rendering into intelligible form of the reconfigured experience to match its new context.

In his emblem books and in his visual and verbal collages, Ashbery lays out how time becomes space. The emblem books, poetry that is paired with images that sometimes correlate directly with the text as illustrations but do not always bear any connection with it, set up a constant spatial movement between the text and the image.[2] In looking at the images, the eye needs to move; in "seeing" the text, the eye also needs to move. Because of the image-text pairing, sight is called on to create space in roving across the page planes and back through the text.

The poem *Fragment* is an example of an emblem book in which Ashbery lays out his sense of Being as a "field of presence."[3] In an interview with Janet Bloom and Robert Losada, Ashbery talks about the form of this poem and his intentions for it:

> I had been reading Maurice Scève, the sixteenth-century poet who wrote in dizains and I was impressed by the fruitful monotony of his form, as over and over again he says very much the same thing in the hundreds and hundreds of ten-line stanzas, constantly repeating the form and yet adding something a little new each time, and the ultimate cumulative effect of these additions is something I was aiming at, although I didn't use the ten-line stanza with any very definite aim in mind or desire to imitate Scève particularly. It also seemed like a good in-between length; lacking the in-the-round effect of a sonnet and longer than a quatrain; a purposely stunted form which is ideal for these repetitions with minimal variations."[4]

John Shoptaw points out that the work of Scève that Ashbery knew best was his emblem book, *Délie*, which contains close to 450 dizains, regularly interspersed with fifty emblems, woodcuts in the form of elaborately framed pictures, the images of which do not necessarily bear any relationship to the content of the poem.[5] Representative examples are shown in figures 4.1 and 4.2. The words of the poem in stanza VI read, as translated:

Freely I lived in the April of my days,
Exempt from every care my adolescence,
Until my eye, unschooled in pity's ways,
Was surprised by that sweet presence,
Which by its high divine excellence
So stunned my soul and what sense I prize,
That the cruel archer of her eyes
Ever stole my freedom, so continually
That from that very first sunrise,
My life and death lie in her beauty.[6]

The stanza depicts a self-described innocent youth who is so enraptured by a woman that the experience becomes one of negativity rather than the expected joy of first love.[7] Instead of being happily immersed in this experience, he finds himself "stunned" and therefore incapable of self-defense. Normally in a new love experience, it is possible to feel safe in spite of the vulnerability of the exposure of one's feelings, but the case here betrays that open disclosure through the theft of the youth's "freedom" by the impalement inflicted by his beloved's eyes. The archer of love transverses here into a "cruel" act, not by a god but by her personal attack. Scholarship on Scève's life suggests that he had a brief and unhappy relationship when he was around twenty years old and then a longer and more intense relationship with a married woman twenty years younger than him when he was in his mid-thirties.[8] He appears to have had an additional mistress at an overlapping time.[9]

The image accompanying the stanza depicts a young girl with a unicorn. The Lady and the Unicorn story derives from hunting mythology of the Caucasus region.[10] According to Christian myth, the unicorn represents the Incarnation and Jesus Christ, God becoming flesh in being born as Jesus Christ.[11] Also according to myth, only female virgins (representing the Virgin Mary), because of their sexual purity, have the capability of capturing the most elusive unicorn, but once captured, the unicorn places its head on the virgin's lap and falls asleep. Myths vary on the outcome of this scene, whether the virgin lures the unicorn and keeps it in captivity or whether she is the lure to draw the unicorn in for hunters to kill it.[12]

There are two versions of *Délie*, one from 1544 and the other from 1564. In the 1544 version, the image of the Virgin and the Unicorn appears to rely on both of these myths, as the emblem presents a young girl seated on the ground with a unicorn's head in her lap, but protruding out of the unicorn's rear end, in nearly the reverse angle of its horn, is an arrow, lodged firmly in its flesh. However, the 1564 version, while still showing the arrow set in the unicorn's haunch and in the same reverse angle as its horn, and a tree similarly placed just behind them as a barrier, represents a distinctly different relationship between the unicorn and the virgin. Rather than depicting the unicorn as submissive to and tamed by the virgin, with its head in her lap, this version shows the virgin reclining at ease with the unicorn's front legs and hooves across her hip. Their heads are now level with each other, with the virgin pulling the unicorn's head to make eye contact with it and the unicorn's eyes cast down. While the unicorn's averted eyes and the lodged arrow still suggest its submission, this scene is more sexually charged than the earlier one, and the virgin is much more assertive and physical.

The image matched with these lyrics is encircled with a phrase that translates as: "To gaze on this I lose my life,"[13] suggesting that love will not necessarily lead to the youth's death but certainly to his loss of himself, particularly represented in the later emblem where the unicorn tries to avoid the direct gaze

Figure 4.1. Emblem 1: "The Lady and the Unicorn," Maurice Scève, *Délie*, 1544.

Figure 4.2. Emblem 1: "The Lady and the Unicorn," Maurice Scève, *Délie*, 1564.

of the young woman. However, and most essential, the emblems in *Délie* are not illustrations. Sometimes they refer directly to the text, but not always. In fact, even though two of the emblems depict scenes with unicorns, Scève never mentions these creatures in this entire poetry cycle. Emblems are therefore not illustrations in the sense that they are not meant to explain the poem's text. In emblem books, as such, the emblems exist as art on their own, the texts exist as words on their own, and the interactions between the emblems and the texts range from the immediate to the impossible. Because emblems are interspersed with the text of a poem, however, they modify time and the present in that the "reading" is not simply an examination of the text and the effort to come to terms with it, but now a movement between the text and the image with the attempt to make sense out of why the image was created for this section of the poem and what there might be about it that will explain what the poem is trying to say; that is, the reader looks to the emblem as an illustration that will support the interpretation of the text, but this act attenuates time and the interpretation through setting up this interchange, one that is often impossible to complete.

Since, as quoted previously, Ashbery revealed the influence of Scève's *Délie* on *Fragment*, it is not a surprise that his poem appeared as an emblem book. Ashbery and Alex Katz collaborated on such an edition of *Fragment*, published by Black Sparrow Press in 1969 with twenty-five of Katz's illustrations (ink-wash drawings), each placed opposite two of Ashbery's stanzas.[14] Emblem books are inherently collaborative, as in most cases the illustrator and the writer are not the same person. Collaboration is the culmination of the phenomenological effort to transcend one's own self, and not just to recognize the other but to engage with and intermingle with the other, shifting perception into a newly configured sense of the self.

Laurence Lieberman describes Ashbery's reliance on fragments in his poetry as a method to use the fragment synecdochally, whereby one small instance of experience can be used to represent the whole of a life. Lieberman comments on "Ashbery's remarkable theory that our wholeness of self can be assembled and contained in a poem by isolating a single fragment of our living, a living sample evoking the whole life of which it is the emblem. . . . By inspecting a freely scattered assortment of fragments selected from a few hours—or days—of a life, gradually, the continuity of the whole inner life is added up and, at some unexpected, chance moment in the trance of composition, emerges complete."[15] Emblems are, therefore, compressed representations of the larger world of experience; their composite, if one is successful, might come to depict the entirety of a person's existence.

The first image-text pairing in *Fragment* sets up the expectation that the emblems are illustrations, explanations, or supports of the text, as the image is of a woman and appears next to references to a woman.

The text on this page states: "You / See the intrusion clouding over her face" with a link to the "you" addressed, "As in the memory given you" and transferred to "your face."[16] In this case, therefore, the image supports the impulse to "see [that] intrusion clouding over her face" as depicted and to relate "her face" to the later "your face." However, the image presented here neglects to explain anything about what is most important: "a moment's commandment."[17] This rupture introduces time into space in the emblem

Figure 4.3. John Ashbery and Alex Katz, *Fragment*, 8.

book, where the spatial interaction of the text and the image and the time involved in relating them to each other spirals into a field of presence, a never-resolving, ever-perpetuated lack of stability.

An example of this disjunction between the image and the poetry is the ninth image in the series, which is of a male head with a female torso rising out of its top. The text in the first stanza paired with this image is on the seasons of the year, and it talks about pictures as if they really exist. The second stanza on this page concentrates on personal anecdotes, "Recounted in touching detail."[18] The image has nothing apparent to do with either of these stanzas, creating not an alignment with them but instead a resonating vibration through and across space, the literal space on the page and the figurative space where sense is made, of the poem and of its relationship with the image. The image here is baffling, though, as the expression of the face on the large head is perfectly calm despite the woman erupting from it. The serenity of Katz's images in this book, regardless of their improbability, support and transcend the languid monotone of the text.

The lack of linkage between the images and the text, the nonillustrative function of the images, becomes the norm in the poem cycle, so that when the twenty-third image appears, the reader will assume that the image will bear no clear relationship to the text. Yet this pairing disrupts the pattern of nonrelationship. The image on this page is of a small-scale sailboat on a

Figure 4.4. John Ashbery and Alex Katz, *Fragment*, 24.

blank page, as if the water and sky have merged to erase the horizon, and as if the weather is perfectly still. The paired text in the first stanza talks about "impossible oceans" and a "lake opening out broader than the sun!"[19] The second stanza says, "The boat stood hieratically still / On the unread page of water."[20] The image, in this case, is a boat that is not moving. Because the background is perfectly blank, even though it is framed in black line, it merges into and becomes the page; page and water are the same. Here, too, however, the image is tranquil. The boat is not adrift, it is just not attempting progress, just as the text calmly goes nowhere.

When Bloom and Losada asked Ashbery in their interview with him about the content of *Fragment*, he said:

> I don't remember it very well. I think what I said before about its taking up again and again a single situation and repeatedly developing and then in a way casting aside what has been developed to start over again is the content in this particular case. I think it's like maybe all of my poems, it's a love poem; Scève's "Délie" was a long cerebral love poem; and the actual situation isn't apparent in the poem, but it's what is behind it and is generating these repeated re-examinations and rejections and then further examinations.[21]

Important in this interview is Ashbery's concern with repetitions, their accumulations with little to no variation, and this cycle of examination,

Figure 4.5. John Ashbery and Alex Katz, *Fragment*, 52.

rejection, and reexamination. These are the efforts to address time and perception and how experience of them leads to a comprehension of human existence through orientation in space. "Slowly," the poem says, "as from the center of some diamond / You begin to take in the world as it moves / In toward you...".[22] Movement in space is apparent here, as is perception's connection to that spatial organization. This stanza clearly addresses the importance of intentional perception of external phenomena: "Seen from inside all is / Abruptness. As though to get out your eye / Sharpens and sharpens these particulars; no / Longer visible, they breathe in multicolored / Parentheses, the way love in short periods / Puts everything out of focus, coming and going."[23] We therefore hone in on specific elements, but since perception is so fleeting, our cognizance of them devolves instantly from this "sharpness" of our primary perception into the fuzzier transient remnants of the past experiences. These little "parentheses" remain in us, as the poem says: "Thus your only world is an inside one / Ironically fashioned out of external phenomena."[24]

It is essential to persist in this effort to perceive, however, and to be open to multiple perceptions because this endeavor will lead, ideally, to comprehension, in this case of the interlocutor: "hesitations, reverse darts, the sky / Of your plans run through with many sutured points. / Only in this way can a true basis for understanding be / Set up,"[25] and only in this way is it possible to achieve meaning and a sense of Being, as in "This time / You get over the threshold of so much unmeaning, so much / Being, prepared for its event, the active memorial."[26]

Perception leads to the experience of time: "The sense of that day ... Its landscape puts toward a pointed roof / Continuing inquiry and reappraisal of always new / Facts pushing past into bright cold / As from general spindles a waterfall of data / Is absorbed above by command. Whether construed / As lead or gold it leaves a ring / On the embellished, attendant time."[27] Perception is apparent in this portion of the poem in "sense," the awareness of a "landscape," and most particularly in this "Continuing inquiry and reappraisal of always new / Facts." Each of these elements "leaves a ring," an impression or mark, on time. That is, each perception is an instant of the present; the overaccumulation of them, that "waterfall of data," creates the "field of presence."

The poem dwells on time, particularly on time passing and occurrences evolving into memories. "But why should the present seem so particularly urgent?," the poem asks, "A time of spotted lakes and the whippoorwill / Sounding over everything? To release the importance / Of what will always remain invisible? / In spite of near and distant events, gladly / Built?"[28] We feel like the present moment is very important, and all of our perception occurs in the instant of the present, but truly, it is not ever just the present moment; all "near and distant events" are also in the collocation of experience.

The poem describes this process of the transformation of perception in the present to the layers of memories of past perceptions: "It is that the moment of sinking in / Is always past, yet always in question, on the surface / Of the goggles of memory. Nothing is stationary / Nor yet uncertain; a rhythm of standing still / Keeps us in continual equilibrium ..."[29] The "moment of sinking in" is the instantaneous shift from perception into the gathering of perceptions that will lead to an understanding of human experience; each perception slips immediately into memory, a memory that, in Ashbery's conception, is visual, those "goggles of memory." Goggles are safety glasses, used to protect the eyes in laboratory experiments; they are also used in sports, such as swimming and skiing, designed to seal against the face to protect the eyes from water or snow. Because of this, and perhaps oddly, they are not designed for enhanced vision; more often than not, they distort vision. "Goggles of memory" are suspect, therefore, in the quality of their perception. Perception is distorted; it is distorted once again as it slides from the present into the repository of memory. "So the weather of that day, and scalloped / Appearance of those who went by you / Are changed like mist" by this operation of memory. Mist, like goggles, distorts and impedes our ability to see. We can review perceptions via these memories, but it is difficult to make sense of them: "It was time to compare all past sets of impressions . . . A moment of addition, then one hidden look / At it all, but it is scattered, not the outline / Of your famous openness, but kind of the sleeves / in the weather time after the doubtful present saluted."[30] This present remains "doubtful" in the impossibility of grasping a moment without also "[comparing] all past sets of impressions." We cannot perceive accurately; we cannot capture the moment. However, we can gather those mis- and multiple perceptions into that stratification of the past and the present to immerse ourselves in this "field of presence."

A second emblem book by Ashbery is *The Vermont Notebook*,[31] a collection of pieces written by Ashbery, each of which is paired with an ink drawing by Joe Brainard. Ashbery wrote these pieces first, and Brainard composed the images afterward;[32] because of this, there is some sense that this work might not be the result of a true collaboration. I suggest, however, that while it was not all composed while Ashbery and Brainard were physically together, at the very least it was composed as a call and response, that Brainard was reading the text by Ashbery and responding directly to it, what Jess Cotton refers to as a "collaborative notion of self."[33]

As noted earlier, the impulse with emblem books is to consider the image in terms of the text. That is, since humans are visual creatures, we look at the image first and then "look" in the text for the corresponding reference to it. However, as with the other emblem books discussed here, a consideration of the image as an illustration, as a picture that will illuminate or explain the text, is an approach leading only to confusion, or at the very least to less clarity. It is as if the visual artist seeks out amusement at the expense of the reader.

A look at the first few pairings will demonstrate what I mean here. The first image/text pairing is perfectly aligned, as the image is of rain and the text talks about the climate (*CP*, 331).

The next few images identify particular elements in the text, such as the Mobil Oil Company's Pegasus trademark next to a list of companies of different types (*CP*, 334–35); an image of a tape measure next to a list of fashion companies, one of which is called "Tapemeasure," followed by a list of fashion-world colors (*CP*, 336–37); and images of game items like cards, jacks,

Figure 4.6. John Ashbery, *Collected Poems*, 1956–1987, 330.

and dominos next to a list of games that precedes a second list of specific criminal charges (*CP*, 338–39).[34]

Reading the text becomes a sort of game, therefore, to identify the image appearing in the text: the beaver's face, the newspaper, the coffee. The reader is set up for this pattern: see the image, find the reference to it in the text, and somehow feel confirmed by this connection, as if it leads in any way to comprehension of the work as a whole. The texts and the images are neutral in tone and subject matter, suggesting the blandness of the travel and the relatively dull and matter-of-fact experience. It is not, as Ashbery says earlier of *Délie*, that it is monotonous repetition with small variation, but it approaches that sensibility in its dry tone and topic.[35] These attempts to link the text with the images create a spatial disjuncture between them, the eye moving repeatedly back and forth between them and never finding a place for repose.

This process works fairly well until the sixteenth image, where it starts to break down. The image appears to be six plates of food seen from overhead (*CP*, 358).

The text is a mix of landscape description and an extended polite farewell

Figure 4.7. John Ashbery, *Collected Poems*, 1956–1987, 334.

Figure 4.8. John Ashbery, *Collected Poems*, 1956–1987, 358.

Figure 4.9. John Ashbery, *Collected Poems*, 1956–1987, 360.

of the kind expressed by a small hotel owner. The next pairing shows an image of a television next to text appearing like a diary entry (*CP*, 360).

The twenty-first image, as well, fits oddly with the text: a hanging button-down shirt opposite lengthy disquisition on sideburns, on doing nothing, and then "Little nuts, big nuts," clearly a sly testicle reference but at once, because of the insipid text, also just food items (*CP*, 370–71).

The next image as well creates an odd juxtaposition, with the text talking creepily about water, "sliding, now crawling delicately under the wax surface of the ice," and then: "Her only food in five days: a dead chicken that floated by her on the water, which she ate raw" (*CP*, 373). The image presents a diner breakfast special with two rashers of bacon nestled into a sunny-side-up fried egg (*CP*, 372).

The twenty-fourth image is of a man and a woman kissing, looking very much like a Roy Lichtenstein *Kiss* cartoon image of a romanticized depiction of a heterosexual relationship, while the text talks about what shoes to wear with orange pants, nose picking, and a man's dream about putting his penis between a woman's breasts, quite unlike the happily-ever-after drawing (*CP*, 376–77).

And finally, but not the final image, is a nude portrait of a man, probably, like many if not all of these drawings, taken from a photograph (*CP*, 382).[36]

Figure 4.10. John Ashbery, *Collected Poems, 1956–1987*, 370.

Figure 4.11. John Ashbery, *Collected Poems, 1956–1987*, 372.

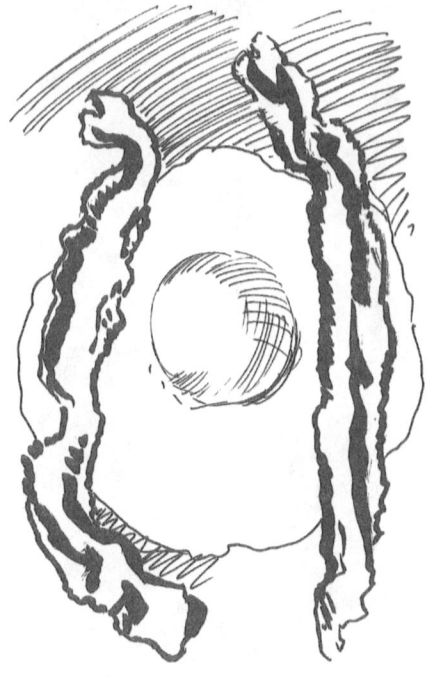

Figure 4.12. John Ashbery, *Collected Poems*, 1956–1987, 376.

Figure 4.13. John Ashbery, *Collected Poems*, 1956–1987, 382.

His languid come-hither pose with averted eyes contrasts sharply with the relatively bland text about Americans' zest for life, as demonstrated by their "retirement communities," lawn mowing, and golf playing.[37] Yet this text evolves into something deeper than the texts in the rest of this volume, as it argues that things "stand for something broader and darker than at first seems to be the case" (*CP*, 383). It lists examples of people's behavior that appear to start out as representative of the goodness of human nature, such as a truck driver who stops to help with a loose swimming pool cover, and people trapped in the elevator who comfort each other by singing songs. However, the third example is of someone who commits a crime, a "nursing home director" no less, and goes to jail. The final example is of looking into the depths of water with a small spot of reflected light and finally only seeing yourself, clearly unrelated to the image.

An activity related to these emblem books and integral to the notion of phenomenological space are Ashbery's visual collages.[38] These collages are lightly made, by which I mean that he takes a strong background and places a few cutouts onto it. The approach stands in contrast with collagists who shape their entire images through elements brought together from other contexts and shaped for the context of the current collage, such as those by Kurt Schwitters or Romare Bearden.[39]

Instead, in many of Ashbery's collages, he will start with a printed background, such as a game board, and add some small elements to it.[40] These collages are, I believe, versions of what Heather Love calls "queer camp," a form that "with its tender concern for outmoded elements of popular culture and its refusal to get over childhood pleasures and traumas, is a backward art"[41]—not, I need to emphasize, backward in a negative sense, but in the sense that it pulls the past into the present. Ashbery's turn to these games, therefore, suggests a nostalgia for his childhood, but it is a nostalgia of mixed feelings, complicated by the contradiction between the desire to remember and to reenter a past of rosy memories, and the loneliness and sense of being a misfit on his parents' farm near Rochester, New York.[42] In addition, Ashbery's younger brother died when Ashbery was twelve, a trauma recounted by Ashbery in his poem "The History of My Life": "Once upon a time there were two brothers. / Then there was only one: myself" (*CP II*, 667).[43] The fairytale opening of this poem suggests the romanticized perfection of his childhood, while the line break and sudden closure of the opening mirrors the tragedy of his brother's death.

But yet, in spite of the link between memory and sadness, whether through the isolation of the rural farm in the 1930s or the loss of his brother, memory of childhood serves essential functions for the poet, in particular from a phenomenological standpoint, with the focus on the experience and the attempt to depict it. As, Rosalind Krauss argues, "[c]ollage can talk about space without employing it," memories from childhood can serve as a repository of experience and sensation that is less considered and self-conscious and create spatial formations within the work of art.[44] When Ashbery takes up game boards not just to serve as the background for his collages but to establish this nostalgic atmosphere and underlying focus, he recalls the "backward" look at pleasures and the sting of solitude. A child will not, as I will argue in my discussion of "Europe," judge these elements of popular culture in terms of their artistic or conceptual merits but will, rather, see them as if they were transparent, the ground for the game, the compass to orient direction through its space.

Three examples of these collages by Ashbery appear in Antonio Sergio Bessa's catalog for the exhibit of Ashbery's collages at the Pratt Institute's Manhattan Gallery.[45] The first of these is based on a board for the Uncle Wiggily game, a swirling passage through a rural woods and farmland setting, complete with a chicken house and a kraken. For the collage *Uncle Wiggily*, interestingly, Ashbery has either cut the board to remove bad characters, such as the wolf and the fox, or stripped them of their aggression by placing a tomato in the alligator's mouth and giving the kraken a rose to juggle. This game is rated for small children, four years old and older, so while the cheerful chickens and welcoming dog are all nonthreatening, many characters are quite disturbing, bearing large teeth or evil smiles. In pulling this game into the present, therefore, Ashbery has clearly acted in ways that we are not able to as children, to modify the "playing field" to render it less frightening for the small child, creating a spatiotemporal construct between the past and the present.

The next collage based on a game board is *Chutes and Ladders III (for David Kermani)*.[46] Ashbery says that many of the materials for this collage were provided by Brainard over the years.[47] The original images on this board (that is, pre-collage) depict children in various activities, such as sitting on a stool wearing a dunce's cap, walking while "dressing up," and skating vigorously. While most of these images are cheerful, many are not: two

Figure 4.14. John Ashbery, *Uncle Wiggily*, 2008. Collage. 16 × 15.875 in. Copyright Estate of John Ashbery, courtesy of the Tibor de Nagy Gallery, New York.

boys are fighting, a child is crying while being dragged along by his mother, another is running from a large adult shoe poised either to kick him or to catch him. To create the collage, Ashbery has taken some square images, that is, that are not shaped or not radically so, and some plant and flower images that are cut to shape, and distributed them around the board, usually but not always avoiding the ladders and slides.

Overlaying the nostalgia of the past, therefore, are the experiences of the present, some flowers, some magazine images of a restaurant interior and a water fountain of male sculptures where the water flows out through their penises, some postcards of city scenes, and some playing cards from a French game called "7 Familles," a game somewhat similar to "Go Fish." The swirls of the slides and the sharp diagonal of the central ladder interact with the wild scatter of the overlaid "disjecta membra," as Ashbery termed it, literally the scattered fragments of imported images.

The interplay between the game's already frenetic presentation and the multiple collaged elements creates not just a juxtaposition between these two categories of the composition but an immersion of the new elements into the

Figure 4.15. John Ashbery, *Chutes and Ladders III (for David Kermani)*, 2008. Collage, 18.5 × 18.375 in. Copyright Estate of John Ashbery, courtesy of the Tibor de Nagy Gallery, New York.

game space. The large ladder might still cross the space, but it is impossible to start climbing it because an upside-down image of the dining room of a hotel refuses access and asserts a downward push when climbing the ladder requires an upward movement. Taking the large slide down is equally compromised, in this case by an enormous violet overlaid with postcard images of a bridge, a church, and several urban scenes.

The third collage, titled *Corona*, is based on the game Chinese checkers. The collage includes several cards from a "Heads and Tails" game, with the lower body of one person presented over the upper body of another one. This secondary game, of these cards, proceeds by matching a lower body to an upper one. The games incorporated in these collages all require at least two players, a condition not always available to a small boy in rural upstate New York in the 1930s, particular a boy like John Ashbery, who showed little interest in sports and farm life. Part of the "nostalgia" apparent here is therefore the sadness about the solitary activity of playing all the sides of the game. The "Heads and Tails" game reinforces this solitude; the only others present are the random and oddly chosen Rembrandt woman, the small girl hanging over a typewriter, and the image of a boy seated in a pool of water that has been negatively developed. He is cheerful, but the question hovers about whether he is placed there as a self-portrait.

The final collage that I want to discuss is based on a reusable bingo card. Titled *Bingo Beethoven*, it has Beethoven's image pasted over several of the number slots with another one at the bottom, and numbers appear in some of the uncovered slots. Bingo, as a game, has a fairly plebian reputation. It requires not just the two to four or so players of these other board games, but a host of people. If Ashbery did play this game as a child, it would have been with a local church group or in a fire hall. Ashbery's poem "Album Leaf" refers to "bingo tables" (*CP*, 12) and also, as David Herd notes, to "'marigolds,' 'cloths,' . . . 'receipts,' and 'sweet peas,'" a list that creates the kinds of collages described here.[48] The bingo table reference in the poem links to the "grounds" and suggests a kind of fair that risks failure from the "rain that fell / All day" (*CP*, 12). Bingo also surfaces in *Flow Chart*, in "What about the spiders that drilled all day, maneuvers / that took up so much time the judge never got around to depositing the check and the / bingo night went kerflooey, what with the sounds of drenching rain, leaks in the shutters, / pivotal oilcloth sentiments peeling, junked party ornaments, a woman who says he's a size 11 / and other

Figure 4.16. John Ashbery, *Corona*, 2011. Collage, digitized print, 16.5 × 16.5 in. Copyright Estate of John Ashbery, courtesy of the Tibor de Nagy Gallery, New York.

gadabouts, listless ones, too revealing to report on?" (*CP II*, 47–48).[49] There is certainly a turn toward the ironic and critical in the "oilcloth sentiments" and the persistent rain, which while not intended in the sense of the uncontrollable nature of the weather, highlight the bedraggled aspects of the decor.

But this isn't just bingo, it's Beethoven Bingo, and the composer's face appears repeatedly across the playing card, eyes forward, jaw thrust forward, classic near-scowl. Here is the direct confrontation between the popular-culture, small-town past time spent in church halls and fire halls face to face, literally, with a symbol of high or elite culture. Bingo is what is said on the

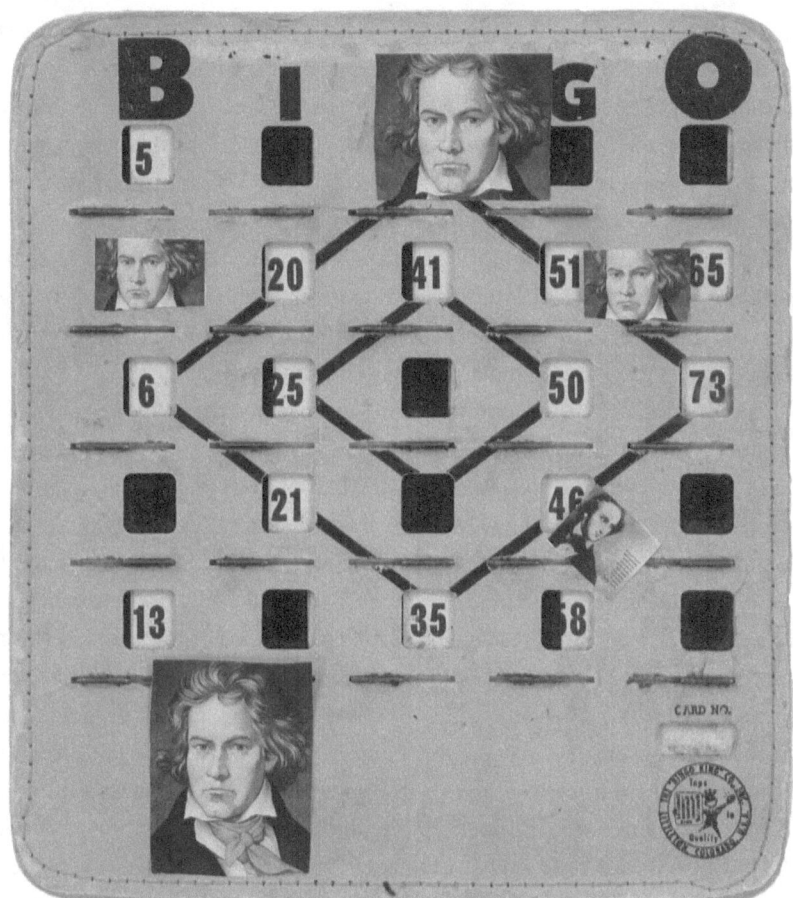

Figure 4.17. John Ashbery, *Bingo Beethoven*, 2014. Collage on vintage bingo board, 8.25 × 7.5 in. Copyright Estate of John Ashbery, courtesy of the Tibor de Nagy Gallery, New York.

achievement of a winning combination; it is also what is said with surprise and happiness on achieving a goal: I got it! This collage sets up the "Bingo!" of finding one's cultural place, launched out of the bingo halls of childhood and into the concert ones of a sophisticated adult.

This collage, as well as the others described here and the others crafted by Ashbery, use his sense of nostalgia, the mixed perception of the childhood past as a safe and pleasant interlude with the recollection of his childhood as uncomfortable and lonely, punctuated with the family catastrophe of his brother's death. The collages, therefore, pull these mixed and conflicting resonances of the past into the present moment and recast them, not simply with a critical eye but with the understanding of how the past is ever present and ever shifting in our experience of the present. Yet, at once, the reconfiguration of the game boards makes it possible to redo the past, to take up images taken at face value at an early age and exert control over them, to erase the scary parts and interfere with the dangerous ones (such as being sent back in Chutes and Ladders by descending a slide), and thereby to strip them of power they might have held over the young child.

Ashbery relied on the technique of collage for his poetry as well, so that the poetry becomes a pastiche of a multitude of elements, phrases seen or heard in random places, never noted in the text of the poems through quotation marks or citations.[50] I have spoken about poetic collage elsewhere, suggesting that the collaged materials, those quotations lifted from one context and placed into the new one of the poem, still bear links to their original context but also become "reshaped" in the new context of the poem, setting up an oscillation between the original meaning and situation and those of the new position.[51] A key example of poetic collage in Ashbery's poetry is "Europe,"[52] a poem that has received a great deal of critical attention and about which Ashbery was asked in multiple interviews.[53] It is well known that a major source for this poem is the 1917 novel for children, *Beryl of the Biplane* by William Le Queux.[54] The novel's subtitle is *Being the Romance of an Air-Woman of To-day*, and it focuses on just that, a romance between a young woman, Beryl Gaselee, and her fiancé, Ronald Pryor. Beryl is a pilot, but while she is permitted to fly in this novel, she only does so for the sake of ease of transport, and it is only at the novel's end that she actually sees some action, flying her lover to safety after he has been wounded in a skirmish in the air. "Ronnie" is a well-to-do and very handsome man who took up flying but was wounded grievously in the early part of the war (World War I), so he has started up an airplane factory and invents improvements for planes, in particular the "silencer," which is a gizmo that, when attached to an airplane, allows it to fly perfectly quietly, an important feature for flying over antiaircraft stations. Beryl is all girl, "devoid of that curious hardness of feature which usually distinguishes the female athlete,"[55] "a charming figure of that feminine type that is so purely English";[56] but, while the novel comments on her "air-woman's" outfit every time she flies, it finally describes her flying clothes as "a warm jersey and a pair of workmanlike trousers, and over them a wind-proof flying suit with leather cap tied beneath her chin, a garb which gave her a very masculine appearance."[57] The novel is composed of six chapters, each of which recounts a thrilling and dangerous incident in Beryl and Ronnie's successful efforts to protect the English from the "Huns." Each chapter stands on its own; that is, rather than being structured around one coherent plot, the novel is episodically structured, as if it had first appeared in serial form.

David LeHardy Sweet describes the poem that Ashbery wrote out of this novel as a "junk" collage, like those created by Robert Rauschenberg: "The relevance of such [junk collages] to Ashbery's poem is the *disorienting* quality of constructed multiplicity—of combing disparate, junk elements and almost casually coordinating them to establish what Rauschenberg has called a 'random order.'"[58] Sweet dismisses the Le Queux novel source as a "patently jingoistic novel for English school girls"[59] and argues that Ashbery's reliance on this source diminishes the poem: "Meaning . . . is what troubles this poem and it is not accident that the literal meanings it sometimes offers are so insipid, drawn from the jingoistic adventure story, the paranoid spy thriller, and the vapid romance."[60]

There is no question that this novel is a little cheap and a little silly and even quite cringeworthy at moments, and these are elements linked to the notion of "camp" raised earlier, that wry tone of irony to call attention to and make fun of cheesy popular culture from previous eras. However, at the same time, this source would have been the type of novel that a young John Ashbery would have encountered in his small, local public library and would have read without irony or question, but with pleasure and excitement. In calling it up in the poem, the irony is met with the sincerity of the child and accepted as such. The notion of the silencer is particularly salient here, for it reduces the danger of these flights to encourage the launching of the child's imagination.

Additionally, these quotations from the novel take on some of the form and function of the readymade: half collage, I would suggest, and half incorporation in an intact state. That is, in this poem in particular, the collage technique that Ashbery uses, as with his visual collages, is a "light" technique in that, rather than adapting and incorporating materials from other sources, he drops them into the text relatively unmodified. Because "Europe" contains multiple small sections, each "collage" element is also a readymade: a stand-alone element presented without adaptation into its new context within the poem. In her essay "Mixed Feelings: Ashbery, Duchamp, Roussel, and the Animation of Cliché," Susan Rosenbaum talks about cliché as a readymade.[61] I am pressed to disagree with this link between these two artistic elements, as the readymade is a mass-produced object; it is designed and manufactured for the use of as many people as possible. In putting a urinal or bottle rack on display as art, Marcel Duchamp was not simply making a statement about how art can be defined but was also insisting that we perceive these industrially fabricated things as designs in their own right, too. Ashbery himself talks about readymades in his essay "The New Realism," saying that they are important to art because "they are a common ground, a neutral language understood by everybody, and therefore the ideal material with which to create experiences which transcend the objects."[62] He argues that the artist, in using these readily recognized objects, can assume that everyone will access them and their functions immediately, and through that connection, the artist can link the audience to experience beyond the object itself.

Ashbery relied on collage across the breadth of his poetic career. In 1981 in a letter to Helen McNeil, he wrote: "[W]hen writing I sometimes use as bits of collage things that happen to be lying around my desk or that I hear over the radio. There are very few such elements in 'Litany,' but that passage comes from an autobiographical story by [Giacomo] Leopardi, 'The Woman Whom [sic] Cannot Be Found,' page 48 in his *Selected Prose and Poetry* translated by Iris Origo and John Heath-Stubbs. I had Xeroxed that page for use as some sort of exercise for my writing students. . . . It happened to be next to my typewriter as I was writing and got sucked into the poem."[63] In Rich Kelley's interview of him, Ashbery said, "Collage-making using words seemed to come naturally to me, as I mentioned before about my experiments in Paris. It seems a prototypically modernist strategy—placing something next to something else to see what unexpected result might emerge—as in Lautréamont's oft-quoted 'chance encounter of a sewing machine and an umbrella on a dissecting table.' (I hope I'm getting that right.)"[64] In another interview not long before Ashbery's death, Charles Bernstein asked about collage: "But you don't really work that way after those early poems when you are writing.

My sense is that when you write, it's not necessarily using a source extensively," and while Ashbery responded by saying, "I do a lot now but it's from my own stuff that I collage," in a poetry reading at the University of Massachusetts in 2014, he spoke about using text from sources such as advertisements in his work, so I believe that he never ceased working with collage elements in his poetry.[65]

Ashbery himself refers to "Europe" as "a lot of splintered fragments,"[66] and it is certainly that, but the movement between these chopped bits of text creates tension and energy, and ultimately energizes Le Queux's mundane prose so that it becomes poetry as well. In fact, while several incorporations of the novel into the poem are in prose form (e.g., sections 8, 22, and 23), most of them appear with line breaks, a clear transformation of prose into poetry: "I had come across / to the railway from the Great North / Road, which I had followed up to London" (*CP*, 93). The line break forces emphasis where it normally would not fall, on "cross" and "North," and creates an awkward caesura after "Road."

The anxiety appears in the nausea of section 2 and in the "What might have . . . This could have been done— / This could not be done" of section 7 (*CP*, 92). There are many instances of crisis, such as "that surgeon must operate" (*CP*, 93); the "razor today engraved sobs" (*CP*, 94); the "wounded carrying dying" (*CP*, 94); and the "snapshots offal in the wind / that's the way we do it terror" (*CP*, 98). These are primarily crises of war, in keeping with the Le Queux novel, but in their juxtaposition with the novel, these words of fear and massacre are sharpened, for the novel is breezy in tone. Beryl and Ronnie face danger, but even when Ronnie is injured and Beryl is flying him home across the British Channel, it is clear that we can count on her, with her "marvelous judgment and foresight" and her "pluck—the pluck that had come to the female sex in these days of war."[67] Even with that sharpness of contrast, the excerpts from the novel might serve to make us feel better; that war might be utterly ghastly, but valiant heroes are there to defend us and to win that war or at least do their best.

The final section of the poem is only excerpts from one page of the novel but in poetic form (that is, with line breaks). The passage is from just before Ronnie and Beryl prevail over the wicked spies from Germany, and it consists of a series of signals in Morse code in the form of lights flashing from a searchlight. As far as I can tell, the "N.F." that is flashed refers to the German

Nachtflug, for night flight. The abbreviation SSS probably refers to Special Service Selection, though I am unclear here. It is not the equivalent of SOS for a call for help, but a signal to call a plane overhead. The message does not refer to where the landing field is, since the protagonists already know that it is in Yorkshire. Perhaps it is merely an agreed-upon signal. I see these signals as connected to the silencer, that mechanical add-on to the plane that permits it to fly silently. Signals are abbreviated efforts to communicate; a silencer permits us to do things quietly so that we will not be caught doing them, but it also prevents us from speaking, from communicating. It could be that the poem is saying that it is impossible to talk about war, that all we can do is to signal our horror: "N.F.," "N.F."

Whether in the form of emblem books or collages, Ashbery pulls us across time and texts in making space out of time. When he inserts the past directly into the instant, that "field of presence," perception can come into itself, drawing on the activations of multiple senses and re-forming memories. The disjunction between elements in the poems, whether in images mismatched to the texts or in incorporated textual fragments, forces clear and focused attention to the present but also a call to what in the past might support a comprehension of experience.

Chapter 5

Memory
"That Stalled Moment"

PHENOMENOLOGY IS, AS Merleau-Ponty asserts, a "philosophy of reflection" (*VI*, 32). Reflection carries within it two primary concerns, that of memory and that of the consciousness of memory. The consciousness of memory entails as well how we make sense of memory, that we are not simply conscious of memories, but we persistently rethink them and reprocess them. Ashbery considered the function of memory and reflection in his work at great length; it persists in just about every poem he wrote.

In his consideration of memory, Merleau-Ponty argues that the present always interacts with and modifies memory. "Reflection," he says, "is only the perception returning to itself, the conversion from the knowing of the thing to a knowing of oneself of which the thing was made, the emergence of a 'binding' that was the bond itself" (*VI*, 37). This consciousness of the act of perception and its quality is not the end of the reflection process, however. It contains within it the interest in comprehension of present and past experience, but this comprehension, while the effort to gain it energizes us, is never complete or adequate. The "light" of comprehension that we receive back from our reflection on our memories is simply that, a pale reflection not bearing the light of understanding or knowledge. Merleau-Ponty argues that "[w]hat is given [through the act of reflection] is not a massive and opaque world, or a universe of adequate thought; it is a reflection which turns back over the density of the world in order to clarify it, but which, coming second, reflects back to it only its own light"(*VI*, 35). This inadequacy of reflection shapes our position in the world as a more "muted" one, as Merleau-Ponty says: "The relation between a thought and its object, between the *cogito* and the *cogitatum*, contains neither the whole nor even the essential of our commerce with the world[,] and . . . we have to situate that relation back within a more muted relationship with the world, within an initiation into the world upon which it rests and which is always already accomplished when the reflective return intervenes" (*VI*, 35). It is not just that reflection is weaker than experience, this quotation suggests, however; it is rather that perception, that "relation between a thought and its object," is always partial, and it is upon that partiality that reflection comes to rest.

Still, and even so, reflection is necessary for some sense of "energy" and "recovery." Because we need to exert ourselves to comprehend existence by being conscious of it, and therefore by reflecting on it, we gain "energy" through what Merleau-Ponty calls "inspiration" from our knowledge of the past: "As an effort to found the existing world upon a *thought* of the world, the reflection at each instant draws its inspiration from the prior presence of the world, of which it is a tributary, from which it derives all its energy" (*VI*, 34). Merleau-Ponty sees reflection as an "act of recovery" (*VI*, 38), therefore, as it literally recovers the past, as in bringing it back and revealing it to the present, but it also makes things better as in a recovery of health by supporting the impetus to make sense of the present through the persistent dredging up and rethinking of the sediments of the past.

Additionally, reflection is a creative function. Facing the fragmentation of memory and attempting to retrieve it activates innovative capacities in the reflective person. Merleau-Ponty describes this process by saying that "we must consider reflection to be a creative operation that itself participates in the facticity of the unreflected. This is why, of all philosophies, phenomenology speaks of a transcendent field. This word signifies that reflection never has the entire world and the plurality of monads spread out and objectified before its gaze, that it only ever has a partial view and a limited power. This is also why phenomenology is a phenomenology, that is, the study of the *appearance* of Being to consciousness, rather than taking for granted its possibility in advance" (*PP*, 62). Phenomenology would have it, therefore, that even though access to memory is only "partial," the important, the most essential feature of turning to memory is that it makes perception a conscious act; that is, that there is not only human awareness of perception but human effort to "make sense" of that perception. Thus, "[t]he task of a radical reflection," Merleau-Ponty argues, "that is, a reflection that attempts to understand itself, consists paradoxically in recovering the unreflective experience of the world in order to import the attitude of verification and reflective operations back into this experience, and in order to reveal reflection as one of the possibilities of my being" (*PP*, 251). In order to be reflective, we must tap back into unretrieved memories and endeavor to come to terms with them, specifically to understand them and their role in our existence. Also, because our present is not the time of the events creating any memory, this retrieval pulls these memories into a different time and our different person, creating a reflection that is also shaped by this distinctly different context of the present.

Crucial in the act of reflection is communication about it, and for my evidence for this point I turn to Jacques Derrida, for he talks about reflection in terms of how it connects not just to a reconsideration of memory but to the creative act itself. In "Meaning as Soliloquy," Derrida says: "There is a double effect of the medium, a double relation between logos and sense: on the one hand, it is a pure and simple *reflexion*, a reflection which respects what it receives and returns, *de-picts* the sense as such in its original colors and re-presents it in person. This is language as *Abbildung* (copy, portrait, figuration, representation). But, on the other hand, this reproduction imposes the blank imprint of the concept. It forms the sense in the meaning, it produces a specific nonproduction, which, without changing anything in the sense, *pictures* something in it."[1] Although translated into English here, his use of the word "de-picts" (the original was probably *dépeindre*) is interesting. The prefix "de-" refers to a "removal" or "negation."[2] However, the word "depict" comes intact from Latin *depictus*, which means "to portray, paint, sketch, describe, imagine," where "de-" can also mean "down." That is, depict means to "get down" as in portraying something, usually an image, but at once the "de-" of depict also suggests a stripping away of the image. In "de-picting" the memory, its image is removed, but then it is re-presented, that is, shown or accessed again but via reflection. This re-presentation is how a memory appears in reflection;, it is not the memory itself but rather this "copy, portrait, figuration, representation," this incomplete and inaccurate portrayal of that elusive memory, reconstituted through an act of communication, this representation, whether visual or verbal.

Marcel Proust's concern with the impact of memory is, of course, legendary, but, as interpreted by Georges Poulet, the operation of memory is not as simple as eating a madeleine cookie and being transported to the past. According to Poulet, "When in the depth of memory, some image of the past offers itself confusedly to the consciousness, there still remains a task to be accomplished which consists, says Proust, 'in learning what particular circumstance, what epoch of the past is in question.' This task bears a name. It is called *localization*. Now, in the same way that the mind localizes a remembered image in duration, it localizes it in space."[3] That is, orientation in time and place are necessary for memory to serve its function as a transporter to another moment. The moment must be determined with exactitude. Yet, this exactitude is never possible to attain because of the "affective" nature of memory, its entanglement with emotion, which is linked to the original moment and those attached to the remembrance. What is retrievable through memory is always incomplete: "What [memory] restores is restituted only in a provisory fashion," Poulet argues, "so that the partial restoration realized by the memory has for effect only the substituting for the spatial discontinuity, a discontinuity this time temporal . . . [a] progress interrupted by gaps.[4] The effort to bridge these gaps is ceaseless and attenuates memory and the emotions connected to it, what Poulet calls a "force [that] stretches out in Proustian space. It is accompanied by an incessant murmur of words. Continuous movement, incessant murmur!"[5] The novelist fills the temporospatial fissure with the words that try and try to link the trigger for the memory to the actual event in the past.

Ashbery read Proust before college and then again in college. He refers to Proust in his art criticism[6] and in interviews, such as with Ross Labrie: "The value of Proust. I suppose we all know time is the main subject of his writing, and it's something that has preoccupied me";[7] and with Peter Stitt, during which he talks about a "Proustian excursion" and how he read Proust in a "course with Harry Levin."[8] In the same interview, Ashbery describes the impact reading Proust had on him, that it left him "feeling sadder and wiser" and that Proust's fiction "seizes the way life sometimes seems to have of droning on in a sort of dream-like space."[9] Stitt asks, "Who is your favorite novelist of all time?" and Ashbery answers, "Proust."

At least two poems of Ashbery's show explicit links to Proust, though I would argue that many of them betray an interest in this experience of life as on and on into a kind of meditative state. "Bird's Eye View of the Tool and Die Co." starts with a reference to Proust's *Swann's Way* (the first volume of *Remembrance of Things Past*):[10] "For a long time I used to go to bed early" becomes in this poem, "For a long time I used to get up early" (*CP*, 507). The

"Overture" to Proust's novel, from which Ashbery pulled this quotation, focuses on sleep and the lack thereof, and becomes a lengthy discourse on dream and memory, what Proust calls "shifting and confused gusts." Both this section of the Proust multivolume novel and Ashbery's short poem concern time and its constraints, for Proust refers to "the chain of the hours" and Ashbery's poem talks about "the / Enclosure of time" (*CP*, 507). By inverting the time in the poem from going to bed to waking up, Ashbery shifts immediately not just from the first person to the third but to details of human life ("20–30 vision, hemorrhoids intact"), but then he brings in dreams as another nod to Proust.[11]

Where Proust focuses on social moments with relatives, Ashbery pulls in "meditated / Gang-wars, ice cream, loss, palm terrain" (*CP*, 507), random elements floating to the conscious through those "confused gusts" of memory. More closely aligned with Proust is "The force of / Living hopelessly backward into a past of striped / Conversations" (*CP*, 507), that constraint not just of time but of the inescapable power of memory to pull us into the past, and these are conversations, like Proust's, that are never complete but rather fragmentary and imperfect, warped by time and emotionally veiled resurfacing. "It has become a stricture" (*CP*, 508), this poem closes, in talking about the constraints of social interaction and the time ordering and confining our existence.

Ashbery's poem "Proust's Questionnaire" is another overt nod to Proust.[12] By starting the poem with "I am beginning to wonder / Whether this alternative to / Sitting back and doing something quiet / Is the clever initiative it seemed" (*CP*, 773), Ashbery appears to be saying that he (or rather, this first-person narrator) has decided to take a different approach to life than Proust did, to stay as quietly as possible in reclusion for as long as possible. The second stanza responds to the poem's title: "It's a question of questions," that there are different kinds of them, one of which is "The nuts-and-bolts kind you know you can answer" (*CP*, 773) and others of which are "the impersonal ones" (*CP*, 774) that launch memory, so that "Someone is summoned to a name, and soon / A roomful of people becomes dense and contoured / And words come out of the wall . . ." (*CP*, 774). However, the poem suggests, it is "up to" the poet to make sense of memory and experience ("the luck of uncoding / This singular cipher"), that mash of sensations that are, as Proust said, "shifting and confused."

Poetry must not just turn to memory, however, but to the notion of reflection that is situated on memory and launches beyond it into a consciousness and "making sense" of it. Charles Bernstein calls reflection the act of "language turning upon itself"[13] and argues in "The Objects of Meaning: Reading Cavell Reading Wittgenstein" that poets "literally make the world come into being by giving voice to it, by our (re)calls."[14] Nothing, James McCorkle argues, is possible for Ashbery's poetry in particular without the act of reflection, what he calls the "force of remembering," and it is these acts of reflection that "integrate the past with the present: In Ashbery's poetry, presence and memory depend on each other; no assemblage of the present, of the very momentum of thought and perception with language, can be void of memory or the force of remembering.... Ashbery's poetry is particularly important in that it reintegrates our mnemonic processes, eros, and the everyday."[15]

Jody Norton insists that reflection is an essential, and probably the essential, function at work in Ashbery's poetry. She argues that "an attempt to produce a formulation of subjectivity is necessarily reflective—that is, distanced from both the materiality and the experience of the individual"[16]—and that, therefore, Ashbery's intent is to "explore the shifting configuration of subjectivity."[17] Doing so requires a reflective turn in pulling away from experience in order to acquire a sense of it. "Poetic thinking," therefore, Norton argues, "for Ashbery, is reflection: the subject, as thinking being, reflects on his own subjectivity, and in doing so reflects that subjectivity—which is no more fixed or consistent than thought itself."[18] Reflection, in these terms, is not necessarily objective, but it certainly requires the effort to decouple from experience as it constitutes oneself to consider it and recount it. In so doing, the reflection enables poetry to effect this recursion between current experience and memory, however fragmentary, and back into the present in the form of language. "Sense," Ben Lerner suggests, "is a value of retrospection, a backward motion that forces the speaker to identify with his speech. ... A demand for sense pins the poet to the past, but understanding can ... be dissolved into the flow of language, enabling a kind of presence."[19] In his interview with Bloom and Losada, Ashbery himself concurs with these appraisals of his approach, that "[a]t the end a person is somehow given an embodiment out of those proliferating reflections that are occurring in a generalized mind which will eventually run together into the image of a specific person."[20]

Reflection permeates Ashbery's poetry, and in ways that are not always traceable, but that do not require tracking. By this I mean that these "gusts" of memory surge up and receive the poet's consideration and incorporation into the text of his poems in another state, that is the state of having been remembered, inadequately and fragmentarily, and having been reflected upon, and so reconsidered and regurgitated into another form. It is, therefore, not necessary to look into his poems for instances of the true past, but instead to think about these small elements, each statement, as something out of the banks of his memory. There are, of course, identifiable instances in his poems, such as those recollections probably based on his brother's death, as in "Our Youth": "He is dead. Green and yellow handkerchiefs cover him" (CP, 72); and in "Rain": "And the little one / the hooded lost one / near the pillow // A fine young man" (CP, 62). "The Picture of Little J. A. in a Prospect of Flowers" talks explicitly about memory, too, in Ashbery's close examination of a photograph of himself as a child positioned before blooming phlox. Here the poem argues that the "comic version" of the poet as depicted in this image is the "true one," and that it is only by reaching back to that "version," to those "lost words," that the poem can "find words" (CP, 14).[21]

It is only later in poems like "Syringa," "Blue Sonata," and "A Wave" that Ashbery permits himself to become more explicit in his poetry about the function of reflection.[22] In a clear nod to the previous poem, in "Syringa" he writes, "For although memories, of a season, for example, / Melt into a single snapshot, one cannot guard, treasure / That stalled moment. It too is flowing, fleeting" (CP, 535). Here he questions what he had previously affirmed, that while the photograph might appear to crystallize an instant, time makes it impossible to do so. The passage of time away from that "stalled moment" changes perception of that second in the past. Ashbery also takes up this question of reflection in "Blue Sonata" when he writes,

> The things that were coming to be talked about
> Have come and gone and are still remembered
> As being recent. There is a grain of curiosity
> At the base of some new thing, that unrolls
> Its question mark like a new wave on the shore.
> In coming to give, to give up on what we had,
> We have, we understand, gained or been gained

> By what was passing through, bright with the sheen
> Of things recently forgotten and revived.
> Each image fits into place, with the calm
> Of not having too many, of having just enough.
> We live in the sigh of our present. (*CP*, 533)

We might "live in the sigh of our present," but we forget and remember and "revive" elements of the past that float into this present. And, he suggests, the poet does not simply dredge these elements up as is but processes them through the activity of reflection: "It would be tragic to fit / Into the space created by our not having arrived yet, / To utter the speech that belongs there, / For progress occurs through re-inventing / These words form a dim recollection of them, / In violating that space in such a way as / To leave it intact. Yet we do after all / Belong here, and have moved a considerable / Distance; our passing is a facade. / But our understanding of it is justified" (*CP*, 533). Essential here are the references to "re-inventing" and "dim recollection," that reflection takes up those "dim" and fragmented memories and reconsiders them, reshaping them for the present.

While "A Wave" is largely a consideration of the nature of love, embedded within it are clear statements of how important the past is in understanding the present and also how reflection modifies those recollections. As this poem states, the past is essential to consider: "past experience matters again" (*CP*, 788). The poem uses an analogy of the beach at low tide for memory, saying that the receding sea exposes odd bits of debris, each of which represents something that happened in the past: "As with rocks at low tide, a mixed surface is revealed, / More detritus. Still, it is better this way / Than to have to live through a sequence of events acknowledged / In advance in order to get to a primitive statement. And the mind / Is the beach on which the rocks pop up, just a neutral / Support for them in their indignity. They explain / The trials of our age, cleansing it of toxic / Side-effects as it passes through their system. / Reality. Explained. And for seconds / We live in the same body, are a sibling again" (*CP*, 790). Memory is, therefore, a repository more for instants than for this "sequence of events," each exposed rock representing something in the past. These "rocks" become the fodder for poetry, that "dream of rubble" (*CP*, 793), for "That memory contains everything" (*CP*, 798). All that persists from the past is the memory, but it is the clear evidence that the past happened at all: "surely / The slightly sunken memory that remains, accretes, is proof / That there were doings" (*CP*, 801). Yet this past, these memories, are always incomplete: "And as it / Focuses itself, it is the backward part of a life that is / Partially coming into view" (*CP*, 789).

The past alone is not sufficient for poetry, for poetry requires reflection on the past in order to produce energy, the force of the imagination to recover and remember the past. This process is a cycling through of observation and speculation, repeated multiple times (*CP*, 795–96), in which the poet perceives, remembers, and considers what that memory might signify. "So," therefore, "the voluminous past / Accepts, recycles our claims to present consideration" (*CP*, 797). Reflection is beyond simply memory, but it involves a "[transposition]" that takes the poet past what memory had been ("The spirit that was to occupy those times / Now transposed, sunk too deep in its own reflection / For memory" [*CP*, 805]) and renders the memory that the poet reconfigures into a more robust entity: "And we can get back to that raw state / Of feeling, so long deemed / Inconsequential and therefore appropriate to our later musings / . . . What is restored / Becomes stronger than the loss as it is remembered" (*CP*, 796). By "getting back" to that memory fragment, the poet is able to achieve what is essentially a better memory, one reconstituted for the present moment and, especially, one bearing the nuance of interpretation: "In falling we should note the protective rush of air past us / And then pray for some day after the war to cull each of / The limited set of reflections we were given at the beginning / To try to make a fortune out of. Only then will some kind of radical stance / Have had some meaning . . ." (*CP*, 806–7).

The poem talks repeatedly of this "making sense," not just of these memories, of course, but also of human experience and, in this poem in particular, of the human experience of love: "But for the tender blur / Of the setting to mean something, words must be ejected bodily, / A certain crispness be avoided in favor of a density / Of strutted opinion doomed to wilt in oblivion: not too linear / Nor yet too puffed and remote" (*CP*, 789); "And the issue / Of making sense becomes such a far-off one" (*CP*, 789); "I think all games and disciplines are contained here, / Painting, as they go, dots and asterisks that / We force into meanings that don't concern us / And so leave us behind. But there are no fractions, the world is an integer / Like us, and like us it can neither stand wholly apart nor disappear" (*CP*, 790); "And though there are some who leave regularly / For the patchwork landscape of childhood, north of here, / Our own kind of stiff standing around, waiting helplessly / And mechanically for instructions that never come, suits the space / Of our intense, uncommunicated speculation . . ." (*CP*, 795); and "everything, in short, / That makes this explicit earth what it appears to be in our / Glassiest moments . . . / celebrates us / And what we have made of it" (*CP*, 796). Essential here in this list of evidence demonstrating Ashbery's devotion to memory and to "what we have made of it" is the sense of effort involved not just in recalling memories but in working to figure out what they might do to help us understand our present. In particular, too, is the sense in this poem, and in much of Ashbery's work, I would argue, that this is how poetry comes about, that it is the articulation of these memories, fragmented "gusts" of imperfect "rock" resting on the beach at low tide, and the reconstruction of them, not into what they were, for that is not possible, but into our sense of what they might be for the present.

"What Is Sequestered": Mirrored Perception

A second type of reflection (in contrast with a turn toward memory) is that of the mirroring of an image, the reproduction of the image created by its bouncing back from a surface that is flat and smooth and accommodates reflection, such as a mirror, but also a still pool of water or a sheet of polished metal. A flat mirror will reflect a relatively exact image. A concave one pulls light in and concentrates it, so it is used for telescopes (a frequent Ashbery image). A convex mirror reflects light outward, giving a fish-eye view of what is reflected, useful for security cameras or for situations where a photographer cannot back up far enough to include an entire scene in one shot. Ashbery's "Self-Portrait in a Convex Mirror"[23] is devoted to this last type of reflection, one that distorts both literally and figuratively.[24]

In 1524, Parmigianino painted a self-portrait through the distorted reflection created by a convex mirror.[25]

Ashbery's poem is the poetic equivalent of a line-by-line "reading" of the painting, another "image" of the painter, doubly reflected, doubly warped, because he will never accurately depict what he is seeing; his words cannot re-create the painting, even in our mind's eye, but also, he cannot mimic the manner in which others would encounter the painting, not only through the

Figure 5.1. Parmigianino, *Self-Portrait in a Convex Mirror*, 1524. Kunsthistorisches Museum, Vienna.

looking at it but particularly not through the conceptual and/or emotional responses to it. Ashbery's continual awareness of this contortion of what he sees is apparent in "Lithuanian Dance Band," where he says, "Perhaps another day one will want to review all this / For today it looks compressed like lines packed together / In one of those pictures you reflect with a polished tube / To get the full effect" (*CP*, 463).[26]

The poem starts out with a sentence fragment, "As Parmigianino did it..." The unstated but concluding part of this sentence is, "so shall Ashbery"; that in this poem he will do what the painter is doing in this self-portrait.[27] That is, as self-portraits are not just about the painter but about art in general, the poem is about poetry, about its function and purpose, and also about human existence and everyday experience.[28]

The guiding principle for this poem is the sphere.[29] It is a metaphor of the self, of the individual life "englobed." Merleau-Ponty argues that "[u]niversality and the world are at the core of individuality and of the subject. We will never understand this as long as we turn the world into an ob-ject; but we will understand it immediately if the world is the field of our experience, and if we are nothing but a perspective on the world" (*PP*, 428). The "ob-ject," in this case the sphere, represents the world, therefore, and Ashbery's approach to it is the effort to communicate as this "field of experience" becomes the poem.[30]

In this englobing, Ashbery suggests that there is some kind of entrapment, that we would "like to stick [our] hand / Out of the globe, but [it] will not allow it" (*CP*, 475), and we are "restless . . . Longing to be free, outside" (*CP*, 474), but we are "captive" (*CP*, 474). Encapsulated within this rounded space is "our moment of attention" (*CP*, 475), the instant of perception; it is "contained," yet "transparent." The sphere's surface, that "skin of the bubble" (*CP*, 478) is what we perceive: "The surface is what's there/ And nothing can exist except what's there" (*CP*, 476). Yet, it is what is outside the sphere that is the most important; as the poem says, "Each person / Has one big theory to explain the universe / But it doesn't tell the whole story / And in the end it is what is outside him / That matters" (*CP*, 486). The sphere is "a metaphor / Made to include us" (*CP*, 481), "glazed, embalmed" (*CP*, 474), "In suspension" (*CP*, 474). As such, it is essential that it remain immobile: "it must stay / Posing in this place. It must move / As little as possible" (*CP*, 474–75).

The poem becomes, then, a resistance to what is inside the sphere and an appeal to escape it. Still, as a truncated sphere, the convex mirror has its benefits. It is "organizing" (*CP*, 477, 484), a "mapped space" (*CP*, 480) that orders this "magma of interiors" (*CP*, 477) just as the artist "weaves [his] delicate meshes" in the painting (*CP*, 475). Even though it is a reflection of a reflection (that is, the painter painting, creating a reflection of his reflected image), and so at a greater remove from himself, it is "lively and intact" (*CP*, 474), "a spark or star" (*CP*, 475).

Attention, therefore, emphasizes the sphere in "Self-Portrait in a Convex Mirror," becoming an extended metaphor in the poem. Because of the roundness of these images, perhaps, time, especially experience over time, takes on roundness as well, a call back to the round motif in "Clepsydra." Thus, there is a "carousel" (*CP*, 477), a "balloon" (*CP*, 476), and a "waterwheel of days" (*CP*, 484). Time here becomes a "concentric growing up of days /

Around a life" (*CP*, 481). While the surface of this mirror provides only "velleities" (*CP*, 479), there is pressure for movement and change. The roundness evolves into an oscillation, where "in and out, back and forth" (*CP*, 482) become a part of the present: "these are things as they are today / Before one's shadow ever grew / Out of the field into thoughts of tomorrow" (*CP*, 477). Like everyday experience, "In the present we are always escaping from / And falling back into" (*CP*, 483–84) what are "ordinary / Forms of daily activity" (*CP*, 485).

The poem focuses clear and direct attention on the present and on the experience of the moment: here, we perceive the "strewn evidence" (*CP*, 477) of perception that "[flows] like an hourglass" (*CP*, 478). Here, too, time is like weather (*CP*, 476), where it is a state of change. The present appears in the poem as the moment of experience, "the present we are always escaping from / And falling back into" (*CP*, 483–84), and it considers the idiosyncrasy of individual experience: "I used to think they were all alike, / That the present always looked the same to everybody / But this confusion drains away as one / Is always cresting into one's present" (*CP*, 483).[31] Preceding this statement is a description of the present, "that special, lapidary / Todayness that the sunlight reproduces / Faithfully in casting twig-shadows on blithe / Sidewalks" (*CP*, 483). The jewel-like moment of the present instant slides into this sense of the present as a wave or as an arrival at a height, that "cresting," with such an awareness of the flash of time as if all drops away from us. It is as if, at this moment, we rise above the morass of the "chaos" (*CP*, 477) of the reflection and experience a momentary clarity.[32]

This reflection is also attention to the past in a recognition of the impact of the memory of past events on the experience of the present.[33] Memories become in the poem those "forgotten / Things that don't seem familiar when / We meet them again, lost beyond telling, / Which were ours once" (*CP*, 479).[34] As described earlier in this chapter, access to and dredging up of memory is imperfect. Merleau-Ponty says to that effect that "[t]here is no real coinciding with the being of the past: if the pure memory is the former present preserved, and if, in the act of recalling, I really could become what I was, it becomes impossible to see how it could open to me the dimension of the past. And if in being inscribed within me each present loses its flesh, if the pure memory into which it is changed is an invisible, then there is indeed a past, but no coinciding with it—I am separated from it by the whole thickness of my present in making itself present anew. As we never have at the same time the thing and the consciousness of the thing, we never have at the same time the past and the consciousness of the past" (*VI*, 122). Memory is, therefore, "fleshless" and "invisible"; access to it is imperfect. Memories might, as the poem says, have been "ours once," as in our experiences, but when we turn to them, we cannot see them as they were when they occurred, so they are no longer "familiar."

The poem repeats this point, that "we can no longer return to the various / Conflicting statements gathered, lapses of memory / Of the principal witnesses" (*CP*, 483).[35] We cannot go back to the past; no one remembers perfectly. The past is, therefore, hardened; memory is not directly accessible. As a part of the painting motif, the past has a "gray glaze" (*CP*, 484). In a sense of the randomness of experience and how we retain elements of it in the form of memory, the poem describes "memories [as] deposited in irregular / Clumps of crystals" (*CP*, 476), a metaphor for memory as little, odd fragments of materialized structures with inherent patterning. This conception of memory provides a link to the distortion of light passing through it, reshaping it as it is pulled into the present experience, the allusion to Emily Dickinson in "a peculiar slant of memory" (*CP*, 476).

It is not a surprise, given the poem's topic of the deformity of an image created by a reflection on a convex surface, that it would take up questions of perception and its inaccuracies.[36] There are repeated references to "distortion" (*CP*, 479) and to "perspective" (*CP*, 477), and there are very careful verbal renderings of what happens to the image when seen this way: that enormous hand in the foreground that "loom[s] large / As it retreats slightly" (*CP*, 475), "Roving back to the body of which it seems / So unlikely a part" (*CP*, 475), "that / Sliver of window or mirror" (*CP*, 476), this "pinpoint of a smile" (*CP*, 475).

The distortion of the reflection becomes symbolic of the distortion of perception.[37] It is possible to discern the landscape (*CP*, 477, 480), but as with all of these efforts, perception reaches its limits in the form of the horizon: "our / Landscape sweeping out from us to disappear / On the horizon" (*CP*, 478). This limit means that comprehension of existence through experience is always "sequestered" (*CP*, 474), "veiled, compromised" (*CP*, 484), and tucked into "recesses" (*CP*, 481) much like those "alcoves" visible in the artist's studio behind his body. There is always in perception, therefore, "something that can never be known" (*CP*, 482). Reflection becomes only a matter for "speculation / (From the Latin *speculum*, mirror)" (*CP*, 475).

This inability to "see" accurately becomes in the poem the inability to say exactly what we mean exactly how we mean it, and it is here in the poem, too, that there is an explicit turn to philosophy:

> . . . as the principle of each individual thing is
> Hostile to, exists at the expense of all the others
> As philosophers have often pointed out, at least
> *This* thing, the mute, undivided present,
> Has the justification of logic, which
> In this instance isn't a bad thing
> Or wouldn't be, if the way of telling
> Didn't somehow intrude, twisting the end result
> Into a caricature of itself." (*CP*, 485)

"The way of telling" here distorts the recounting of the present much the way the convex mirror distorts what it reflects. In equating language to a game of "Whisper Down the Lane" immediately following this quotation, the poet suggests that in the translation from the experience of the moment into poetry, the words of the poem become corrupted by signal interference, like a misheard whisper passed along from one person to the next, so that the final result may bear no resemblance to the actual experience.

Ultimately, the poem turns away from this "gibbous / Mirrored eye of an insect" (*CP*, 487) and turns toward movement. While gesture has been apparent across the work (*CP*, 480, 482), gestures largely of the artist as shown in the self-portrait, it finally appears as a "frozen gesture" (*CP*, 487), and the poem resists this turn. The gesture, even "frozen," like the convex mirror, serves as a focal point around which all experience clusters. Merleau-Ponty says that this

> abstract movement is thus inhabited by a power of objectification, by a "symbolic function," a "representation function," or a power of "projection" that, moreover, is already at work in the constitution of "Thing" and that consists in treating the sensory givens as representatives of each other and, when taken together, as representatives of an "*eidos*."

> It consists in given them a sense, in animating them from within, in organizing them into a system, in centering a plurality of experiences upon a single intelligible core, and in making an identifiable unity appear in them under different perspectives. In short, it consists in arranging behind the flux of impressions an invariant that gives the flux its reason and in articulating the material of experience. (*PP*, 123)

The abstract movement here is the gesture. In this quotation, Merleau-Ponty is talking about objects, how the gesture supports the perception of them, and the "making sense" of that perception. Graham Harman says that "[t]he term 'object' . . . means anything that exists. The term 'relation' means any interaction between these objects. . . . [S]uch interaction is always a kind of translation or distortion" of the kind created by the rounded surface of the mirror.[38] Harman focuses on the "assemblage theory of objects" in which the whole impression is greater than the simple summation of the parts, that is, the myriad, minute impressions of each element of an object.[39] "Real objects," he says, therefore "withdraw from mutual contact and encounter each other only as translations or caricatures. They somehow come into relation through a vicarious medium, and I have said that this medium can only be the *interior* of some other object—a perceptual space filled with intentional objects rather than real ones."[40] This "assemblage" of Harman's is equivalent to Merleau-Ponty's "flux of impressions" that coalesce into experience.[41]

"Shuttlings" (*CP*, 480), "enactments" (*CP*, 480), and "change" (*CP*, 481) are simply elements in what becomes highly charged language. This is language that pursues the achievement of what are prefatory in "intentions" (*CP*, 477).[42] In the poem, this implementation appears in the form of an "explosion" (*CP*, 484) and culminates in the narrator adjuring the artist/depiction to "withdraw that hand" (*CP*, 487) that is "big enough / To wreck the sphere" (*CP*, 475). All that is left in this effort to escape this "[confinement]" (*CP*, 487) are those "distorted" "whispers out of time" (*CP*, 487), elusive and transitory mistransmissions of experience.

In one of his collages, Ashbery took the image of Parmigianino's self-portrait for its base and laid over it a hand holding a bunch of grapes. The hand overlaps the artist's hand in the reproduction of the painting as if to suggest two things at once: that the artist's hand was in fact able to burst through the "globe" encasing him to offer these grapes to the audience, and

Figure 5.2. John Ashbery, *Still Life*, 2016. Mixed-media collage, 11 × 8.5 in., signed and dated verso (Inv. no. 7854). Copyright Estate of John Ashbery, courtesy of the Tibor de Nagy Gallery, New York.

that the audience's hand, the poet's hand in this case, was able to push beyond the mirror's glass to give the painter the grapes. In either case, the collage enacts the poet's desire to "wreck the sphere" by "[sticking] one's hand / Out of the globe" and pierce "the skin of the bubble," and in doing so, to flatten the mirror and erase these reflective distortions.

Sometimes these inaccuracies, we might call them, relate less to literal mirrors and more to misperceptions or inconsistencies in other poems by Ashbery. In "Polite Distortions," for instance, the narrator talks about how "the same old story is different / With each new telling," how "We linger against a pattern / Of hills ... and everything comes / To sway in our sense (well with it)" (CP, 858).[43] In the distinctly different retellings of this "same old story," the memory of the story and of incidents reconfigures and reshapes according to the narrator's faulty recollection, but also to the story's audience. In "Down by the Station, Early in the Morning," Ashbery also writes, "There's the moment years ago in the station in Venice, / The dark rainy afternoon in fourth grade, and the shoes then, / Made of a dull crinkled brown leather that no longer exists. / And nothing does, until you name it, remembering, and even then / It may not have existed, or existed only as a result / Of the perceptual dysfunction you've been carrying around for years" (CP, 743).[44] Here, the "perceptual dysfunction" suggests not just that memory is accessed at different times and in different ways, but that the physical tools supporting perception themselves are flawed and therefore inaccurate. And finally, in "Grand Galop," Ashbery writes, "Too bad, I mean, that getting to know each other just for a fleeting second / Must be replaced by imperfect knowledge of the featureless whole, / Like some pocket history of the world, so general / As to constitute a sob or wail unrelated / To any attempt at definition" (CP, 438). In this case he reflects on the encounter of an instant that is "replaced" with the recollection of it that is fragmentary and "imperfect."

Memory serves an essential function as considered by phenomenology. People turn outside of themselves to take in sensory data. They experience a multitude of things and other people at each moment. They pull this information back into themselves and check it against the repository of memory and cultural and historical artifacts. If the current experiences match up with what is stored, then the repository remains as it is. However, if, as often happens, these experiences present a mismatch with stored materials, then articulation is required to reset this repository. Yet, because the repository is inaccurate and because the articulation can never quite encompass the experience, memory and the reflection onto it are always equally distorted. These are the issues of memory that Ashbery addresses in his poetry in multiple ways.

Chapter 6

Motility and Motricity

I am not in space and in time, nor do I think space and time; rather, I am of space and of time; my body fits itself to them and embraces them.[1]

MOVEMENT IS CRUCIAL to phenomenology because (1) we need to "move" outside of ourselves in the act of sensing what and who are around us, and (2) perception works through contrasts, through what is different from another thing and in what ways it differs from that thing. Movement is apparent in Ashbery's poetry in the form of literal movement, particularly in travel experiences, but it also appears more figuratively, in what Merleau-Ponty refers to as abstract and concrete movement, in the case of this poetry, in particular, in the form of cliché.

To Merleau-Ponty, movement is integral with and essential to perception and in fact takes primacy over language in its ability to grant and shape meaning. Perception cannot occur in absence of a state of flux. He writes that

> for the normal person[2] every movement is indissolubly movement and consciousness of movement. This can be expressed by saying that, for the normal person, every movement has a background, and that the movement and its background are "moments of a single whole." The background of the movement is not a representation associated or linked externally to the movement itself; it is immanent in the movement, it animates it and guides it along at each moment. For the subject, the beginning of kinetic movement is, like perception, an original manner of relating to an object. (*PP*, 113)

The body in movement makes perception possible; it is through our awareness of the world moving around us that we perceive. The movement of the world is also the movement of the body. Essential here, too, is the notion of orientation. By insisting on a background for every movement, Merleau-Ponty integrates the act of situating the movement, and of linking that situation to the consciousness of movement and so of oneself. At its core, phenomenology is the consciousness of perception accessed through perpetual shifts and changes.[3]

Movement can be broadly broken down into two categories: motility and motricity. Motility is the motion of the individual body, its ability to move on its own. Examples of this are sperm and the intestines. They operate without external direction or compulsion. Motricity constitutes the movement between things, such as objects and/or bodies, responses or reactions of one body to the movements of another or others. An essential aspect of movement is the constant recalibration of one's body's positioning, an orientation and reorientation in perpetual refinement.

One method of movement is through travel, a theme of many of Ashbery's poems, including his early poem "And You Know" (*CP*, 29–30)[4] and "The Skaters" (*CP*, 147-78).[5] As Christopher Macann says, "Dynamic motility . . . being in the world . . . has to be understood in terms of tasks, actions to be accomplished, a free space which outlines in advance the possibilities available to the body at any time. In turn, these possibilities have to be understood not as the possibilities of a perceptual presentation or conceptual representation of the world but as the possibilities of action in a world . . . [that] we find in oriented space."[6] Much of what Macann says here has to do with not actual action but the potential for action, these "possibilities," these "actions to be accomplished."

Merleau-Ponty argues that the ability to perceive "forms, distances and objects" and to understand how to act on them "require[s] the same power of marking out borders and directions in the given world, of establishing lines of force, or arranging perspectives, of organizing the given world according to the projects of the moment, and of constructing upon the geographical surroundings a milieu of behavior and a system of significations that express, on the outside, the internal activity of the subject" (*PP*, 115). Essential here, therefore, is not just external movement or orientation but the movement occurring within, the organization of perceptions that shape understanding and responses to the outside world.

The poem "And You Know" posits that potential, that notion of "tasks . . . to be accomplished," as travel: "We are pointing to England, to Africa, to Nigeria; / And we shall visit those places . . . and other places . . ." (*CP*, 29). These are the dreams of childhood in the classroom, and while part of the point of this poem is about the schoolmaster left behind in the dusty, stifling classroom, the poem also emphasizes the imperative of travel: "we must travel on, not to a better land, perhaps, / But to the England of the sonnets, Paris, Colombia, and Switzerland / And all the places with names, that we wish to visit—" (*CP*, 30). Less important than actual travel is the belief that it could happen, that the thought of this type of movement sets up virtual if not actual transience.

As Merleau-Ponty says, "The normal person *reckons* with the possible, which thus acquires a sort of actuality without leaving behind its place as a possibility" (*PP*, 112). The potential for movement not only is apparent to the individual but supports the idea of movement as if it were actually occurring, allowing the production of meaning in the absence of actual events. Douglas Low argues that, "for Merleau-Ponty, where the active, lived-through body meets the patterned structures of the world, there meaning is formed. The structures of the world fold in upon the body just as the body's favored frameworks fold back upon the world. In fact, the framework for experience is created in this lived interaction. In this lived interaction, meaningful perceptual gestalt structures are formed."[7]

Movement is not simply a constant state of flux but contains within it the shift from one state to another, from one place to another. Merleau-Ponty describes this approach by saying: "If we want to take the phenomenon of movement seriously, we must imagine a world that is not merely made up of things, but also of pure transitions" (*PP*, 288). These transitions occur in "And You Know," not just in the form of travel potential but in shifts in time from day to night, as in "At night, comets, shooting stars, twirling planets, / Suns . . . Some find the summer light / Nauseous and damp . . ." (*CP*, 29); in state, as in the contrast between the "onrushing students" and "The girls [who] live in an atmosphere of vacuum"; and in time, as in the teacher "sitting, / Like a great rock, through many years. / It is the erratic path of time we trace . . ." (*CP*, 29).

These moments of perception do not require actual movement but can be triggered by a provocation similar to that which leads to movement.

Merleau-Ponty argues that "[e]ach bodily stimulation for the normal subject awakens, not an actual movement, but a sort of 'virtual movement'; the part of the body addressed escapes from anonymity, appears through a strange tension, and as a certain power for action within the frame of the anatomical apparatus. The normal subject's body is not merely ready to be mobilized by real situations that draw it toward themselves, it can also turn away from the world, apply its activity to the stimuli that are inscribed upon its sensory surfaces, lend itself to experiments and, more generally, be situated in the virtual" (*PP*, 111). The virtual movement is like the potential tasks earlier described but can have a real moment of incitement. Such a moment occurs in "And You Know" when the children "trace / On the globe, with moist fingertip, and surely, the globe stops . . ." (*CP*, 29). Nothing truly happens at this moment other than a tap on a globe with a finger, but it sets off the possibility for adventure and opens the door to a fantasy in which the narrator and his companion will be the king and queen of Naples.

And while "it is too late," as the poem says, to travel to any of these places, the option still exists to go to "the nearest star, that one, that hangs just over the hill, beckoning, / Like a hand of which the arm is not visible" (*CP*, 30).[8] The potential of imagination becomes reality at this moment, when "we fly to the nearest star," an emblem of shift from patterns of classroom lessons to life experiences.

The poem supports movement through its contrast between activity and stillness. The verbs are largely in the "-ing" form, creating adjectives or the present continuous, as in "onrushing," "shooting stars," "twirling planets," "going out," "flaming," "invading," and so on. The action of these verbs is vigorous and unconstrained by time. These planets will twirl forever; that star will always beckon.

Set against them are the deep pockets of silence and motionlessness. The weather is "nauseous and damp" and "humid" and "muggy," a type of "great heat" that enervates the human body. There is no air in this poem—the atmosphere in the classroom is "breathless"; it is a "vacuum." Unlike the whirling dervishes of the students, the teacher is inert, "like a great rock" "on the vast vapid bank," and the children "must rest here." Merleau-Ponty says that "the perception of the body and of objects in contact with the body is confused for the normal subject . . . when there is no movement" (*PP*, 110). The poem periodically slows to a stop in terms of time but also in terms of space, sound, and even air in order to force the children through their perplexity to arrest their thoughtless rushing and to permit the "quiet feeling [that] pervades the classroom," a calm that permits conscious experience.

Merleau-Ponty distinguishes between what he calls "abstract movement" and "concrete movement":

> Within the busy world in which concrete movement unfolds, abstract movement hollows out a zone of reflection and of subjectivity, it superimposes a virtual or human space over physical space. Concrete movement is thus centripetal, whereas abstract movement is centrifugal; the first takes place within being or within the actual, the second takes place within the possible or within non-being; the first adheres to a given background, the second sets up its own background.... The distinction between abstract movement and concrete movement is thereby clarified: the background of concrete movement is the given world, the background of abstract movement is, on the contrary, constructed. (*PP*, 113–14)

Centripetal force keeps an object at a constant speed on a circular path—like an orbit. In terms of concrete movement, this means that by keeping to its path, in this case, the object sticks to its normal pattern of action or behavior. Centrifugal force, on the other hand, is not a force but rather the tendency of an object to fly off a circular path, much like children on a roundabout.[9] Abstract movement is centrifugal, therefore, because it consciously adheres to an action rather than being forced by an external agency to do so. The daily patterns of the classroom, in that case, would adhere to concrete movement, in which the schoolmaster is "not merely / Asking questions and giving answers, but grandly sitting" (*CP*, 29), the present continuous verb form indicating repeated and similar behaviors. Concrete movement does not require thought or consciousness; it is a simple indicator of habit.

Abstract movement, however, transpires within consciousness—the awareness of perception and the effort to make sense of it. This type of movement appears in the poem in the touch of the globe and the fantasy of going to Naples as royalty, which develops because of the tap, "the erratic path of time we trace / on the globe..." (*CP*, 29). It also appears in the final action of "fly[ing] to the nearest star... into the forever" (*CP*, 30). It is constructed, as

Merleau-Ponty argues, through fantasy or exceptional transition; it creates its own space. It has the potential to occur but does not necessarily need to happen.

I argue that, contrary to its reputation, cliché is a form of abstract and concrete movement at once. Taken from printing like the word "stereotype,"[10] "cliché" is a term from the French language that originally referred to a type of printing in which a mold was taken of a typeset page so that multiple editions could be printed more easily, type was freed up for other projects, and printers no longer needed to contend with the instability of the typeset page.[11] Interestingly, as these terms migrated from the print shop, they took on differing usages, so that "cliché" came to refer to old and tired phrases scarcely offering any meaning of any kind (while "stereotype" is now how we describe fixed and overly general depictions, usually of people or groups of people).

Clichés, in spite of their reputation as the mark of the grindingly prolix bore, do have their uses, for, as Orin Hargraves suggests, they "signal the familiar" and in so doing provide a certain grounding, a footing, that is often required in social intercourse.[12] A cliché is, therefore, an instance of concrete movement, for it behaves linguistically in the same way that habitual behavior does in the sense that it presents an expected phrase in an expected situation and with the expectation of an expected response. A cliché is a concrete movement because it arises out of habit.

Because of its recursive nature, a cliché is as well an instance of what Robert Porter calls "ideological patterning" from the theories of Gilles Deleuze and Félix Guattari.[13] For Deleuze and Guattari, the slogan is the smallest enunciation possible, and so its core unit: "The elementary unit of the utterance is the slogan."[14] Other translations used for Deleuze and Guattari's term for ideologically embedded phrases, *mot d'ordre*, are the literal "word order" cited by Jean-Jacques Lecercle, and the more figurative "watchword," "plan," and "policy," but Porter uses "slogan" and links the notion of slogan to cliché.[15] In doing so, Porter sets cliché up as a part of what Deleuze and Guattari call the "collective assemblage of enunciation" that can "ideologically pattern social action."[16] Sayings of this type, therefore, are proclaimed not by the individual but by the collective body; in proclaiming them and reproclaiming them (and an important feature of cliché is its repetition), the sayings reinforce proscribed patterns of thinking and behaving.

Less important than the actual substance of the cliché is its function in creating an opportunity for change and questioning. Clichés consolidate concrete movement, therefore, but they are also disruptive and bear the important function of abstract movement, as well, to produce meaning. Deleuze and Guattari suggest, therefore, that "[t]he only way to . . . revamp the theory of ideology [is] by saying that expressions and statements intervene directly in productivity, in the form of a production of meaning or sign-value."[17] Any utterance, no matter how vapid or seemingly devoid of anything new to say, contains the ability to participate in a critique of the prevailing ideology.[18] Porter calls this ability a "micro-political" critique. As he says, "A slogan/statement does not represent something or mean something, as much as it functions by intervening in the social body or micro-political conjunctive. A slogan is not a claim to transcendence or universality, so much as a singularly useful intervention that changes things."[19]

The cliché can operate in this way through two avenues: situational and recursive. Clichés are situational in the sense that each time they are repeated, the repetition is modulated by the context; the repetition can never be delivered in exactly the same way or under the same circumstances. In speaking directly about the body but talking in general about movement and how important the context is, Merleau-Ponty says that "my body's spatiality is not, like the spatiality of external objects or of 'spatial sensations,' a *positional spatiality*; rather, it is a *situational spatiality*" (*PP*, 102). This perpetual shift in delivery creates the opportunity for reevaluation and resynthesis, not only of the banal platitude but of the ideology that orchestrated it.

The recursive nature of the cliché saps all meaning, so that an enunciation devoid of meaning serves as a linguistic and social black hole that essentially erases, momentarily, the structures that conceived and constructed it. Therefore, as Porter argues, "[t]he micro-political critique of ideology implies a cleaning or emptying out of the clichés that play through the canvas of our socio-political world."[20] In his discussion of the body and movement, Merleau-Ponty concurs with the necessity of inversion for meaning creation: "[I]n order to possess my body independently of all urgent tasks, in order to make use of it in my imagination, and in order to trace in the air a movement that is only defined by a verbal instruction or by moral necessities, I must also invert the natural relation between my body and the surroundings, and a human productivity must appear through the thickness of being" (*PP*, 115).

For the cliché to produce meaning and to question prevailing ideological proscriptions, the concrete part of the movement must occur in order to make movement possible at all, but in so doing, the recursion of the movement provides space for an inversion, the instant of rethinking and of focused consciousness that engenders meaning.

Ashbery relies extensively on clichés in "Variations, Calypso and Fugue on a Theme of Ella Wheeler Wilcox," partly probably to talk about Wilcox's poetry and its truly insipid and embarrassingly fervent tone, but also, I argue, to provide a moment to reconsider the function of clichés.[21] Wilcox recognized that her poetry is permeated with clichés and defended her reliance on them in her poem "Women Who Want to Succeed": "We are given to sneering at platitudes in this age, and we sometimes forget that principles are platitudes."[22] Principles could be seen as the instrument of ideology—right thinking and right behaving dictated by external social forces, Deleuze and Guattari's *mots d'ordres*. In Ashbery's poem on Wilcox, which he begins with a long quotation from her poem "Wishes," the narrator states that "it is a good experience, to divest oneself of some tested ideals, some old standbys" (*CP*, 190), thereby announcing his intention to take up these platitudes and evacuate them, permitting the production of meaning and a critique of ideology.

In "John Ashbery and the Challenge of Postmodernism in the Visual Arts," Charles Altieri refers to Ashbery's "flatness of voice": "I suggest that this 'flatness' is the result of the effort to merely describe, to remove hierarchy. Refusing any irritable reaching after depth and significance, the poet can rely on a casual surface as a workable pretext for a plausible density of metaphor," says Altieri. "Or," he goes on, "to put the same point another way, cliché enables, tempers, contains and releases lyrical energy while allowing the poet a strangely exact means of expression."[23]

It is a gamble to focus a poem on clichés, as the poet risks having the audience take them at face value: as oft-repeated, insipid, and meaningless bromides.[24] Because clichés bear such negative connotations in the world of poetry, where the "make it new" approach prevails, if the poet does not make it explicitly obvious that the point of the poem is to decry reliance on cliché, the audience might miss that part of the poem's point; in order to escape this fate, the poet is forced to flirt with heavy-handed or obviously sarcastic tones.

However, Ashbery openly declares that clichés have their function in poetry. In his interview with Richard Jackson, for instance, Ashbery says, "My mind wants to give clichés their chance, unravel them, and so in a way contribute to purifying the language of the tribe. . . . And I think [clichés] have a beauty because of being hallowed somehow by so much use. . . . Thought has taken this form again and again, and that should be respected."[25] This "[purification of] the language of the tribe" is the work of articulation. In working through perception, the poet maps what has been experienced to what has been experienced and articulated in the past. In cases of mismappings, the poet adjusts the past articulations to fit the context of the present. In the case of clichés, however, the articulation remains intact, but the context around it in the poem shifts it in order to "unravel" it and reestablish how it worked in the past and how it might serve as is in the present.

In addition, the regular, dependable pattern created by clichés can serve to provide stability in daily irregular, disordered experience. *The Recital* states, for instance, "'once burned, twice shy'; one proceeds along one's path murmuring idiotic formulas like this to give oneself courage" (*CP*, 322). Repeating these "idiotic formulas" is not idiotic if they ensure that the poet does not become overcome by the never-ceasing abundance of the flux of experience.

Ashbery employs multiple tactics in his effort to wield clichés as meaning production while avoiding either looking like he values them or resorting to sarcasm. The first is stretched metaphors. While these do not, in my opinion, attain the wildly odd and elaborate comparisons of the metaphysical poets, they are jarring and disjointed enough that they force attention to them, a tactic that renews or reshapes those "old standbys," as in the phrase in "Variations, Calypso and Fugue," "the acorns / Lie around on the worn earth like eyeballs" (*CP*, 190).

This rather grisly comparison of the dark brown and hard acorn with the gelatinous globes of human eyes is an instance of how Merleau-Ponty says that people derive meaning from their surroundings. "[F]or the normal person," he says, "the subject's intentions are immediately reflected in the perceptual field: they polarize it, put their stamp on it, or finally, effortlessly give birth there to a wave of significations" (*PP*, 133). In the case of this metaphor, the narrator is reflecting back to his childhood, playing army under an oak tree with toy soldiers. The large tree links to Wilcox's poem that is partial inspiration for this one, in which she argues that a simple act of planting an acorn could have an enormous impact on the future, on those people who are provided with its "[shelter] from the sun."[26] Beneath the oak tree becomes this "perceptual field" for the narrator, where even in the absence of his body and those soldiers who "shrug and slink off," the acorns remain to "see" and create signification within the tree's shelter.

As well, the past, present, and future are incorporated with each other through a movement of time rather than space, or perhaps, in addition to space. The narrator regards his childhood at play under the tree as a safe and unquestioning time of acceptance of aphorisms as fact; that past provides a launching point for the dismissal of each of these platitudes in turn, not to erase them but to devise a structure with which to resist the ideology embedded within them and from which to launch into the future. Merleau-Ponty describes this passage as follows:

> At each moment in a movement, the preceding instant is not forgotten, but rather is somehow fit into the present, and, in short, the present perception consists in taking up the series of previous positions that envelop each other by relying on the current position. But the imminent position is itself enveloped in the present, and through it so too are all of those positions that will occur throughout the movement. Each moment of the movement embraces its entire expanse and, in particular, its first moment or kinetic initiation inaugurates the link between a here and a there, between a now and a future that the other moments will be limited to developing. (*PP*, 141)

A second and probably more salient metaphor is developed as a result of one of the main points of this, the first section of the poem. In order to establish the importance of letting go of accepted rather than considered knowledge, those "old standbys," the narrator inserts a cliché that he can immediately reconfigure: "all good things must come to an end" (*CP*, 190). When these "things come to an end," however, the poem asserts twice that something must come in their place on their culmination: "one must move forward / Into the space left by one's conclusions," and "even finding nothing to put in their place is a good experience, / Preparing one, as it does, for the consternation that is to come" (*CP*, 190). Relinquishing these happy, safe times and their concomitant platitudes is uncomfortable, for the stable footing enabled by never having to think or question is disrupted by just that: thinking and questioning and not simply accepting broadly general statements about life. By stepping out of the safety of cliché, by "mov[ing] into the space left by one's conclusions," the narrator can, as Merleau-Ponty argues, "[place] his own thoughts in the world" through a "dialogue between the subject and the object, where the subject takes up the sense scattered across the object and the object gathers together the subject's intentions, namely, physiognomic perception, arranges a world around the subject that speaks to him on the topic of himself and places his own thoughts in the world" (*PP*, 134).

The stretched metaphor is then applied to provide a sense of how difficult it is to let go of these accepted notions: "the ideas were good only because they had to die, / Leaving you alone and skinless, a drawing by Vesalius" (*CP*, 190). Stripped of platitudes, the youth is as exposed and vulnerable as if flayed alive. Skin is the sheltering carapace that protects against having to think anew. When we think for ourselves, we might not even be able to replace those mindless statements of accepted "fact" with anything. We might never have a new skin to succeed the old one. The metaphor is extreme, somewhat violent in fact, in order to stress the depth of the pain experienced by stripping cliché of its content; the poem is firm, though, in emphasizing the significance of this rejection of past patterns of thought.

Another method that Ashbery employs to sap cliché of meaning in order to produce new and more relevant meaning is to introduce clichés that start out like clichés, like statements that we have heard repeatedly and with great affirmation, but then to make them take odd turns, undermining the platitude's trajectory. This tactic recurs in the middle section of the poem, a long series of rhyming couplets largely in iambic tetrameter. The first few couplets employ the tone and poetic skill of a child,[27] and the set of couplets is riddled with cliché, from "snug as a bug" to "act according to the dictates of your art" (*CP*, 191).[28] However, with the couplet on the Great Wall of China, the clichés start to break down, and it becomes increasingly apparent that many of them appear to be accepted clichés that Ashbery has modified, thereby evacuating and reconstituting them. The Wall of China cliché is, "It cleaves through the air like a silver pill" (*CP*, 191). Possibly, "pill" refers to bullet, but the idea that the wall is like a pill is quite odd. "Pill" could refer to the wall serving as an antidote, to block marauders from entering the Chinese state and to unify those within its borders.[29] This dual purpose is perhaps why Ashbery selected the word "cleave," which refers at once to a splitting and a consolidation. The oddness of this "cliché" links as well to other ones, like the trapeze artist who "flies through the air with the greatest of ease." Uniting the pill and "cleaves the air" is Edmond Temple's *The Life of Pill Garlick; Rather a Whimsical Sort of Fellow*. In that book, the narrator erupts into very bad and sarcastic verse: "Let never bird that cleaves the air with wing, / Except the owl, be that day heard to sing!"[30]

Other malapropisms include "There is a hole of truth" (*CP*, 191), which links to Alfred North Whitehead's aphorism, "There are no whole truths: all truths are half-truths"; "act according to the dictates of your art" (*CP*, 191), which comes from Thomas Jefferson's "Everyone must act according to the dictates of his own reason" and/or from Anna C. Ellis-Reifsnider's *Unforgiven*, "Act according to the dictates of your heart";[31] and "I felt the tears flow forth with all their might" (*CP*, 190), possibly coming from James Beattie's *The Minstrel; or, The Progress of Genius* with "Tears flow forth with all their might."[32] In modifying these clichés, Ashbery sets them up for greater attention, so that they do not sweep by with a simple nod of the head and in fact are the focus of some humor.

In tweaking the form of a cliché, Ashbery sets up movement that provides the opportunity for the production of meaning. As Merleau-Ponty says, "Movement is a modulation of an already familiar milieu" (*PP*, 288). In addition, the movement generated through undermining and refashioning cliché transforms how we perceive. Merleau-Ponty argues that "[w]hat we have discovered through the study of motricity is . . . a new sense of the word 'sense'" (*PP*, 148). By "sense," he means not just what and how we perceive but what meaning we derive from that perception and how we derive it.

These pseudo- or stretched clichés are utterly broken down by the end of the rhyming couplet section of "Variations, Calypso and Fugue," largely because the calypso influence in the poem erupts through increasing and rather wild syncopation, as in "snug as a bug," "Which is why nobody is sending you flowers," "And that person isn't likely to be you," and "And trust in the dream that will never come true" (*CP*, 192). Having set up the rhyming couplet section of this poem as excited and inspired by travels and the links between these places and history, such as Mount Ararat and the Flood, the poet leads us into the later section with reasonable trust. We can see that the persona of the early narrator is young and somewhat unsophisticated, so we are thrown by the later one's disillusionment and cynicism, marked by the skipping beat and lengthier lines. As with the cliché adjustments, the metrical shifts away from the insipid ballad form provide the opportunity to pay closer attention and to question what they are really saying rather than simply accepting them at face value.

I use the term "recursion" in order to emphasize that there is not simply repetition in the poem but a loop through which the poem cycles, each time with modified content. Part of the poem's title invokes the fugue, a form of music that takes up one or more themes and uses distinctly different voices to develop them, culminating in a finale for closure.[33] This poem's form is fugal as it contains three separate sections: free verse, rhyming couplets, and prose poetry with an emphasis on the prose. While the free-verse section focuses on the narrator's youth, the rhyming couplets section on his travels, and the prose section on the urban life of New York City, each develops the theme of memory of experience: how it felt to be a child under the oak tree or in the sandlot, and how much more salient experience is if it is heartfelt.

In addition to its relevance in music, a fugue functions in the field of psychiatry. A fugue state occurs in a person when they experience a sudden memory loss and often submit to a compulsion to travel from home.[34] The rhyming couplet section of the poem involves a long sequence of voyages that terminate back at home. The close of this poem links the musical fugue to the psychological one through a scene of a man, clearly in a fugue state, being questioned by a friend. The scene concludes with the man's hysterical response, a rousing climax for the musical fugue: "peering fearfully into the shadowy corners of the room. 'I will tell you nothing! Nothing, do you hear?' he shrieked. 'Go away! Go away!'" (*CP*, 194).

Recursion occurs in the poem as well through spatial shifts away from one position and back: "Do you step out from under the shade a moment, / It is only to return with renewed expectation, of expectation fulfilled" (*CP*, 189); "the hand keeps brushing away a strand of chestnut hair, only to have it fall back into place again" (*CP*, 190); "such affirmation in the way the days goes 'round together" (*CP*, 190). Each time these actions recur, they are different—the hand brushing the hair away moves slightly differently; the hair falls back into a different "place" in a different arrangement.[35] More importantly, the "renewed" and "fulfilled" expectations are not the same and in fact contradict each other, as the renewed one means that the expectation is still an unrealized hope and the fulfilled one means that it has been accomplished and the narrator is not hoping for some kind of extra culmination.

This type of recursion, and in fact all of these tactics that Ashbery deploys in these poems to make it possible to produce meaning, are also a part of Merleau-Ponty's notion of "abstract movement." "Abstract movement," he argues,

> is thus inhabited by a power of objectification, by a "symbolic function," a "representation function," or a power of "projection" that, moreover, is already at work in the constitution of "things" and that consists in treating the sensory givens as representatives of an "eidos." It consists in giving them a sense, in animating them from within, in organizing them into a system, in centering a plurality of experiences upon a single intelligible core, and in making an identifiable unity appear in them under different perspectives. In short, it consists in arranging behind the flux of impressions an invariant that gives the flux its reason and in articulating the material of experience. (*PP*, 123)

In taking up these multitude of experiences—realized, imagined, and potential—and in reshaping platitudes to provide a reimagining of them, Ashbery can create this "intelligible core" from which to examine life from multiple angles and perceptions. Doing so permits him to "[arrange] behind the flux of impressions an invariant that gives the flux its reason" and ensures the ability to "[articulate] the material of experience" (*PP*, 123). This act is the purpose of poetry, to take up the strands of experience in all of their fluidity and ephemerality, and to make sense of it, that "[materiality] of experience."

Chapter 7

Order and Meaning

The Transcendence of the Everyday

[T]he whole landscape is overrun with words as with an invasion.[1]

You limit me to what I say.
The sense of the words is
With a backward motion, pinning me
To the daylight mode of my declaration ("Measles")[2]

THE MAIN PHILOSOPHICAL source for this book on John Ashbery's poetry is clearly the work of Maurice Merleau-Ponty. Other, equally forceful phenomenological theorists include, in particular, Martin Heidegger and Edmund Husserl. Heidegger, in fact, focused on poetry quite particularly, especially in *Poetry, Language, Thought*. I have opted to rely on Merleau-Ponty, who did not often talk explicitly about poetry in his work, for two main reasons. First, Heidegger is less apt for a poetry like Ashbery's because he contends that the language of poetry falls into a different category than everyday language, that it is a special kind of language.[3] I do not think that this approach works in a consideration of Ashbery's poetry, because his language is specifically NOT special; it is the language of the quotidian, making me believe that a reliance on Heidegger's conceptual framework of poetic language to explain Ashbery's oeuvre would overlook or ignore this essential quality in his work. Second, part of why Merleau-Ponty talks less about poetry and more about painting is because, for him, the primary sense to be activated in the act of perception is sight, and this, I believe, is the primary sense for Ashbery, for his is a poetry of description. However, I also believe that in composing a poetry of description in everyday language Ashbery enacts the process of phenomenology: to see what surrounds us, to take it into us in order to consider it in terms of what perceptions have occurred in the past, and to articulate that perception. In turning outside ourselves, we must transcend ourselves; requisite for perception is transcendence.

Core to Merleau-Ponty's notion of phenomenology, and therefore to this transcendence, is the visible, what we can perceive, attested to by his book devoted to that sense: *The Visible and the Invisible*. He argues, for instance, that "[w]e must habituate ourselves to think that every visible is cut out in the tangible, every tactile being in some manner promised to visibility, and that there is encroachment, infringement, not only between the touched and the touching, but also between the tangible and the visible, which is encrusted in it, as conversely, the tangible itself is not a nothingness of visibility, is not without visual existence" (*VI*, 134). "Tangible" suggests two qualities: that which can be touched, and which therefore has material essence, and that which is real and definite. In making the tangible reliant on the visible, Merleau-Ponty suggests that we cannot use our sense of touch, nor can we determine manifest properties of the perceptible, in the absence of sight. I take his notion of the visible in a metaphoric sense of comprehension, too, that we cannot comprehend in a dearth of manifestation. "Tactility" is of equal importance here as well, in emphasizing the quality of that touch, that the material essence is touchable, and so that we predict what that touch might entail. However, here too, in Merleau-Ponty's statement, is the attitude toward the visible, that it intrudes into other senses ("encroachment") and modifies it negatively ("infringement"). That is, it is evident here that the sense activated by the visible predominates to the point where other forms of perception cannot exist without it, even reshaping those perceptions so as to diminish them.

Phenomenology conceives of perception as transcendent partly because it is possible for people to "sense" beyond what they access perceptually at a particular instant. By this I mean that when we perceive something, like a house, we also understand that there are aspects of the house to which we do not have access at any particular moment; we can only see it from one vantage point at a time, but it is as if we can take on a cubist perspective and perceive across time and space in knowing that those other sides of the house exist and even what they might look like. Merleau-Ponty explains this transcendent capacity by saying that "it is the same world that contains our bodies and our minds, provided that we understand by world not only the sum of things that fall or could fall under our eyes, but also the locus of their compossibility, the invariable style they observe, which connects our perspectives, permits transition from one to the other, and—whether in describing a detail of the landscape or in coming to agreement about an invisible truth—makes us feel we are two witnesses capable of hovering (*survoler*) over the same object, or at least of exchanging our situations relative to it, as we can exchange our standpoints in the visible world in the strict sense" (*VI*, 13). We compile our perceptions, therefore, to establish a clearer sense of the "whole" of what surrounds us.[4]

Vision is, therefore, crucial to our ongoing encounter with experience, not just with the outside world but within our own being. Merleau-Ponty argues, thus, that "[t]hought is a relationship with oneself and with the world as well as a relationship with the other; hence it is established in the three dimensions at the same time. And it must be brought to appear directly in the infrastructure of vision. . . . [We] are asking precisely what is that central vision that joins the scattered visions, that unique touch that governs the whole tactile life of my body as a unit, that *I think* that must be able to accompany all our experiences" (*VI*, 145). It is the visible, above all other senses, that guides perception and that, in fact, pulls them together, coordinates and orchestrates them, and even provides a framework to support the comprehension of experience.

Launched out of this perception, driven by the visible, is poetry. Merleau-Ponty says: "A vision or an action that is finally free throws out of focus and regroups objects of the world for the painter and words for the poet" (*S*, 56). Here, he adds the motility so core to perception to a possible engagement with experience that makes poetry, or any art, possible. This perception does two things: it removes "focus," and it "regroups" our access to what we perceive. This loss of clarity, I argue, links to how we gain meaning out of experience, through what Merleau-Ponty calls the "Invisible." The "regrouping" is, I believe, the ordering effort that the artist embarks on in order to communicate perception, addressed in this chapter after the invisible.[5]

Ashbery's affinity with the Romantic poet John Clare demonstrates this investment in experience and in the description of what is around us. Stephanie Kuduk Weiner devotes a chapter in her book *Clare's Lyric: John Clare and Three Modern Poets* to John Ashbery, in particular to his poetry book *The Double Dream of Spring*, which includes his prose poem "For John Clare."[6] Weiner links Ashbery's description of Clare, "Being immersed in the details of rock and field and slope," to Ashbery's own poetry by saying that both "employ the words and cadences of everyday speech in the service of a literary art that arranges words and patterns of sound and meaning in ways that endow them with a significance that is simultaneously aesthetic and referential."[7]

In "For John Clare," Ashbery proclaims the emphasis on the visible so important to Merleau-Ponty. He writes that "there is so much to be seen everywhere" but then how it is impossible to transform what we see accurately into words: "There is so much to be said, and on the surface of it very little gets said" (*CP*, 198). Even looking is never quite comprehensive: "You are standing looking at that building and you cannot take it all in, certain details are already hazy and the mind boggles" (*CP*, 198). Even photographs of a scene, if we have access to them, are inadequate in supporting the effort to use that immersion in visible detail to render the scene verbally.

In this poem, Ashbery turns directly to perception and its imperfections: "we perceive them if at all as those things that were meant to be put aside" (*CP*, 198). The poem ends by talking about "the whole history of probabilities" that fill in the gaps created by articulation's inadequacies. Therefore, the metaphor linking "probabilities" to "a sail" in the "upper left-hand corner" of the page establishes the notion that it is these fissures in description that launch the poem, those words starting in the upper left of the page that "sail" through this raft of experience floated by the poet.

The other side of the visible is, therefore, the invisible, and this is where meaning resides.[8] Merleau-Ponty argues, therefore, that "[m]eaning is *invisible*, but the invisible is not the contradiction of the visible: the visible itself has an invisible inner framework (*membrure*), and the in-visible is the secret counterpart of the visible, it appears only within it, it is the *Nichturpräsentierbar*, which is presented to me as such within the world—one cannot see it there and every effort to *see it there* makes it disappear, but it is *in the line* of the visible, it is its virtual focus, it is inscribed with it (in filigree)" (*VI*, 215, emphasis in the original).[9] The translation for the original French of *membrure* is given here as "framework," which is absolutely accurate. However, what is missing here is the sense of the linkage of the interrelated parts. That is, when *membrure* is used in a literary context, it refers to the coupling of the limbs of a body; it suggests not just, say, the framework of a house but the elements of the framing at once. This translation is essential to consider, for it is not that Merleau-Ponty places the invisible on another side from the visible, as if to suggest that there is some kind of wall dividing us from what we can perceive and what we can only guess at, but rather that "within" the visible there exists a framework that coexists and is utterly integrated with the visible: that is the invisible.

Since Merleau-Ponty was not given to reliance on German terms, in spite of his clear allegiance to Husserl and Heidegger, and since *The Visible and the Invisible* was translated only from the French, the German term *Nichturpräsentierbar* appears untranslated in this work and means roughly "not possible to represent." Completely incorporated within the perceptions linked to our consciousness are those that we cannot access, and this is where the meaning of perception resides. This is the goal of the poet, to gain entrance to this "invisible inner framework" and to attempt to represent it, to read and communicate these inscribed elements of "filigree." Filigree is an interesting combination of thread and seed, from the Latin, suggesting that the invisible, the "seeds" of meaning, are interlaced within the visible.[10]

While interviewing Ashbery, Peter Stitt asked, "Is the issue of meaning or message something that is uppermost in your mind when you write?" Ashbery responded, "Meaning yes, but message no. I think my poems mean what they say, and whatever might be implicit within a particular passage, but there is no message, nothing I want to tell the world particularly except what I am thinking when I am writing." A bit later in the interview, when Stitt asked about the line "Daffy Duck in Hollywood," Ashbery explained, "'The allegory comes unsnarled too soon,' that might be my observation of poetry and my poetry in particular. The allegory coming unsnarled meaning that the various things that make it up are dissolving into a poetic statement, and that is something I feel is both happening and I don't want to happen." Stitt asked, "So for you a poem is an object in and of itself rather than a clue to some abstraction, to something other than itself?" Ashbery said, "Yes . . ."[11] In drawing a clear distinction between a "message" and the "meaning" of a poem, Ashbery is, I believe, adhering to Merleau-Ponty's notion of the invisible. A message would indicate that the artist was trying to push forward a particular point: here is what you need to learn from this work of art. Meaning, in contradistinction, is what comes out of simply experiencing and what that experience might come to intimate.[12]

The second aspect of meaning comes out of the artist's impulse to order. In his essay for a catalog of Fairfield Porter's work, Ashbery feels some compulsion to apologize for the lack of abstraction in Porter's painting. How can he place Porter in the same rank with his contemporaries, the abstract expressionists like Willem de Kooning and Jackson Pollock? He does this by arguing that Porter is a natural descendent of American artists of multiple media, so that his paintings are "intellectual in the classic American tradition . . . because they have no ideas in them, that is, no ideas that can be separated from the rest. They *are* idea, or consciousness, or light, or whatever. Ideas surround them, but do not and cannot extrude themselves into the being of the art. . . . He painted his surroundings [therefore] as they looked."[13]

How "his surroundings looked," however, relates to Porter's sense of order that he derived from Ludwig Wittgenstein, who said, "Every sentence is in order as it is."[14] Porter believed that he could unveil this order in describing what he saw through the medium of paint. "The truest order," Porter said, "is what you already find there, or that will be given if you don't try for it."[15] Ashbery responds to this artistic enterprise by ending his essay on Porter with a clear paean to Wallace Stevens: "We must [be] prepared to find the order that is already there, not the one that should be but the one that is."[16]

The quotation from Wittgenstein is from *Philosophical Investigations*. It might help here to start with what immediately precedes and follows it to establish the context for this idea. Wittgenstein says:

> Thought is surrounded by a halo.—Its essence, logic, presents an order, in fact the *a priori* order of the world: that is, the order of *possibilities*, which must be common to both world and thought. But this order, it seems, must be *utterly simple*. It is *prior* to all experience, must run through all experience; no empirical cloudiness or uncertainty can be allowed to affect it—It must rather be of the purest crystal. But this crystal does not appear as an abstraction; but as something concrete, indeed, as the most concrete, as it were the *hardest* thing there is. . . . On the one hand it is clear that every sentence in our language "is in order as it is."

> That is to say, we are not *striving after* an ideal, as if our ordinary vague sentences had not yet got a quite unexceptionable sense, and a perfect language awaited construction by us.—On the other hand, it seems clear that where there is sense, there must be perfect order.—So there must be perfect order even in the vaguest sentence. . . . Here it is difficult as it were to keep our heads up,—to see that we must stick to the subjects of our everyday thinking, and not go astray and imagine that we have to describe extreme subtleties, which in turn we are after all quite unable to describe with the means at our disposal. We feel as if we had to repair a torn spider web with our fingers.[17]

Wittgenstein's assurance here is remarkable, that sense might actually exist, and so might this "perfect order."[18] Here, too, Wittgenstein turns to multiple and overlapping metaphors, each of which finds resonance in Ashbery's poetry: the halo, the crystal, the spider web. To find this "order" within these analogies, we need also to think about "everyday" things. This "halo" around thought links to Merleau-Ponty's concern for the past and its impact on the present, that the "field of the present" exists here in a kind of aura surrounding all of our present experience that includes within it activations of past experience and reshaped remembrances of it.

In Wittgenstein's idea of order, four ideas stand out: simplicity, preexistence, concreteness, and what he refers to as crystallization. This latter idea, "crystallization," was an issue of clear concern to Ashbery, who says in "Dreams of Adulthood," "What is needed is a disparate account of the thing happening just now, / To have it sink finally into print, from which there is no escape, no / Never" (*CP*, 815).[19] Print, the final publication of a poem, becomes the poet's version of crystallization: the immutable form of the poem. Wittgenstein talks about the hardness of crystal, the impermeability, but also that fixity to which Ashbery refers. However, crystals are matrices; they have an internal structure composed of repeated three-dimensional patterns of molecules in perfect and regular geometric relationships. The laciness of snow is a form of crystallization, too, one whose fragility and ephemerality contrast with the toughness of mineral or more permanent frozen forms. Not only that, but the crystal, while it is set in a particular form, permits the transmission of light—and does not just permit it, but changes light's path through the refraction that is created by crystal's inherent structure.

Wittgenstein argues that, if there is sense, there must be perfect order. This is a sense that exists, that is not laid out. It is not that the artist is trying to shape the world; it is not that the artist is looking for patterns in the world. Wittgenstein says in *Philosophical Investigations*, "But since [an exclamation] is the description of a perception, it can also be called the expression of thought. —If you are looking at the object, you need not think of it; but if you are having the visual experience expressed by the exclamation, you are also *thinking* of what you see."[20] Clearly, to him, speaking of what you see is an indication, a verification, of what you are thinking about, and that is linked to what you perceive, so expression becomes essential to the thinking.

Ashbery might list what he sees in poems, therefore, but in seeing these things, he is thinking about them and therefore also rendering them into perception. In "On Autumn Lake," for example, he explains the importance of small detail: "By air from other places to here isn't much, but / It doesn't count, at least not the way the / Shore distance—leaf, tree, stone; optional (fern, frog, skunk); / And then stone, tree, leaf; then another optional—counts" (*CP*, 460).[21] What is important, he indicates here, is less getting to a place or the overview of a place once he is there, than the minute and particular items that he finds there. Here, in addition to this notion of value, of degree of importance, count establishes the poet's role as the counter, the one to keep track of things by literally counting them, by accounting for them in the sense of taking into account, including, but also rationalizing their existence. By enumerating them, the poet makes them exist, as well, but this existence appears related to the truth of experience that Wittgenstein describes, and it seems especially connected to that rendering of events of the present into crystalline form as they transform themselves into the past.

The work of the poet is to capture experience as accurately as possible and with as little ego or intentional shaping as possible. In "Down by the Station, Early in the Morning," Ashbery says, "It all wears out. I keep telling myself this, but / I can never believe me, though others do. Even things do. / And the things they do. Like the rasp of silk, or a certain / Glottal stop in your voice as you are telling me how you / Didn't have time to brush your teeth but gargled with Listerine / Instead. Each is a base one might wish to touch once more / Before dying" (*CP*, 743).[22] Each memory and each perception, therefore, becomes a part of what impels expression, the ordering of experience.

It is, however, I believe, impossible to relinquish control in the transformation of lived experience into art forms. The visual artist makes clear decisions that undermine that effort to merely see and replicate what is there: composition, palette, subject matter all rest in the artist's hands. The artist makes decisions, as well, that are less visible. Porter, for instance, selects what to place in the center of a painting, what details to bring out and which ones to exclude. There may be a lot of clutter that he excised from the porch for his *Iced Coffee* (1966). Other boats could have been in the water when he painted *Still Life with White Boats* (1968), and other items could have been on the table next to those selected for the interior section of that still life. What is certain is that he chose to depict Maine vacation life, that summer respite for the well-to-do.

The verbal artist faces greater obstacles. While some poetic movements, such as those of the futurists and concrete poets among others, tried to enact an explicit rejection of hierarchy and to create simultaneity, as seen in their efforts to lay out their work in asequential systems, whether in printed or verbal form, language is sequential. As shown by the synchronous poems *Litany* and "To the Same Degree," it is impossible to read or articulate more than one word at once or to comprehend multiple words spoken at the same time. The problem with this, as Ashbery indicates in "Finnish Rhapsody," is that "There is no time for anything like chance" (*CP*, 822).[23] Even what Wittgenstein calls "the vaguest sentence" must have been created by a human who, however badly, selected and ordered the progression of words. In elucidations of any sort, it is impossible to remove the operations of agency entirely. For both the visual and verbal arts, therefore, selection is a control process. Artists like Porter and Ashbery are aiming for letting everything in, but it is impossible to do that. Art is, after all, motivated by what Charles Peirce called precision, "that which arises from attention of one element and neglect of another."[24]

The other point raised by Ashbery in his essay on Porter's painting is apparent in his statement that his paintings "*are* idea, or consciousness, or light, or whatever, [that] Ideas surround them, but do not and cannot extrude themselves into the being of the art.... He painted his surroundings as they looked."[25] Porter is, like Ashbery in his own poetry, attempting to render experience as it occurs. Mixing the efforts of the painter together with those of the poet, Wittgenstein says in *Philosophical Investigations*: "But if a sentence can strike me as like a painting in words, and the very individual word in the sentence as like a picture, then it is no such marvel that a word uttered in isolation and without purpose can seem to carry a particular meaning in itself."[26] Wittgenstein speaks here of the articulation that is necessary for perception, for the attainment of meaning.

However, words do not stand alone but rather appear within their context of the situation of their present and of their cultural and historical implications. Merleau-Ponty says, therefore, that "that there could be a language of coincidence, a manner of making the things themselves speak—and this is what [the philosopher or poet] seeks. It would be a language of which he would not be the organizer, words he would not assemble, that would combine through him by virtue of a natural intertwining of their meaning, through the occult trading of the metaphor—where what counts is no longer the manifest meaning of each word and of each image, but the lateral relations, the kinships that are implicated in their transfers and their exchanges" (*VI*, 125). This statement clearly points to the notion of "finding the order that is there," and the order that is there comes out of the intermingling of experiences both past and present and the articulations that rise out of those meshes.

Merleau-Ponty conceptualizes a "'chiasmic' intersection between humans and the world."[27] Ashbery's poetry explores this decussation but also the intersections perpetually forming and closing between self and other and self and world. It is in these interstices created by this "interweaving" where imagination foments to occlude these gaps and fashion relationships between them and where it erupts in this effort in the form of poetic language.[28] Merleau-Ponty explains the chiasm, as shown in chapter 3, by saying that "a sort of dihescence opens my body in two, and because between my body looked at and my body looking, my body touched and my body touching, there is overlapping or encroachment, so that we must say that things pass into us as well as we into the things" (*VI*, 123).

Merleau-Ponty's description of this chiasm appears in Ashbery's "Rivers and Mountains" in his map metaphor in which mapping takes on elements of raw nature and orients and organizes it.[29] "Gray-brown quills like thoughts," the poem says, "In the melodious but vast mass of today's / Writing through fields and swamps / Marked, on the map, with little bunches of weeds" (*CP*, 126). In mapping, the land becomes paper, paper that comes to represent the land: "you found / It all on paper but the land / Was made of paper processed / To look like ferns, mud or other . . ." (*CP*, 126); and "It worked well on paper" (*CP*, 127). Similarly, the reproduction of the landscape on a stamp miniaturizes it but also institutionalizes it, so that the landscape becomes emblematic of the nation: "So that a stamp could reproduce all of this / In detail, down to the last autumn leaf" (*CP*, 128). Chiasms are here, therefore, in the split between nature and depictions of it, and between the two factions described in the poem, that "enemy [separated] into two groups" (*CP*, 127), oneself and other. However, the chiasmic structure does not simply exist in the form of a split, but in the overlapping and concentric forms of existence. As the map overlays and intertwines with the land that it is meant to represent, consciousness of existence overlaps and interweaves with and into the moments of perception.

Ashbery functions on this level when he says in "Disguised Zenith," "All the beautiful crafts, the tint choicer / Than the rest, are available 'at all times,' but / We decode them backwards, / Their meaning is *for* our meaning, and where / Is the meaning in that?" (*CP*, 835).[30] This "backwards" "decod[ing]," turning to past perceptions and attempting to understand them, never provides us with a perfect mirror, either to the past or to the present. Ashbery writes in "October at the Window," "One must always / Be quite conscious of the edges of things / And then how they meet will cease / To be an issue . . . / That there are flowers in shacks, broken / Mirrors among fallen doorposts / Doesn't trip us up so much, rather / It's the lesson, unlearned, whose wry whimper, / Hidden among congruent pages, tells / The story of how we were and how we were meant to be" (*CP*, 837–38).[31] The edges of things, like those horizons of intention so prevalent in Merleau-Ponty's approach, are where we need to focus our attention, to what might really be there and to how an understanding of that might provide us with a sense of our existence. As well here is the urge to look very closely in order to discern that nearly unglimpseable moment of meaning, this "whimper [that is] Hidden."

The poem "By the Flooded Canal" reveals the process of sorting and ordering and seeing what is there: "And I shift, arranging the pieces / In a cardboard drawer. No two are alike, and I like that . . . I don't expect thanks / And am happy in the small role assigned me, / Really. I think I'll go out in the garage" (*CP*, 877–78): the poet in the act of seeing what is there, these "subjects of our everyday thinking," those things "[awaiting] clarification, or [being] swept aside as rubbish."[32]

Once the poet has discerned pattern in the "filigree" of meaning, it is essential to figure out how to transmit the recognition of that invisible material into language, to express experience as it transpires. In *The Prose of the World*, Merleau-Ponty distinguishes between "language as an institution" and spoken language (*PW*, 10).[33] Institutional language, he says, is "sedimented" and "effaces itself in order to yield the meaning which it conveys" (*PW*, 10). The effacement occurs because in the course of its transmission between experience and meaning, little attention can be paid to the elixir that transports it. The sedimentation is the layers of language that develop over time as it evolves and mutates, each element still lingering in the amber of the past.

Hugh Silverman contends that, for Merleau-Ponty, literary expression involves the entanglement of both of these types of language, "institutional" and spoken:

> In literary experience, expression belongs to both spoken language and speaking language. But pure, spoken, conventional language is not one thing and the living, speaking, literary language something else. They are both aspects of expression. Aesthetic experience can never be uniquely one or the other but is always infused with both. The meaning produced by literary uses of speech can also be found in everyday language. Both involve the production and expression of sense, namely the embodied enactment of language. Literary language drives speaking subjects to express themselves in new ways, and yet there is an ambiguity to their expressivity.[34]

In fact, I would like to suggest that aesthetic language, particularly poetry, rather than effacing itself, risks drawing attention to itself, making itself a part of the transmitted meaning. It is possible, therefore, that Ashbery, in turning to the language of the everyday, is trying to ensure that his language maintains this expressive wallpapering.[35]

In one of his rare explicit statements about poetry, Merleau-Ponty argues that it actually changes existence itself, not simply how we experience it. "[P]oetry," he says, "is essentially a modulation of existence. The poem . . . employs language . . . such that the existential modulation . . . finds in the poetic apparatus the means to make itself eternal. . . . [L]ike every work of art, the poem too exists in the manner of a thing" (*PP*, 152). In repeating "modulation," Merleau-Ponty emphasizes that poetic language moderates existence, not in order to dampen our experience of it but in order to recalibrate how language matches what we experience. By saying that poetry "exists in the manner of a thing," the philosophy suggests that poetry renders existence as nearly as it can.[36]

Poetic language must push against institutional language in order to reset this mapping to experience. Ashbery's poem "Idaho" takes on this reconsideration of institutional language frontally in its integration of punctuation and symbols into the poem.[37] Strings of question marks, commas, hash symbols, exclamation points, and single quotation marks permeate the text, not to create images or to demarcate the text but rather, I believe, to say what cannot be expressed textually. These textual markings, for so they become in losing their functional positions, might express complete lack of understanding, of the situation, of how to talk about it, of what it might mean: "???????? ???????????????????????????????" (*CP*, 119). The number of question marks arrests movement through the poem and expresses incredulity in addition to the simple question asked: "Can this be the one time" (*CP*, 118). The hash marks have interestingly changed meaning in a time of Twitter; at the time of Ashbery's writing, they would simply have indicated a number. In positioning them between the curtailed text, "the piece of crude blue paper that is a French telegra" and the utterly unrelated text, "The mouth of weeds," "# # # # # # # # # # # # #" becomes a visual barrier while we complete the first phrase and try to "say" the hash marks, creating that mouthful of weeds, an unutterable utterance (*CP*, 119). And finally, the double series of single quotation marks indicates what is not said between Jim and Carol:

Jim was pouring himself another glass of port as she came down.
"""""""" "I won't be very long,"""""""" she said. # # (*CP*, 120).

These marks, much like the colon discussed in chapter 3 above, render language as a material entity, but they lose its sound.[38] Merleau-Ponty argues, "[A]ll that is required is to meet the phrase ready made in the limbs of language, to recover the muted language in which being murmurs to us" (*PW*, 6).

"[Recovering] the muted language," according to Merleau-Ponty, grants us access to meaning, but it is as if meaning is unattainable, simply something for language to gesture at: "[I]t seems that *language never says anything; it invents a series of gestures, which between them present differences clear enough for the conduct of language, to the degree that it repeats itself, recovers and affirms itself, and purveys to us the palpable flow and contours of a universe of meaning*" (*PW*, 32, emphasis in the original). These are the gestures afforded out of experience, that "remnant / Of a memory, a gesture time made / To no one in particular, to itself / Or not even to itself" (*CP*, 589) that Ashbery calls to in *Litany*.

This "series of gestures" that language provides in its inability to "say anything" becomes, in that effort to say but never saying, a transcendental moment. Merleau-Ponty describes this moment as a sort of "*hyper-reflection.*" In reflection, the individual pulls experience inside and considers it, setting it against what has happened before that resides in the repository of previous perception, assessing misalignments with these previous instances, and rearticulates it, thereby shifting the contents of the repository. Yet in the act of hyper-reflection, the individual is capable of keeping track of the thing perceived, what Merleau-Ponty calls the "brute thing," and of how perception shifts itself in this changed articulation. That is, it is essential, he argues, to maintain the link between the thing seen and the reflection about that seeing, as it provides a clear consideration of existence. In thinking about that link, he believes, the individual transcends the self and, in this reflection, transcends perception. Transcendence is, therefore, discerning and communicating "the secret of our perceptual bond" with the world (*VI*, 38).[39]

This is not a transcendence that is special to particular experience or to poetic language, but is rather one that Merleau-Ponty refers to as "consciousness," the awareness and the questioning of perception:

> The acts of the I are of such a nature that they transcend themselves and that there is no private sphere of consciousness. Consciousness is entirely transcendence, not a transcendence that is undergone—we have said that such a transcendence would be the end of consciousness—but rather an active transcendence.... Vision is an action, that is ... an operation that holds more than it promised, that always goes beyond its premises, and that is only inwardly prepared for by my primordial opening to a field of transcendences, or again through an ecstasy. Vision is accomplished and fulfilled in the thing seen. (*PP*, 395)[40]

Core to his approach, therefore, is this view of perception and vision in particular that is explicitly not a passive human characteristic. That is, we do not sit around and wait for our senses to be activated; rather, we engage with the world through intentional perspicuity, link our reception of it to our remembrance of all of our past experiences, and search for understanding of it with those in mind. Amplifying that recursive absorption is the necessary impulse to impart our sense of this understanding, an additional assertion of our agency in perception.

We use ordinary language in this communication, according to Merleau-Ponty: "The same transcendence which we found in the literary uses of speech can also be found in everyday language. This transcendence arises the moment I refuse to content myself with the established language" (*PW*, 20). This focus on everyday language, I believe, provides one approach to Ashbery's poetry: the possibility to attain transcendence through simple experience and the effort to recount it.[41]

Ashbery's poem "Soonest Mended"[42] has received extensive critical attention, much of which talks about it in terms of poetry and largely about nonconformity.[43] This perspective is reasonable, given the poem's beginning with the notion that the first-person-plural narrator is "barely tolerated" and the later statement that we must "[conform] to the rules," read by these scholars as rules for behavior and belief by society.

In turning the lens of phenomenology onto this poem, I do not suggest that these analyses are invalid. I do, however, believe that this poem is talking about experience and perception through its proclaimed effort to find meaning in existence. The poem talks about "information" that arrives and how "[confusing]" it is, and whether even to take it as information ("*Was* it information?" [*CP*, 184]). This information arrives in a "rustling of coils," with images from high (Ariosto poetry, Ingres painting) and low (*Happy Hooligan*) art. That is, sensory data is flooding in, and the "we" of the poem is not sure what to do with it. With all of the things that flow into our lives, the poem asks, how are we to organize it and establish hierarchy when our minds have "room enough and to spare for our little problems (so they began to seem), / Our daily quandary about food and the rent and bills to be paid" (*CP*, 184).

What the group narrator wants is not to have to worry about these things, but to consider the vast horizon of the "gigantic plateau" and "to be small and clear and free" (*CP*, 184). Part of this freedom has to do with the acquisition of simple sensations: "a robin flies across / The upper corner of the window, you brush your hair away / And cannot quite see, or a wound will flash / Against the sweet faces of the others..." (*CP*, 185). These are visual and tactile moments of seeing the bird and feeling the hair on the head and on the hand. The wound could be physical, but it also could refer to the emotional shift in people's faces, when they suddenly express feeling pain. These are "dream[s,] ... vision[s]"; because of that, they must be experiences from the past, held in the memory. Over time, these experiences and memories build up in us, these "faces, namable events, kisses, heroic acts" (*CP*, 185).

Joined to these memories are behavior regulations, these "rules." Included in the repository for our perceptions are patterns for behavior and recognizing what behavior might represent what culturally according to the context. We are inculcated in these behavioral patterns through our childhood (and sometimes as adults). We should not walk around outside in our underwear, much less naked; we should not randomly strike people with our fists; we should not (although we sometimes do) run over people while driving our cars. While we had thought that we were playing the "game" of life, the poem says, we come to discover that it is the rules that are playing the game, and "we... / Were merely spectators."[44] We bowed to the rules for behavior, and because we did so, we have become "'good citizens'" who "[brush our] teeth ... and [learn] to accept / The charity of the hard moments as they are doled out" (*CP*, 186).

Certainly, as I said earlier, the poem is not thrilled about this "conforming to the rules." However, embedded within these rules are impulses toward perception, in particular, the passage of time, "These ... moments, years," when each new moment changes what had been understood in the past: "Tomorrow would alter the sense of what had already been learned, / That the learning process is extended in this way, so that from this standpoint / None of us ever graduates from college" (*CP*, 186). "[T]ime is an emulsion" in that all things that have ever happened become incorporated in the amalgamation of perception.

In this drive to perception, there is also a compulsion to speak, that articulation that makes sense of experience. "We are all talkers," says the poem. In "The being of our sentences, in the climate that fostered them," is the way to articulate what accords with the moment that shaped it. These "flash[es]," these "vision[s]," these "flickering bulbs of the sky" make visual sense difficult, so that "You ... cannot quite see"; this impediment is not simply that sight is impaired, but that meaning, that visible, is hard to come by.

For while this poem worries that meaning "Has somehow come to nothing," it is the need to attain meaning that is at its core: "underneath the talk lies / The moving and not wanting to be moved, the loose / Meaning, untidy and simple like a threshing floor" (*CP*, 185). The mess that is experience is inherently passive. It is up to the poet/philosopher to make sense of it. This effort never stops during life, "But [is] like the friendly beginning of a geometrical progression / Not too reassuring, as though meaning could be cast aside some day / When it had been outgrown" (*CP*, 185). Growth from childhood, with its requisite adherence to rules, makes it feel like adulthood will bring a release from the need for meaning, but the "as though" here suggests that this urge cannot be relinquished "until the end that is past truth," that mortality.

The "fence-sitting / Raised to the level of an esthetic ideal" (*CP*, 185) becomes, therefore, the act of hyper-reflection, when the perceiver sits between the thing that is seen and the thing that is reflected upon. In closing the poem with "For this is action, this not being sure, this careless / Preparing, sowing the seeds crooked in the furrow, / Making ready to forget, and always coming back / To the mooring of starting out, that day so long ago" (*CP*, 186), the poet argues that all we can do is experience, that our form of agency derives from "this not being sure," this persistent lack of certainty and failure to achieve meaning. Instead, our actions are this kind of cultivation, a metaphor for laying out and finding order in the "untidy and simple" mass of experience.

Ashbery's everyday language, his poetry of the description of everyday experience, becomes emblematic of Merleau-Ponty's approach to phenomenology. In this life-long extended effort to say what he experiences, Ashbery brings forth this very "wild meaning," this "expression of experience by experience." There is in this quest, as Ashbery says in *Litany*, "No half-naked limit, / And, in the orange light that the sun succeeds nevertheless / In shedding all over this terrestrial ball, to avert / One's gaze no longer and no less time than is intended / By the illuminating party to be your account / Of yourself, here on earth and for all time" (*CP*, 591). Here is the perception of the visible; here, too, is the accounting, that rendition of the perceived into the poetic, the poetics of the everyday.

Notes

Introduction

1. John Ashbery to R. Joseph Adams, n.d., John Ashbery Papers, MS AM 3189, Houghton Library, Harvard University.
2. John Ashbery to George Bowering, September 13, 1978, John Ashbery Papers, MS AM 3189, Houghton Library, Harvard University.
3. John Ashbery to Stephen Berg, n.d., John Ashbery Papers, MS AM 3189, Houghton Library, Harvard University.
4. John Ashbery to Charles Altieri, May 2, 1979, John Ashbery Papers, MS AM 3189, Houghton Library, Harvard University.
5. For more detailed information about Merleau-Ponty's life and work, see, among others, Stewart, *The Debate between Sartre and Merleau-Ponty*; Crossley, "Phenomenology, Structuralism and History"; and Carman and Hansen, introduction to *The Cambridge Companion*.
6. Morris, *The Sense of Space*, xiii.
7. Carman and Hansen, introduction to *The Cambridge Companion*, 1.
8. See, in particular, Romdenh-Romluc, "Maurice Merleau-Ponty," 103, for a list of influences on Merleau-Ponty's development.
9. Priest, *Merleau-Ponty*, 9–11.
10. My description of these philosophies and the ways in which they differ from Merleau-Ponty's is meant to provide basic context for Merleau-Ponty's brand of phenomenology. For more in-depth analyses, see, for example, Priest, *Merleau-Ponty*; Mallin, *Merleau-Ponty's Philosophy*; and Madison, *Phenomenology of Merleau-Ponty*.
11. Riukas, "The Problem of the Transcendental Ego," 501–2.
12. Priest, *Merleau-Ponty*, 34.
13. Carman and Hansen, introduction to *The Cambridge Companion*, 22.
14. Priest, *Merleau-Ponty*, 54.
15. Ibid., 38, 46.
16. Stewart, *The Debate between Sartre and Merleau-Ponty*, xiv.
17. Priest, *Merleau-Ponty*, 49.
18. For more detail on distinctions between Merleau-Ponty and Sartre, see, in particular, Stewart, *The Debate between Sartre and Merleau-Ponty*.
19. Carman and Hansen, introduction to *The Cambridge Companion*, 10.
20. Ibid.

21. Crossley, "Phenomenology, Structuralism and History," 110.
22. Carman and Hansen, introduction to *The Cambridge Companion*, 19, 25, 16.
23. Crossley, "Phenomenology, Structuralism and History," 88.
24. Most of the poetry under analysis in this book is Ashbery's longer poetry, most of it written before 1987. The longer poetry is my main focus because it is in these works that he takes the time to explain his poetic approach. The earlier poetry (that is, from the first of the two Library of America volumes) is also my focus because here I see him working out his poetics most explicitly.
25. Kostelanetz, "How to Be a Difficult Poet," 24.

Chapter 1

1. *CP*, 520. "What Is Poetry" appeared in the *Vanderbilt Poetry Review* and was included in *Houseboat Days* (New York: Viking Press, 1977).
2. Mallin, *Merleau-Ponty's Philosophy*, 45.
3. Madison, *Phenomenology of Merleau-Ponty*, 13.
4. Hass, *Merleau-Ponty's Philosophy*, 130.
5. Dastur, "World, Flesh, Vision," 28–29. David Cerbone argues that "perceptual experience involves the ideas of both figure and ground"; because of this, perception includes the recognition of space ("Perception," 124).
6. Pietersma, *Phenomenological Epistemology*, 166. Samuel Mallin and Taylor Carman concur with our imperfect perceptual abilities. Mallin says that "our single world is necessarily vague and perpetually indeterminate" (*Merleau-Ponty's Philosophy*, 68); Carman explains that "perception is hard to describe, or even think about clearly, for it is part of its nature to *deflect* thought. The phenomenal field is elusive . . . precisely because its function is to draw us out into the world. The phenomenal field pushes us away from itself" ("Between Empiricism and Intellectualism," 56). Merleau-Ponty writes that "[p]erception hides from itself" (*PP*, 58).
7. Hass, *Merleau-Ponty's Philosophy*, 59–60.
8. Carman, "Between Empiricism and Intellectualism," 53.
9. Mallin talks about the conglomerate of clearings that are ever present: "The interchanges between a multiplicity of clearings make possible the presence of the world with such a degree of determinateness and stability; that is to say, many clearings determine and expand one another's present spatial grasps and confirm and preserve one another's past determinations of the world. . . . Our lived natural world as it is phenomenologically given is essentially an intersubjective one, and it can only be founded on and manifest a Being that is constituted by a multiplicity of interrelated clearings" (*Merleau-Ponty's Philosophy*, 258).
10. Maldiney, "Flesh and Verb," 60.

11. Ibid., 58.
12. Cerbone says that "[t]o perceive, to be embodied, to be 'at grips with the world,' are not three separate or separable notions for Merleau-Ponty, but are three overlapping, interconnected, internally related aspects of our existence. The 'return to phenomena' reveals this overlapping and interconnected unity of consciousness, embodiment and the world made manifest through our embodied experience" ("Perception," 129).
13. Mallin, *Merleau-Ponty's Philosophy*, 37.
14. Ibid, 38.
15. Hass refers to *écart* also as "dehiscence, shift, fundamental fission" (*Merleau-Ponty's Philosophy*, 129); and "gap, spacing, rift, [and] dehiscence" (136).
16. Ibid., 137.
17. Ibid., 132.
18. Ibid., 132, 137. Henri Maldiney writes: "Reversibility is the very principle of experience. Perceiving, I am in a situation of 'total part' open to the entire world. The reciprocal intrication and dissimulation of the perceptive moment and of the apparitional moment are those of the openness of and openness to the world: essentially inseparable and essentially never appearing together" ("Flesh and Verb," 60).
19. Maldiney, "Flesh and Verb," 60. Translation differences create interesting complications around this notion. The translation cited by Maldiney, by Colin Smith, quotes Merleau-Ponty as writing: "We are involved in the world and with others in an inextricable tangle"; the Donald Landes translation has that phrase as, "We are mixed up with the world and with others in an inextricable confusion" (*PP*, 481).
20. Transcendence is a core feature of Merleau-Ponty's thinking, but it is important to state here that the use of this word is in no way an attempt to link Ashbery's poetry with the transcendentalists. Gary Brent Madison talks about the verticality of transcendence when he says: "The dialectic which constitutes human behavior is a *dialectic of transcendence* and . . . the structure is a vertical circularity. Human existence thus bears witness to a power of transcendence (of *écahappement* . . .) embedded in it" (*Phenomenology of Merleau-Ponty*, 13).
21. Ted Toadvine describes this paradox as the "contradictory intertwining of immanence and transcendence that is the perceived world" ("Phenomenology and 'Hyper-Reflection,'" 29).
22. Madison, *Phenomenology of Merleau-Ponty*, 70. Madison explains this paradox and how transcendence works by saying: "It is a truly insurpassable fact when man sees the world and sees himself in it—for as the actualization of a movement of transcendence, this is a fact which surpasses all others. A world wherein consciousness, even a single conscious being, exists transcends by this very fact and by an infinite distance a world which is plunged into the night of

the unconscious; and thus this essential, qualitative difference is itself insurpassable" (105).
23. Ibid., 70.
24. Toadvine, "Phenomenology and 'Hyper-Reflection,'" 20.
25. Hass, *Merleau-Ponty's Philosophy*, 33. Hass continues: "The living body plies itself to a rich, overflowing world in which there is always more than can be grasped in any perception.... [T]his open relation generates a two-fold dynamic between the impersonal-biological layer of one's body and one's personal-intentional projects.... In the ebb and flow between these layers, the living body is able to acquire or incorporate new forms or habits" (153).
26. Davis, "Reversible Subjectivity," 45n36.
27. Madison, *Phenomenology of Merleau-Ponty*, 58.
28. Mallin, *Merleau-Ponty's Philosophy*, 67.
29. Madison, *Phenomenology of Merleau-Ponty*, 202. In explaining this mediation, Madison says that "language must not be an intermediary between thought and silence; it must rather be the mediation of the two, the realization of silence as meaning" (202).
30. Madison argues that "[t]his movement of active transcendence is precisely what is eminently attested to by the *phenomenon of expression*" (*Phenomenology of Merleau-Ponty*, 71). He later argues that "language is the transcendence of merely lived experience, for it is the way the subject mediates that experience" (120).
31. Davis, "Reversible Subjectivity," 31.
32. Barbaras, "Perception and Movement," 79.
33. Harry Adams argues that "[m]eaning emerges through a dynamic process whereby linguistic signs of the past (whose meanings have become sedimented and whose differential relations have become systematized) metamorphose anew through current and spontaneous speech acts" ("Expression," 158).
34. Waldenfels, "The Paradox of Expression," 94 (emphasis in the original).
35. Madison, *Phenomenology of Merleau-Ponty*, 58.
36. Hass, *Merleau-Ponty's Philosophy*, 7.
37. Madison argues, therefore, that "[e]very idea is a cultural object and rests on a spoken or written tradition" (*Phenomenology of Merleau-Ponty*, 59).
38. Hass, *Merleau-Ponty's Philosophy*, 192.
39. Waldenfels, "The Paradox of Expression," 92.
40. Madison, *Phenomenology of Merleau-Ponty*, 139.
41. Mallin, *Merleau-Ponty's Philosophy*, 195–96.
42. Hass argues that "[t]he work of expression is contingent ... upon the people who labor through the trauma of expression to transfigure what has been given to them, contingent upon their ability and commitment to being creative, when so much around them is mimetic" (*Merleau-Ponty's Philosophy*, 160).
43. Mallin, *Merleau-Ponty's Philosophy*, 196.

44. A slightly extreme view of the function of poets comes from Max Scheler, as quoted by Gary Brent Madison: "As Scheler remarks, 'An emotion, for example, which everyone can now perceive in himself, must once have been wrested by some "poet" from the fearful inarticulacy of our inner life for this clear perception of it to be possible'" (*Phenomenology of Merleau-Ponty*, 58).
45. Switzer, "Tactile Cogito," 270.
46. Madison, *Phenomenology of Merleau-Ponty*, 85. Madison is quoting from Merleau-Ponty, *Signs*, 52.
47. Ibid., 104.
48. Hass, *Merleau-Ponty's Philosophy*, 60.
49. Mallin, *Merleau-Ponty's Philosophy*, 234.
50. Madison, *Phenomenology of Philosophy*, 128.
51. Ibid., 89. Madison says further: "Truth thus has a bipolar nature: it is at one and the same time the truth of what is revealed and something which is realized by saying itself. Truth does not precede reflection; it is a result of it. But, *once it has appeared*, it presents itself as that which preceded and motivated reflection. The problem lies entirely in the 'retrospective reality' [VI, 252], this 'retrograde movement' of the truth.... Truth appears as truth only by means of the mediation of reflective expression which, in transcending, in doubling back on existence, renders itself capable of being its truth. Existence is not true in itself, for its truth is precisely reflection" (*Phenomenology of Philosophy*, 137, 140).
52. Madison, *Phenomenology of Merleau-Ponty*, 111.
53. Ibid., 129. Madison argues further: "One discovers the meaning of lived experience only by transcending it through reflection, through language.... Existence is that which demands transcendence, reflection, of us in order to be understood" (141).
54. Waldenfels argues that "experience does not seize upon the word, but rather experience awakens the word.... Translation—the expression of experience ... signifies the work of translating or deciphering.... Experience [is] not ... invented by the writer, but translated by him" ("The Paradox of Expression," 99, 95).
55. Ibid., 96.
56. Mallin, *Merleau-Ponty's Philosophy*, 30.
57. Ibid., 252.
58. Ibid., 98.
59. Madison, *Phenomenology of Merleau-Ponty*, 201. Other descriptions of Being include "visibility, articulation and separation" (Mallin, *Merleau-Ponty's Philosophy*, 34). Mallin describes "Being [as] *nothing*; it is nothing but explosion, radiance of opening and thus ... 'never fully is'" (142). Madison suggests that "Being ... is the world appearing.... Being is nowhere else than in the fact that the world is, is present; it is not the world as a fact, but it is that which makes

the world 'be' a fact; it is the 'facticity' of the fact, its presence.... Being is the very phenomenality of the phenomenon, that which gives it the power of shining forth" (*Phenomenology of Merleau-Ponty*, 218).
60. Mallin, *Merleau-Ponty's Philosophy*, 253.
61. Mallin's complete text is: "[I]t is through this relationship [of two subjects] that Being makes itself maximally explicit. First, it is because the subject thus becomes fully visible to itself; second, because its field gains added determinateness through the specifications which the other contributes; third because its horizons are deepened and extended by being in contact with the other's horizons; fourth because expression becomes possible through this interchange, such that a socio-cultural world can come into being, which in turn gives rise to an intersubjective world of ideas; and finally, because Being can now begin to explicate itself historically. It is for all of these reasons that it is necessary for Being to split itself into a multiplicity of subjects or clearings" (*Merleau-Ponty's Philosophy*, 253).
62. Madison, *Phenomenology of Merleau-Ponty*, 196.
63. Ibid., 250, 103.
64. Mallin, *Merleau-Ponty's Philosophy*, 262.
65. Madison, *Phenomenology of Merleau-Ponty*, 103 (emphasis in the original).
66. Ibid., 209 (emphasis in the original).
67. Barbaras, "Perception and Movement," 83.
68. Ibid., 82–83 (emphasis in the original).
69. Ibid., 85.
70. Waldenfels, "The Paradox of Expression," 96.
71. Priest, *Merleau-Ponty*, 184, 134.
72. Ibid.
73. Mallin, *Merleau-Ponty's Philosophy*, 33. Heidegger writes in *Being and Time*: "We therefore call the phenomena of the future, the character of having been, and the Present, the 'ecstases'' of temporality" (377). "The root-meaning of the word 'ecstasis' (Greek ἔκστασις; German, 'Ekstase') is 'standing outside.' Used generally in Greek for the 'removal' or 'displacement' of something" (*Being and Time*, 377n2).
74. Mallin's complete text is as follows:

> We traced otherness to temporality's future, which we also found to merge with the inexhaustibility of every present. The source of this *ekstase* is Being's essential becoming, which can be conceived as its drive to articulate itself or as the finitude which prevents it from ever fully accomplishing itself. We find that we can trace subjectivity's transcendence, projection, or freedom to this same *ekstase* and thus can meaningfully grasp the way in which otherness and subjectivity merge. We can equally understand their independence by locating subjectivity within

the past as well. This past consists of those previously acquired structures which are used in every present and already determine the outline of any future. Or it can be located to that side of Being which contains the dimensions that have already been determined. The distinction is between that which articulates and that which is articulated, but both are aspects of one and the same movement. Hence subjectivity is a drive that is perpetually ahead of itself into a future, a future that it attempts to make present and non-other to itself and does so by means of capacities that it has already acquired or which were originally given to it. (*Merleau-Ponty's Philosophy*, 33)

75. This quotation is from the 1962 Smith translation of Merleau-Ponty's *Phenomenology of Perception* (269/197). The Landes translation of the same text is: "[E]verything that we live or think always has several senses" (172).
76. Waldenfels, "The Paradox of Expression," 94.
77. Hass explains Merleau-Ponty's notion of the flesh by saying that "[t]he other's self is not reductively equivalent to his/her behaving body. Rather, Merleau-Ponty says, the selfness of the other is 'a certain absence' in the flesh, a 'hollow' that is 'sketched out' behind their behavior. . . . This means the other is not utterly present in his/her flesh, but *beyond* it" (*Merleau-Ponty's Philosophy*, 128). Flesh in these terms means "distance/proximity," "paradox," and "style." Flesh is at once the body, "reversibility"; the "element of being," of "experience" (139–40).
78. Madison, *Phenomenology of Merleau-Ponty*, 248.
79. Priest, *Merleau-Ponty*, 220, 78.
80. Hass, *Merleau-Ponty's Philosophy*, 190.
81. See Ashbery, interview with Louis Osti; and Roffman, *The Songs We Know Best*, for details of Ashbery's early life.
82. See, in particular, Ashbery, interview with Ron Padgett.
83. Ashbery, interview with Michael Silverblatt.
84. Ashbery, interview with Ron Padgett.
85. Epstein, *Beautiful Enemies*.
86. Ashbery said that Auden "was my favorite poet"; Ashbery, interview with Ron Padgett.
87. Ashbery, interview with Brett Lauer.
88. Ibid.
89. Ashbery, interview with Michael Silverblatt; and Ashbery, interview with Charles Bernstein.
90. Ashbery, interview with Brett Lauer.
91. Ashbery, interview with Charles Bernstein.
92. Ibid.
93. Ashbery, interview with Michael Silverblatt.

94. Ashbery, interview with Brett Lauer.
95. Ibid.
96. Epstein, *Beautiful Enemies*, 62.
97. Ibid.; see also Cotkin, *Existential America*.
98. Ashbery, interview with Michael Silverblatt.
99. Bergman, introduction to *Reported Sightings*, xi.
100. Ibid., xiv.
101. E.g., Ashbery, interview with Brett Lauer.
102. Ashbery, interview with Michael Silverblatt.
103. Ashbery, interview with Brett Lauer.
104. Ibid.
105. Epstein, *Attention Equals Life*, 3, 5.
106. Ashbery, interview with Brett Lauer.
107. Ashbery, *Selected Prose*, 201.
108. Ashbery, interview with Charles Bernstein.
109. Matthew Carbery says that Olson read Merleau-Ponty in 1963 (Carbery, *Phenomenology*, 23); Robert Duncan's reading journals, housed in the State University of New York at Buffalo poetry collection, show him reading Merleau-Ponty as well.
110. Jackson, *Acts of Mind*, 70.
111. Ashbery, *Reported Sightings*, 317. See chapter 7 for more extensive discussion of Wittgenstein's influence.
112. Epstein says, in this light, "I am less interested in proving that the poets I discuss actually read or are directly influenced by these philosophers than in arguing that everyday-life theory and everyday-life aesthetics emerge from the same intellectual and cultural preoccupations" (*Attention Equals Life*, 17). See also Ariane Mildenberg's chapter in which she uses Merleau-Ponty's approach to phenomenology to analyze and compare Joseph Cornell and Ashbery's work (Mildenberg, "Through the Wrong End of the Telescope").
113. Ashbery, *Selected Prose*, 209.
114. Epstein, *Attention Equals Life*, 19.
115. Ashbery, interview with Tom Smith.
116. Hulse, "John Ashbery."
117. Ashbery, interview with Janet Bloom and Robert Losada, 123. David Fite sees this aspect of poetry as a reflection of the "flux of experiential consciousness" ("John Ashbery: The Effort to Make Sense," 123). Epstein connects it to everyday experience and sees poetry as focused on the intersection between consciousness and experience: "[P]oetry has staked out as its own special province the complex interaction between mind and world, between individual consciousness and immediate, concrete experience" (*Attention Equals Life*, 11).
118. Ashbery, interview with Brett Lauer.
119. Patrick McGuinness argues, in concurrence, that "[t]racking down the 'I' of

Ashbery's poetry and trying to deduce from it a kind of lyrical starting-block of a stable subject becomes a matter of tracking down the means of its own abnegation. Like the Parmigianino portrait it is at once trapped and transcendental, immanent and excluded, but while Ashbery's work undermines any unified conception of a stable self as poetic 'position,' it does so not to abolish it but to extend the bounds of the self, its field of experience" (McGuinness, "Ashbery").

120. Jackson, *Acts of Mind*, 73.
121. Ibid., 74. Epstein argues that "poetry steps forward as perhaps the quintessential genre for the rendering of concrete, everyday experiences and objects, for an investigation of the workings of attention, and for a method of responding to the moment-by-moment unfolding of time," leading to the notion "that poetry itself might be defined as a form of attention, a heightened mode of attentiveness to the world" (*Attention Equals Life*, 12).
122. "Grand Galop" was first published in *Poetry* (April 1974): 1–8, and then included in *Self-Portrait in a Convex Mirror* (New York: Viking Press, 1975).
123. Stephen Ross describes an essay Ashbery wrote while in college, stating that Ashbery's "method . . . is to write about the object as if he were both within it and without it" (Ross, *Invisible Terrain*, 16n60; from the Ashbery essay "Nature Images in the Poetry of Vaughan and Marvell," John Ashbery Papers, MS AM 3189, Houghton Library, Harvard University). Ross argues that, for Ashbery, "[Henry] Vaughan's 'double vision of nature' gives us nature as it really is, something experienced outwardly and inwardly, objects mediated by subjects which reflect on their mediation" (Ross, *Invisible Terrain*, 16). "The Bungalows" first appeared in *Paris Review* 10, no. 40 (Winter–Spring 1967): 49–51, and was included in *The Double Dream of Spring* (New York: E. P. Dutton, 1970). *Fragment* first appeared in a volume illustrated by Alex Katz (Los Angeles: Black Sparrow Press, 1969) and was included in *The Double Dream of Spring*. *The System* was included in *Three Poems* (New York: Viking Press, 1972).
124. Jackson, *Acts of Mind*, 75.
125. Fite, "John Ashbery: The Effort to Make Sense," 128.
126. Ashbery, *Selected Prose*, 251.
127. Ashbery, *A Worldly Country*, 70.
128. Jackson, *Acts of Mind*, 73. In the same interview, Ashbery also says that "thought created by language and creating it are the nucleus of the poem" (71).
129. Ashbery, interview with Brett Lauer.
130. Ashbery, interview with Alfred A. Poulin Jr., 245.
131. Lieberman, *Unassigned Frequencies*, 20.
132. Ashbery, interview with Janet Bloom and Robert Losada, 79.
133. Ashbery, *Selected Prose*, 75; and Epstein, *Attention Equals Life*, 26.
134. Fite, "On the Virtues of Modesty," 65.
135. For more on space and proximity, see my discussion of Merleau-Ponty earlier in this chapter. Perception requires a sense of space through foreground and

background—that is, the focus of the perception and what is around it. Space sets up questions of distance, where what is perceived must be close enough to sense but not too close to merge with the one doing the perceiving.

136. Ngai, *Ugly Feelings*, 267; and Ross, *Invisible Terrain*, 95.
137. "French Poems" appeared in *Art and Literature* and was included in *The Double Dream of Spring*.
138. Jackson, *Acts of Mind*, 70.
139. Ibid., 71. David Fite argues: "The proverbial knowledge that Ashbery gives us in poems like 'As We Know' and 'Soonest Mended' is not a knowledge based on the lightning bolt of transcendent Romantic truth suddenly wrested from on high. Rather, the proverbs participate fully in the world of Ashbery's fence-straddling aesthetic, an aesthetic of flux which . . . warns us . . . to resist the stiffening formulations of 'always deducing the general from particulars'" ("On the Virtues of Modesty," 76), later mentioning "long cultivated tactics against transcendence" (81).
140. "Tapestry" first appeared in the *New Yorker*, May 21, 1979, 34, and was included in the volume *As We Know* (New York: Viking Press, 1979).
141. Certainly, a part of this overlap would be due to the American devotion to pragmatism and its emphasis on process.
142. Carbery, *Phenomenology*, 6.
143. Ross, *Invisible Terrain*, 31, 11.
144. Ashbery, interview with Louis Osti, 87.
145. Gilson, "Disseminating 'Circumference,'" 40; Dick, "A Serpentine | Gesture," n. 5; and Howard, "John Ashbery," 40.
146. Jackson, *Acts of Mind*, 75.
147. Epstein, *Beautiful Enemies*, 56–57.
148. Carbery, *Phenomenology*, 19.
149. In *Obdurate Brilliance*, Peter Baker also considers poetry via phenomenology, particularly that espoused by Emmanuel Levinas, with his approach that, as Carbery argues, "ethics is grounded on our encounters with others" (Carbery, *Phenomenology*, 9).
150. Ross, *Invisible Terrain*, 29, 11.

Chapter 2

1. For more consideration of phenomenology and intentionality, see Pollio, Henley, and Thompson, *The Phenomenology of Everyday Life*, esp. 5, 16; Ricoeur, *Husserl*, 7; and Moran, *Introduction to Phenomenology*, 16.
2. Bernstein, *A Poetics*, 9.
3. Ibid., 16.
4. "French Poems" were originally written in French and published in that form

in *Tel Quel* 27 (Autumn 1966). The English translation was included in *The Double Dream of Spring*.
5. Ashbery, interview with Peter Stitt, 43. John Shoptaw, as well, focuses on the relationship between Ashbery's poetry and experience. "Like Stein," he says, "Ashbery is interested not in events 'themselves,' . . . but in the way they happen to us, the way we experience them" (*On the Outside Looking Out*, 3). See also Alfred Poulin's interview of Ashbery in which Ashbery talks about his poem "Leaving the Atocha Station": "The dislocated, incoherent fragments of images which make up the movement of the poem are probably like the experience you get from a train pulling out of a station of no particular significance. The dirt, the noises, the sliding away seem to be a movement in the poem. The poem was probably trying to express that, not for itself but as an epitome of something experienced; I think that is what my poems are about. I mean it doesn't particularly matter about the experience; the movement of experiencing is what I'm trying to get down. . . . Most of my poems are about the experience of experience" (Ashbery, interview with Alfred A. Poulin Jr., 245). Also, see Ashbery, interview with Ross Labrie, 31. See also the depth of criticism linking Ashbery's work to phenomenology, both explicit and implicit: Moramarco, "Coming Full Circle," 38; McCorkle, "Nimbus of Sensations," 114; Norton, "Whispers out of Time," 282; Costello, "John Ashbery and the Idea of the Reader," 493; Longenbach, *Modern Poetry after Modernism*, 93; and Longenbach, "Ashbery and the Individual Talent," 105.
6. Ashbery, interview with Janet Bloom and Robert Losada, 117.
7. Ibid., 127.
8. As Merleau-Ponty puts it, "Perception is like a net whose knots progressively appear more clearly" (*PP*, 12).
9. Ashbery, "A Place for Everything," 75.
10. Ashbery, "Second Presentation of Elizabeth Bishop," 10.
11. Ibid., 11.
12. Other instances of Ashbery's explicit references to poetry and experience include another essay on Bishop, "Throughout Is This Quality of Thingness: Elizabeth Bishop," in which he talks about "[t]his strange divided singleness of our experience," merging our interior selves with the world around us (8); his essay on Pierre Bonnard, in which he talks about how the artist is "attempting to replicate the way phenomena appear to the mind's eye" (*Reported Sightings*, 57); and his essay "The New Realists," in which he talks about how "[t]he phenomena evoked by artists in this show are not phenomena, but part of our experience, our lives—created by us and creating us." "Why *the* object?," he asks. Because "[t]hey are a common ground, a neutral language understood by everybody, and therefore the ideal material with which to create experiences which transcend the objects. . . . The unmanageable vastness of our experience [has] been seized on by the New Realist as the core of a continuing situation;

that of man on the one side and a colorful indifferent universe on the other.... Where the balance of power lies in the yet-one-again altered scheme of things. Today it seems to repose in the objects that surround us; that is in our perception of them or, simply and once again, in ourselves" (*Reported Sightings*, 82–83).

13. "Clouds" originally appeared in *Harper's Magazine*, November 30, 1969, 44, and was included in *The Double Dream of Spring*.
14. Bernstein, *A Poetics*, 64.
15. This notion of "invisible light" links to Merleau-Ponty's notion of the visible and the invisible as well, whereby the perceived is visible and the meaning (this light, in a paradox) is invisible.
16. Bernstein, *A Poetics*, 86.
17. Merleau-Ponty discusses speech and language at great length in all of his works. For the purposes of this study, I am focusing on his attention to literary, and especially poetic, communication.
18. Charles Altieri relates Wallace Stevens's poetry to phenomenology, but in ways that I believe are relevant to a discussion of Ashbery's poetry. Altieri refers to these gaps between the poet and the world as missing anchors: "Stevens could not escape addressing the relation to knowledge that pervades our language about subjects and objects: objects anchor subjects in the world, and the lack of such an anchor is felt in various forms of doubt, insecurity, and what Jacques Derrida would call the endless supplementarity of trying constantly to shore up what will pass as accurate description.... [I]t takes poetry to express how subjects can interact with objects so as to establish 'presences' and challenge reductive accounts of value" (*Wallace Stevens and the Demands of Modernity*, 3–4).
19. In a note in the essay "Three or Four Things I Know about Him," Bernstein confirms poetry's function concerning the articulation of experience by saying, "I don't mean 'experience' in the sense of a picture/image/representation that is calling back to an already constituted experience. Rather, language itself constitutes experience at every moment (in reading and otherwise). Experience, then, is not tied into representation exclusively but is a separate 'perception'-like category (& perception not necessarily as in perception onto a physical/preconstituted world, as 'eyes' in the Olson sense, that is, not just onto a matrix-qua-the-world but as operation/projecting/composing activity). The point is, then, that experience is a dimension necessarily built into language.... [E]xperience is not inextricably linked to representation, normative syntax, images, but rather, the other way around, is a synthetic, generative activity" (*A Poetics*, 35).
20. Morse, "Typical John," 18.
21. As John Shoptaw notes, Ashbery wrote *The New Spirit* between November 1969 and April 1970. It appeared in *Paris Review* 13, no. 50 (Fall 1970): 115–53. He

wrote *The System* between January and March 1971. It appeared in *Paris Review* 14, no. 53 (Winter 1972): 33–73. He wrote *The Recital* in April 1971. It appeared in *Poetry Review* 62, no. 4 (Winter 1971–1972): 351–58, and in *Fiction* 1, no. 1 (1972) (Shoptaw, *On the Outside Looking Out*, 362). See David Graham Parnel Spittle for a complete list of influences on this poem ("John Ashbery and Surrealism," 77–78).

22. Spittle links *Three Poems* to the phenomenology of Merleau-Ponty ("John Ashbery and Surrealism," 80–83).

23. Other instances of this pessimism in the poem concerning art's ability to capture experience include: "Perhaps no art, however gifted and well-intentioned, can supply what we were demanding of it: not only the figured representation of our days but the justification of them, the reckoning and its application, so close to the reality being lived that it vanishes suddenly in a thunderclap, with a loud cry" (*CP*, 322); "the landscape isn't making sense anymore; it is not merely that you have misapplied certain precepts not meant for the situation in which you find yourself, which is always a new one that cannot be decoded with reference to an existing corpus of moral principles" (*CP*, 322); and "we experience the energy and beauty of the others as a miraculous manna from heaven; at the same time our eyes are turned inward to the darkness and emptiness within" (*CP*, 323).

24. Ashbery relies extensively on the passive voice as if to say that no one person is responsible or has agency for these matters of importance in the poetry.

25. I would say that it is this poem, in particular, that Ashbery is addressing to David Kermani, to whom this volume is dedicated.

26. While he does talk about breath and breathing several times in this poem, as in, "that any breathing is to be breathing into each other, and imperfect, like all apprehended things" (*CP*, 250), Ashbery does not make an affiliation with Black Mountain poets clear here, but it is possible that he is connecting the breath with language and with the line as they did. See, in particular, Levertov, "Some Notes on Organic Form"; and Olson, *Selected Writings*.

27. Another instance of this urge to speak, and this shift from exterior sensations to interior reckonings, appears in the line: "[I]n staring too long out over this elaborate view one begins to forget that one is looking inside, taking in the familiar interior which has always been there, reciting the only alphabet one knows" (*CP*, 252).

28. Critical descriptions of *The System* include John Gery's "resistance to reductive thinking" ("Ashbery's Menagerie," 132); John Ernest's "willingness to surround himself in the cacophonous flux of his world" ("Fossilized Fish," 181); and John Shoptaw's "homespun prose poem" ("The Music of Construction," 219). Since the poem recursively lays out its phenomenological approach, it would be very difficult to lift small instances of separate elements of phenomenology for critical analysis. Instead, in explaining how it works repeatedly, the poem links

senses to time, to perception, and to movement, making the quotations for explanation long and repetitive as well.

29. Other instances of direct reference to movement in the poem include: "We know that we are enroute in a certain sense" (*CP*, 295); "we have all our mobility in a word" (*CP*, 296); "the unspoken message that motion could be accomplished only in time, that is in a preordained succession of moments which must carry us far from here" (*CP*, 296); "you are moving much too quickly for your momentum to be halted" (*CP*, 304); and "there is no alternative to remaining motionless you must still learn to cope with the onrushing tide of time and all the confusing phenomena it bears in its wake, some of which perfectly resemble the unfinished but seemingly salvageable states of reality at cross-purposes with itself" (*CP*, 307).

30. The poem refers to this discomfort with the present multiple times: "It could be anything, you say. But it could not have been an exercise in defining the present when our position, our very lives depend on those fixed loci of past and future" (*CP*, 317); "at the blurred edge where life is hinged to the future and to the past" (*CP*, 315); and "given a definitive shape to our formless gestures; we can live as though we had caught up with time and avoid the sickness of the present, a shapeless blur as meaningless as a carelessly exposed roll of film. There is hardness and density now" (*CP*, 315–16).

31. Time passage also appear in the poem in the lines, "The allegory is ended, its coils absorbed into the past, and this afternoon is as wide as an ocean. It is the time we have now, and all our wasted time sinks into the sea and is swallowed up without a trace. The past is dust and ashes, and this incommensurably wide way leads to the pragmatic and kinetic future" (*CP*, 317).

32. Other clear references to order in the poem include: "[W]e might miss out on everything by ignoring its call to order, which is in fact audible to each of us" (*CP*, 291); "What about the morning resolutions to convert all the confused details in the air about you into a column of intelligible figures?" (*CP*, 289); and "It is doing the organizing, the guidelines radiate from its control" (*CP*, 310).

33. The poem is rife with statements of these failures, including: "an amalgam is not completeness either" (*CP*, 291); "to complete the cycle of inertia that we began wrongly supposing that it would lead to knowledge" (*CP*, 292); "the happiness withholds itself" (*CP*, 294); "we, have been waiting all our lives for this sign of fulfillment, now to be abruptly snatched away so soon as barely perceived" (*CP*, 294); "its *nearness* is there, tingeing the air around them, in suspension, in escrow as it were, but they cannot get at it" (*CP*, 294); "in reality the ship is sinking under them" (*CP*, 295); "it all seems meaningless" (*CP*, 301); "it cannot be realized" (*CP*, 302); "details, no matter how complete, can give no adequate idea of the whole" (*CP*, 290); "their nature, which is part and parcel of their existence, is to remain incomplete, clamoring for wholeness" (*CP*, 307);

and "ready to slink back into his inner confusion at the first brush with the outside world, so your aspirations, my soul" (*CP*, 307).

Chapter 3

1. John Shoptaw (*On the Outside Looking Out*, 83, 84–85), Annette Gilson ("Disseminating 'Circumference,'" 502), and Stephen Ross (*Invisible Terrain*, 77) all refer to "Clepsydra" as Ashbery's final France composition. "Clepsydra" was included in *Rivers and Mountains* (New York: Holt, Rinehart and Winston, 1966).
2. Shoptaw also says that "[t]he plot concerns a long-term love affair which started out fresh and became ossified by custom" ("The Music of Construction," 249).
3. For ease of reference here, I am using line numbers for in-text citations for this poem (*CP*, 140–46).
4. For more discussion of gesture in this book, see chapters 5 and 6 on reflection and motility.
5. In talking about linguistic gestures and the truth, Merleau-Ponty argues: "Our present expressive operations, instead of driving the preceding ones away—simply succeeding and annulling them—salvage, preserve, and (insofar as they contain some truth) take them up again; and the same phenomenon is produced in respect to others' expressive operations, whether they be past or contemporary. Our present keeps the promises of our past.... Each act of expression realizes for its own part a portion of this project, and by opening a new field of truths, further extends the contract which has just expired" (*PP*, 95).
6. In a letter to Zali Gurevitch, Ashbery writes, "I am not given to paraphrasing my poems, and I try to write in such a way that they cannot be paraphrased. Also, the utterances in the poetry are not to be taken as general truths, but as valid only within the confines of the particular poem" (John Ashbery to Zali Gurevitch, March 29, 1979, John Ashbery Papers, MS AM 3189, Houghton Library, Harvard University).
7. Friedman, "John Ashbery," 36.
8. Richard Kostelanetz writes that "all of his poems are ultimately about two things: the thoughts in his mind at the moment of composition—a mental self-portraiture—and then the processes of making poems" ("How to Be a Difficult Poet," 33).
9. Ibid.
10. Ibid., 24. This poem has received extensive critical attention, including James Longenbach: "[It is an] attempt to embody [temporal] process within discourse—to 'chew on' the meaning of words rather than escape them.... Nominally [it is] about the way in which one moment supersedes another, slipping from the future to the past without any sense of a teleology" (*Modern Poetry*

after Modernism, 95); Lynn Keller: "Thematic focus [is] the constant evasion of perception and articulation by protean reality or truth.... As the poem goes on to explore the nature of these moments, the question of their permanence and coherence, and the meaning of time that surrounds them, the process of the searching consciousness is reflected in the poem's syntactic structure ... convey[ing] the uninterrupted yet varied flow of experience" ("Thinkers without Final Thoughts," 246); Ben Hickman: "What 'Clepsydra' attempts to represent is the movement and essential ungroundedness of moments of thought" (*John Ashbery and English Poetry*, 37); David Herd: "The relentless speed of the poem's transitions [appears] to leave the reader little choice but to go with the flow.... [T]he purpose of the poem is not simply to chart the speed with which events now appear to flow towards one, but ... to find ways of living with that flow.... For all the relentlessness of its perpetual advance, 'Clepsydra' is an argumentative poem: discoursing on Romantic and modernist aesthetics even as in its practice it is moving dramatically beyond them" (*John Ashbery and American Poetry*, 108–9); and finally, the fine and recent work by David Dick in which he says that the poem is "an argument between [a] resistant, half-formed consciousness ... and the presence of time which insists on this consciousness' renewal to arrive at individuality: the self. Although this self exists in the present, it cannot know itself in the present, or retrospectively in the moment just passed" ("A Serpentine | Gesture").

11. Shoptaw links the poem to the metronome, a clearly dialectical instrument, cycling back and forth ("The Music of Construction," 249).
12. Mallin, *Merleau-Ponty's Philosophy*, 12.
13. Mallin argues explicitly that Merleau-Ponty's phenomenology was able to "overcome Cartesian dualism" (*Merleau-Ponty's Philosophy*, 8). Hass explains, for instance, that "the biological layer sustains the personal layer, and yet the personal folds back onto the biological—weaving through and around it a field of personalized action, or a situation" (*Merleau-Ponty's Philosophy*, 90), and he also argues that "the subjective and objective aspects of a situation cannot be isolated, ... they interweave and are dialectically interconnected" (14).
14. Strogatz, "Why Pi Matters."
15. Here, I am taking the notion of untruth as inadequate mapping between the perception and the articulation of it. It is an "untruth," as opposed to a lie, giving it an unintentional sense of not telling the truth.
16. In his interview with Rich Kelley for the Library of America, Ashbery says that "Clepsydra narrates in real time its own coming into being," and he quotes from another poem, "Saying It to Keep It from Happening": "[There is] something about time / That only a clock can tell you: how it feels, not what it means" (*CP*, 509).
17. David Dick links the colon in the poem directly to time, when he says: "In 'Clepsydra' the sense of the eternity of the moment is muted, building via

colons to an 'unstated circumference,' to examine instead how the self only really has the sensation of the passage of time, swirling around, de- and reconstructing the individual moment-by-moment in the midst of the 'unformed,' 'affected,' and disruptively blank 'white din'" ("A Serpentine | Gesture"). Jasmine Kitses links the colon to the material aspect of language by saying that it bears "visual and spatial connotations to remind us that language is a material object in its own right" ("Round / Shiny Fixed / Alternatives," 279).

18. *Oxford English Dictionary*, 2nd ed., s.v. "colon." "Limb, member or clause of sentence. . . . Its best defined use is to separate clauses which are grammatically independent and discontinuous, but between which there is an opposition or similar relation of sense. Thus it may introduce an antithetic statement" (3:493).

19. Ibid.

20. As Ben Lerner argues about the colons in "Clepsydra": "The successive colons divide the already complicated sentence into a kind of linguistic Zeno's paradox, in which the unit of meaning threatens to break up into infinite sub-distances, and such elaborate sentences are then further ramified by lineation" ("The Future Continuous," 205).

21. Krell, *Lunar Voices*, 200–201 (emphasis in the original).

22. Ziarek, *Language after Heidegger*, 181.

23. Heidegger says that the colon "names the call to enter into that relation between thing and word which has now been experienced" (*On the Way to Language*, 65). Avital Ronell also talks about the colon: "In German, the word for 'colon' is . . . the doubling structure of the hearing and saying which inhabit the call" (*The Telephone Book*, 167), and she links the colon to Heidegger: "The colon, calling, eventually puts us through to speaking, to 'what to speak means'" (Ronell, *The Telephone Book*, 168; and Heidegger, *On the Way to Language*, 95).

24. In writing about George Oppen's poetry, Kitses says that "colons . . . take on a 'definitive physiognomic status,' offering a visible reminder that clarity is inextricably vexed by the opacity of language [and that] the materials of language through which we attempt to see the world hinder our clear vision of it" (Kitses, "Round / Shiny Fixed / Alternatives," 282).

25. Ibid.

26. Any question of order must, of course, call to Wallace Stevens's work, in particular to his poem "Ideas of Order." Ashbery mentioned repeatedly his affinity with Stevens, as he wrote in a letter Lynn Keller: "[I]t seems to me that what pleases me in [Stevens's] work is its unique amalgamating of the power of the unconscious mind (imagination, surrealism or whatever you want to call it) with those of the unconscious, ordering mind." Later in the letter, Ashbery hastens to disavow the impact of Stevens's poetry on his own ("However, this thought of mine which came to me quite recently, is not to be taken as a comment on my perception of Stevens's influence on my poetry"), but LDA analysis

does provide clear relationships between Ashbery's "The Skaters" and Stevens's "The Comedian as the Letter C" (John Ashbery to Lynn Keller, January 15, 1979, John Ashbery Papers, MS AM 3189, Houghton Library, Harvard University).

27. Wolf, "The Lyric," 21.
28. Willis, "The Arena in the Garden," 228.
29. See also Werner Wolf ("The Lyric") and Jonathan Culler (*Theory of the Lyric*), who remark on the "brevity" of the lyric.
30. Willis, "The Arena in the Garden," 228.
31. Vendler, *Invisible Listeners*, 53.
32. McHale, *The Obligation toward the Difficult Whole*; and Keller, *Forms of Expansion*.
33. In *Wallace Stevens and the Demands of Modernity*, Charles Altieri argues for a different conception of the lyric: "Aspectual thinking ... differs from traditional lyricism in its refusal of dramatically developed situations and in its foregrounding of the processes of thinking 'as' situations shift and perspectives open up" (43).
34. Cameron, *Lyric Time*, 203.
35. Ibid., 206.
36. Ibid., 204.
37. Kelly, "The Subject as Time," 154.
38. Cameron, *Lyric Time*, 207.
39. Merleau-Ponty, *Phénoménologie de la perception*, 501.
40. Waldenfels, "Coming and Going of Time," 222.
41. Culler, *Theory of the Lyric*, 91.
42. Willis, "The Arena in the Garden," 229.
43. Cameron, *Lyric Time*, 207
44. Waldenfels, "Coming and Going of Time," 232.
45. Kelly, "The Subject as Time," 159. This metaphor resonates in particular in terms of the discussion above of "Clepsydra."
46. Wolf, "The Lyric," 24.
47. Von Hallberg, *Lyric Powers*, 73n75. Clear here, too, is Merleau-Ponty's influence on postmodern thinkers.
48. Morris and Maclaren, introduction to *Time, Memory, and Institution*, 25.
49. Vendler, *Invisible Listeners*, 47. In his interview of Ashbery, John Koethe asks, "A lot of your work is concerned with time in various ways, such as the passage of time," and Ashbery responds: "Yes, I read Proust at an early age and got involved with the problem about time, and for many years I thought I was writing poetry about nothing, that my poetry didn't have any subject matter. Having reached a fairly advanced age, it seems to me that the subject in my poetry is actually time and getting older" (Koethe and Ashbery, "An Interview with John Ashbery," 182).
50. "Night" appeared in *The Tennis Court Oath* (Middletown, CT: Wesleyan University Press, 1962).

51. "Sunrise in Suburbia" appeared in a stand-alone volume (Phoenix Book Shop, 1968) and was included in *The Double Dream of Spring*.
52. "Definition of Blue" was included in *The Double Dream of Spring*. The Library of America volume states that the poem appeared in the *Times Literary Supplement* previously, but there is no record of it in the *TLS* archives (Ashbery, *Collected Poems, 1956–1987*, 1008).
53. "To the Same Degree" was included in *The Tennis Court Oath*. *Litany* was included in its entirety in *As We Know*, only sixty-eight pages long in the larger-format original appearance. The second half of the poem also appeared in *American Poetry Review* 8, no. 4 (July–August 1979): 17–32.
54. Jackson, *Acts of Mind*, 74.
55. *Merriam-Webster.com Dictionary*, s.v. "litany," https://www.merriam-webster.com/dictionary/litany.
56. Wind appears in this poem, in addition to this example, multiple other times (e.g., *CP* 563, 569, 636, 629, 611, 654). Other motifs include music and dust.
57. Surely Ashbery knew from his time in France that *zeph*, from Zephyr, is a euphemism for a fart.
58. Other references to poetry include one on poetry words (*CP*, 607); "Poetry has already happened" (*CP*, 608); "[poetry] is both too remote and too near to transcend [life], / It is [life] probably" (*CP*, 609); and "But poetry is making things in the past; / The past tense transcends and excuses these grimy arguments" (*CP*, 606).
59. Other instances of circularity in the poem include: "Hole left by the great implosion" (*CP*, 556); "The pancake / Is around in idea" (*CP*, 556); "Surrounding" (*CP*, 557); "Blow around the rest" (*CP*, 557); "Leading outward to encircle the profit / Of laughter" (*CP*, 559); "Who can elicit these possible, / Rubbery spirals?" (*CP*, 563); "The eye / Revolving slowly in the empty socket" (*CP*, 572); "The roundness / Was all around to be appreciated, yet somehow flat / As well" (*CP*, 572); and "Summer night is like a goldfish bowl" (*CP*, 576).
60. In a much later poem, "Uptick," from *Planisphere* (2009), Ashbery writes: "To come back for a few hours to / the present subject, a painting, / looking like it was seen, / half turning around, slightly apprehensive, / but it has to pay attention / to what's up ahead: a vision. / Therefore poetry dissolves in / brilliant moisture and reads us / to us" (128). "Uptick" also appeared in *Poetry* 193, no. 6 (March 2009): 507.
61. Ashbery also links time to water and water flowing here, as he does with "Clepsydra": "the channel of time we were being ferried across" (*CP*, 612); and "for someone / Like me the time flows around again / With things I did in it" (*CP*, 554).
62. In describing the access to the past with every present moment, the poem says, "Yet never was for the seeing, / The tasting that jabs back / Into the past as well, / For what is present savoring?" (*CP*, 565).

63. Note the link to Jacques Derrida with this term. Merleau-Ponty's work influenced Derrida in the development of his theoretical positions.
64. Other examples of thread-fabric-weaving analogies in the poem include: "whose truant / Punctuation resumed again the thread / Of what is outside, outdoors" (*CP*, 612); "at last the thread holds" (*CP*, 579); "Only an aftertaste of medicine / And subtle pressures put / Beyond this lattice that is / As narrow as the visible universe" (*CP*, 567); "thorns in the memory / Of laced paths" (*CP*, 570); "one of the strands / Where one shall encounter this and all the / Other deviating forms of momentary life / In a contradiction which shall make its point" (*CP*, 589); and "The ticking of a clock in the / Background could be / Only the plait" (*CP*, 562).
65. It is unclear to me if this is an error in the text or if it was intentional by Ashbery.
66. This concern is not unlike that of Wallace Stevens, known to be an influence on Ashbery (see note 26 above on this affinity).

Chapter 4

1. John Ashbery Papers, MS AM 3189, Houghton Library, Harvard University.
2. Merleau-Ponty says about emblems: "Painting does not copy movement point by point or by offering us signs of it; it invents *emblems* which give it a substantial presence, presenting it to us as the 'metamorphosis' (Rodin) of one attitude into another, the implication of a future within the present" ("The Sensible World," 10).
3. *Fragment* appeared in *Poetry* (February 1966): 283–98. It was published as a separate volume by Black Sparrow Press (1969) with illustrations by Alex Katz and then included in *The Double Dream of Spring*.
4. Ashbery, interview with Janet Bloom and Robert Losada, 125–26. In a letter to James L. McManus, Ashbery writes, "[T]he ten-line stanza form I used was suggested by the *dizains* of the 16th century French poet Maurice Scève. It appealed to me because it had something of the assertive thrust of the sonnet form without its (for me) often irritating and artificially imposed feeling of 'incompleteness'" (February 6, 1977, John Ashbery Papers, MS AM 3189, Houghton Library, Harvard University).
5. Shoptaw, *On the Outside Looking Out*, 111.
6. Maurice Scève, "Libre viuois en l'Auril de mon aage" (*Délie* VI), trans. A. S. Kline, Poetry in Translation, https://www.poetryintranslation.com/PITBR/French/SceveDelie.php#anchor_Toc503186579.
7. Scève was greatly influenced by Petrarch's *Il Canzoniere*, a collection largely but not exclusively of sonnets that focused on the poet's love of a woman, Laura. Scève discovered Laura's tomb in Avignon in 1533 (Mulhauser, *Maurice Scève*, 24–25).

8. Mulhauser, *Maurice Scève*, 32–33.
9. Ibid., 33.
10. Hunt, "The Association of the Lady and the Unicorn," 75.
11. Roberts, "The Unicorn," 39.
12. Ibid.
13. Maurice Scève, "Emblem 1: The Lady and the Unicorn" (*Délie*), trans. A. S. Kline, Poetry in Translation, https://www.poetryintranslation.com/PITBR/French/SceveDelie.php#anchor_Toc503186578.
14. According to Susan Rosenbaum, Ashbery saw Katz's illustrations before writing this poem ("Permeation, Ventilation, Occlusion," 87). In John Koethe's interview of Ashbery, the poet says that *Fragment* is "fifty ten-line stanzas and I decided that I would do two of them each time I sat down to write and not do any more or less. *Fragment* took about six months to write but of writing every once in a while" (Koethe and Ashbery, "An Interview with John Ashbery," 184). Because of this writing process, as Ashbery says later in this interview, "[t]he long poem seems to gain a kind of richness from being written by not different poets, but a poet who is different each time" (185). I am using the Black Sparrow edition for the citations for this poem, since the images by Katz are not present in the Library of America version.
15. Lieberman, *Unassigned Frequencies*, 18. Lieberman explains that *Fragment* is "modeled after the mode of the atonal twelve-note scale in music. The form does not peak, but slowly accumulates epiphanies, all of about the same weight and mild radiance, all the fragments of experience flattened to the same common denominator of equalizing value" (18).
16. Ashbery and Katz, *Fragment*, 9.
17. Ibid.
18. Ibid., 25.
19. Ibid., 53.
20. Ibid.
21. Ashbery, interview with Janet Bloom and Robert Losada, 127.
22. Ashbery and Katz, *Fragment*, 17.
23. Ibid.
24. Ibid.
25. Ibid., 29.
26. Ibid., 18.
27. Ibid., 21.
28. Ibid., 37. Whippoorwill was the name of Kenward Elmslie's whippet hound. Elmslie was Joe Brainard's partner for many years; Brainard collaborated with Ashbery in *The Vermont Notebook* (Cran, "Men with a Pair of Scissors," 105).
29. Ashbery and Katz, *Fragment*, 41.
30. Ibid., 50.
31. *The Vermont Notebook* was published in 1975 (Los Angeles: Black Sparrow Press).

32. Lewallen, *Joe Brainard*, 36; and Rosenbaum, "Permeation, Ventilation, Occlusion," 61. Josh Schneiderman notes that the lines "This is where we are spending our vacation. A nice restful spot. Real camp life. Hope you are feeling fine" (*CP*, 411) are also on a postcard in Ashbery's materials at the Houghton Library, dated August 23, 1949 (Schneiderman, "Whispers out of Time"). In a letter to Ross Labrie, Ashbery writes:

> *The Vermont Notebook* was an exercise in almost automatic writing. I wrote most of it on buses traveling through New England, though not Vermont. It was a kind of experiment for me in writing in an uncongenial environment and also writing in longhand, which I hadn't done in many years. It's a kind of messy grab bag as the word notebook implies. Generally speaking I guess it's a catalogue of a number of things that could be found in the state of Vermont, as well as almost everywhere else— another "democratic vista." This was also the "idea" behind my poem "Europe." (August 17, 1982, John Ashbery Papers, MS AM 3189, Houghton Library, Harvard University)

33. Cotton, "Joe Brainard's Still-Life Poetics," 91. Note the reverse movement here, too, with Katz's images preceding Ashbery's text in *Fragment*.
34. Jess Cotton argues that "Brainard's work is curative in the sense that it pushes back against a mediated seriality that reduces objects to commercial products and which prevents us from being intimate with them" ("Joe Brainard's Still-Life Poetics," 82). I suggest that this approach is operational as well with these commercial and manufactured images.
35. Rona Cran notes that this work "makes extensive use of lists, bringing each element together to form a new whole—as in traditional collage" ("Men with a Pair of Scissors," 108–9).
36. Ron Padgett says that at least some of the images are from photographs. He found the photograph of the fisherman (*CP*, 398) in Kenward Elmslie's studio in Vermont. He thinks that the others have not survived (Ron Padgett, email message to the author, December 8, 2018). This is important because of what it is doing to time—the artist is at a remove from the moment. Some of these images are also clearly from magazines, too. Nathan Kernan confirms this: "Nearly half of the forty-eight drawings that accompany [this text] depict what might be called . . . pre-existing imagery. . . pictures of pictures" ("Joe Brainard: The Madonna of the Future," 56–57). Kernan notes that Brainard referred to images of this kind as "jack-off" drawings (59), signally the "fuck work" that Nick Strum identifies concerning Brainard, the inclination both to dismiss obligations to work and to regard sex as work (Strum, "Fuck Work").
37. Cran argues that Ashbery "collages found texts, recycles old poems (by

Ashbery), blends intellect with kitsch, mixes homoeroticism with consumerist impulses (and attendant anxieties), and presents, throughout, multi-faceted intersections between word and image" ("Men with a Pair of Scissors," 109).

38. In his Clocktower Radio interview of Ashbery, Charles Bernstein asks him about his collage-making. Ashbery responds by saying, "I started making visual collages when I was in college. My roommate and I . . . I sort of did it through the years . . . This sort of rubbed off on my poetry, especially the years when I was living in France for about ten years. The first year or two I had difficulty writing because of not being surrounded by our language, and I tried to cope with this by using things cut out of American magazines, *Esquire*, and newspapers and then sort of weaving my own stuff into them. It became a method of writing poetry" (Ashbery, interview with Charles Bernstein).

39. Stephen Fredman argues that "assemblage [another term that could be used here for collage, most definitely in terms of poetic collage] involves a poetics by virtue of its objects which bear traces of time and associations with prior functions, and by virtue of rhetorical interchange it sets up between objects" (*Contextual Practice*, 15).

40. Cran refers to collage as a "form of collaboration," partly because many of these materials were shared among Ashbery and his friends, partly because they sometimes worked on them together ("Men with a Pair of Scissors," 105). I suggest, too, that collage is inherently collaborative because in drawing on ready-made materials, the artist is essentially working with the producers of those materials.

41. Love, *Feeling Backward*, 7.

42. See Roffman, *The Songs We Know Best*; and Ashbery, interview with Janet Bloom and Robert Losada, 119, in which he describes the solitary nature of his childhood.

43. "The History of My Life" appeared in *Your Name Here* (New York: Farrar, Straus and Giroux, 2000), and earlier in the *New Yorker*, July 5, 1999, 63.

44. Krauss, "In the Name of Picasso," 19–20.

45. Bessa, *John Ashbery: The Construction of Fiction*.

46. An earlier *Chutes and Ladders* collage by Ashbery was dedicated to Joe Brainard. Cran refers to Ashbery's collages as a "conjuration" of Brainard because of his frequent reliance on collaging materials that had been provided by Brainard over the years ("Men with a Pair of Scissors," 105).

47. Ashbery, "Artist's Statement," 33.

48. Herd, *John Ashbery and American Poetry*, 42.

49. *Flow Chart* was published in 1991 (New York: Alfred A. Knopf). "Album Leaf" was included in *Some Trees* (New Haven, CT: Yale University Press, 1956).

50. Another marked example of Ashbery's collage approach is apparent in *Girls on the Run*, which relied on the outside artist Henry Darger's illustrated novel *The*

Story of the Vivian Girls, in What Is Known as the Realms of the Unreal, of the Glandeco-Angelinian War Storm, Caused by the Child Slave Rebellion. Ashbery talks about his poetic collage in several letters, including one to Charles Altieri quoted above in the introduction (May 2, 1979, John Ashbery Papers, MS AM 3189, Houghton Library, Harvard University); and to Robert Nye: "Incidentally, the quoted passage in the poem 'The Tomb of Stuart Merrill' isn't by Stuart Merrill, but is a passage from a letter I received from a college student about my poetry, and which, compulsory *collagiste* that I am, I incorporated into the poem" (November 14, 1975, John Ashbery Papers, MS AM 3189, Houghton Library, Harvard University).

51. Joyce, *Cultural Critique and Abstraction.*
52. "Europe" appeared in *The Tennis Court Oath.*
53. Included among these are Ross Labrie's interview of Ashbery where he calls the poem "another 'democratic vista'" (33); when Ashbery writes about the poem in *Selected Prose* and calls it "[j]ust a bunch of impressions" (67); and the interview with Louis Osti where he explains that for this poem he was "aiming at making a lot of splintered fragments and collecting them all under a series of numbers" (94). Criticism on "Europe" includes James Longenbach's explanation that the poem's "incoherence is *not* arbitrary or contingent; it is essential to the poem's embodiment of the inherently disorganized nature of experience" (*Modern Poetry after Modernism*, 93); and Ben Hickman's argument that the poem "adopts an Eliotic vocabulary of ruin" (*John Ashbery and English Poetry*, 111).
54. See in particular John Tranter's interview of Ashbery ("John Ashbery in Conversation with John Tranter") and Ashbery's mention of it in his *Selected Prose* (67). Many, many thanks here to the lovely librarians at the Wilson Library of the University of North Carolina, who digitized this book for me.
55. Le Queux, *Beryl of the Biplane*, 8.
56. Ibid.
57. Ibid., 41.
58. Sweet, *Savage Sight/Constructed Noise*, 255.
59. Ibid., 259.
60. Ibid., 260.
61. Rosenbaum, "Mixed Feelings," 104.
62. Ashbery, *Reported Sightings*, 82.
63. John Ashbery to Helen McNeil, John Ashbery Papers, MS AM 3189, Houghton Library, Harvard University.
64. Ashbery, interview with Rich Kelley.
65. Ashbery, interview with Charles Bernstein.
66. Ashbery, interview with Louis Osti, 94.
67. Le Queux, *Beryl of the Biplane*, 166–67.

Chapter 5

1. Derrida, *Speech and Phenomena*, 119.
2. See the *Oxford English Dictionary* for more information on the prefix "de-."
3. Poulet, *Proustian Space*, 16.
4. Ibid., 39.
5. Ibid., 60.
6. In his art criticism, Ashbery mentions Proust repeatedly: "For others, such as Proust and [painter Jean-Édouard] Vuillard, the dull conventions and ceremonies of middle-class existence served as a springboard to a kind of universal vision"; "It was customary for [Pierre] Bonnard to push his figures into the margins of the picture, to leave a vacancy at the center. He was trying, he said, 'to show what one sees when one enters a room all of a sudden,' and the eye has an annoying way of zeroing in on unimportant details and ignoring the business of the day. So, too, does the mind, and in fact Bonnard was . . . attempting to replicate the way phenomena appear to the mind's eye as well. The paintings do not so much reflect reality as the way reality appears to the memory—an enterprise which has often been likened to that of Proust"; and in a review of Yves Tanguy's work (*Reported Sightings*, 53, 57, 21).
7. Ashbery, interview with Ross Labrie, 29.
8. Ashbery, interview with Peter Stitt, 42.
9. Ibid. See also J. Deming, "Ashbery, Proust and Time"; and Ashbery, "John Ashbery: By the Book."
10. Quotations from Proust are from the Project Gutenberg version (https://www.gutenberg.org/files/7178/7178-h/7178-h.htm).
11. A later poem with clear links with Proust is "My Philosophy of Life," in which "a fragrance overwhelms him" and he is transported into the past (*CP*, 467–68). "My Philosophy of Life" appeared in *American Poetry Review* 23, no. 6 (November–December 1994): 64 and was included in *Can You Hear, Bird* (New York: Farrar, Straus and Giroux, 1995).
12. The Flow Chart Foundation quotes David Kermani as saying, "The poem 'Proust's Questionnaire' shares its title with an article in the periodical *Quarto* (Quarto Ltd., London, United Kingdom, 1981-05-00, pp. 1–2), about the quiz famously filled out by Marcel Proust at two separate points in his life. Ashbery commented, 2003-12-29, that he had 'undoubtedly' read the article, which was published in an issue with his own poetry and an interview with him, roughly around the time he composed 'Proust's Questionnaire,' but that while the article may have served as an impetus for the poem, he had 'always' known of the questionnaire in question" (https://www.flowchartfoundation.org/catalog-search). "Proust's Questionnaire" first appeared in the *New Yorker*, February 2, 1982, 44, and was included in *A Wave* (New York: Viking Press, 1984).

13. Bernstein, *A Poetics*, 153.
14. Ibid., 167.
15. McCorkle, "Nimbus of Sensations," 101, 114.
16. Norton, "Whispers out of Time," 291.
17. Ibid., 282.
18. Ibid.
19. Lerner, "The Future Continuous," 202.
20. Ashbery, interview with Janet Bloom and Robert Losada, 131–32.
21. "Rain" and "Our Youth" were included in *The Tennis Court Oath*; "The Picture of Little J. A. in a Prospect of Flowers" appeared in *Some Trees*. "Our Youth" also appeared in the volume *The Poems*, illustrated by Joan Mitchell (New York: Tiber Press, 1960) and in *Poetry* 91, no. 3 (December 1957): 163–64. "The Picture of Little J. A. in a Prospect of Flowers" appeared in *Partisan Review* 18, no. 4 (July 1951): 420.
22. "Syringa" and "Blue Sonata" appeared together in *Poetry* 130, no. 1 (April 1977): 4–8 and were included in *Houseboat Days*. "A Wave" appeared in *American Poetry Review* 12, no. 4 (July 1983): 23–30 and was included in *A Wave*.
23. "Self-Portrait in a Convex Mirror" was included in the volume of poetry by the same name and first appeared in *Poetry* 124, no. 5 (August 1974): 247–61.
24. This poem has received extensive critical attention, including by Herd, *John Ashbery and American Poetry*, 161–86; Shoptaw, *On the Outside Looking Out*, 174–78; Epstein, *Beautiful Enemies*, 128; Hickman, *John Ashbery and English Poetry*, 40–46; and Levy, *Criminal Ingenuity*, 187–98. In writing on this poem, Bonnie Costello says, "Here is not the image of experience but experience itself. . . . Convexity in Ashbery is also the spatial equivalent of his concept of temporality, the present no point in a hierarchy but a moment passed through, receding as it arrives like a point along a convex curve. And it is the temporal condition of art, its frustrating pattern of deferral and belatedness, which Ashbery makes his major theme. . . . [Sources] include Eliot's *Four Quartets*, Yeats' 'The Lake Isle of Innisfree,' Stevens' 'To an Old Philosopher in Rome,' [and] Keats' 'Ode on a Grecian Urn'" (Costello, "John Ashbery and the Idea of the Reader," 493).
25. In his interview with Rich Kelley, Ashbery describes his interest in this particular painting: "Anyway, I had been 'carrying around' with me the image of the Parmigianino painting of the same name for years, with a vague intention of 'doing something' with it, after first seeing a reproduction of it in about 1950 and eventually the original in Vienna in 1959—it is truly a miraculous painting. Finally, during a period of leisure at the Fine Arts Work Center in Provincetown in 1973, which coincided with a time when I wasn't writing art criticism and therefore perhaps felt I had been given permission to write poetry about a painting, I began tentatively to work on it" (Ashbery, interview with Rich Kelley).

26. "Lithuanian Dance Band" appeared in *American Poetry Review* 2, no. 4 (July–August 1973): 39 and was included in *Self-Portrait in a Convex Mirror*.
27. Rosalyn Diprose suggests that "for Merleau-Ponty, I live my body outside of myself through the mirror space of the other's body" (*Corporeal Generosity*, 89). In this poem, Ashbery acts out the experience of this mirror space of Parmigianino.
28. See the quotation earlier in this chapter by Derrida on "de-piction" (*Speech and Phenomena*, 119).
29. John Shoptaw suggests that Ashbery modeled this poem after Raymond Roussel's "The View," a "20,000-line poem [that] described in impossible detail the seaside prospect engraved on a convex lens set into a penholder" (*On the Outside Looking Out*, 177). Ben Hickman talks about this poem in terms of "[s]imultaneous motifs of reflection and circularity" (*John Ashbery and English Poetry*, 40).
30. Merleau-Ponty says in *Signs*, "Since perception itself is never complete, since our perspectives give us a world to express and think about which envelops and exceeds those perspectives . . . why should the expression of the world be subjected to the prose of the *senses* or of the concept? It must be poetry; that is, it must completely awaken and recall our sheer power of expressing beyond things already said or seen" (*S*, 52).
31. According to Diprose, "[i]nteriority, for [Merleau-Ponty], is not characterized by self-reflection, nor by an (unconscious) internalized object-cathexis. Interiority, for M-P, is primordially carnal reflexivity, corporeal self-awareness that emerges 'through confusion' 'between the seeing and the seen, between touching and the touched, between one eye and the other, between hand and hand'" (*Corporeal Generosity*, 102).
32. Jody Norton says that "Ashbery's principal concern . . . is to explore the shifting configuration of subjectivity, which takes place not only in, but as, language. Poetic thinking, for Ashbery, is reflection: the subject, as thinking being, reflects on his own subjectivity, and in doing so reflects that subjectivity—which is no more fixed or consistent than thought itself. . . . An attempt to produce a formulation of subjectivity is necessarily reflective—that is, distanced from both the materiality and the experience of the individual" ("Whispers out of Time," 282, 291).
33. Ben Lerner argues: "Sense is a value of retrospection, a backward motion that forces the speaker to identify with his speech. . . . A demand for sense pins the poet to the past, but understanding can . . . be dissolved into the flow of language, enabling a kind of presence" ("The Future Continuous," 202).
34. And yet we need to turn to the past with every moment of perception, as Merleau-Ponty says: "As an effort to found the existing world upon a *thought* of the world, the reflection at each instant draws its inspiration from the prior presence of the world, of which it is a tributary, from which it derives all its energy[,] [for] reflection itself is a distinct act of recovery" (*VI*, 34, 38).
35. Ashbery, in his interview with Bloom and Losada, says: "At the end a person is

somehow given an embodiment out of those proliferating reflections that are occurring in a generalized mind which will eventually run together into the image of a specific person" (Ashbery, interview with Janet Bloom and Robert Losada, 131–32). Andrew Epstein talks about how Ashbery's "self in his poems is thoroughly enmeshed with other people," these "witnesses" in the poem (*Beautiful Enemies*, 129).

36. Ben Hickman talks about this poem in terms of a "metaphoric mirror of the thinking, reading mind" (*John Ashbery and English Poetry*, 46). In a letter to Ashbery, Robert Creeley quotes Marshall Berman in a portrait of Marx as saying: "There is no poetry in a straight mirror—just a reproduction of life. But what one sees in a convex mirror is a complete picture, a composition, an interior" (Robert Creeley to John Ashbery, n.d., John Ashbery Papers, MS AM 3189, Houghton Library, Harvard University).

37. In his essay on the painter Pierre Bonnard, Ashbery talks about the impact of the mirror on perspective: "Another perspective-fracturing device is the mirror" (*Reported Sightings*, 56).

38. Harman, "Time, Space, Essence, and Eidos," 2. Charles Bernstein argues: "Phenomena . . . do not approximate a displaced 'physical reality.' They are the products of mediation by the membrane of consciousness, which is language, and hence actualizations of such a reality"; and later: "[By] 'sight' I mean something more limited than that word might otherwise permit; I'm referring to the object-focused, extra temporal, singled perspective that is, in actuality, a static idealization of the experience of looking" (*A Poetics*, 137).

39. Harman, "Time, Space, Essence, and Eidos," 12.

40. Ibid., 14.

41. Merleau-Ponty says that "[w]e do not begin by knowing the perspectival appearances of the thing: it is not mediated by our senses, our sensations, or our perspectives; we go straight to the thing, and only secondarily do we notice the limits of our knowledge and of ourselves as knowing" (*PP*, 338).

42. "If we dream of finding again the natural world or time through coincidence . . . or . . . the pure memory which from the depths of ourselves governs our act of recall," Merleau-Ponty writes, "then language is a power for error, since it cuts the continuous tissue that joins us vitally to the things and to the past and is installed between ourselves and that tissue like a screen" (*VI*, 125).

43. "Polite Distortions" appeared in *April Galleons* (New York: Viking Press, 1987).

44. "Down by the Station, Early in the Morning" appeared in the *New Yorker*, February 20, 1984, 50, and was included in *A Wave*.

Chapter 6

1. Merleau-Ponty, *Phenomenology of Perception* (2012), 141.
2. In this quotation and in others, Merleau-Ponty describes people as "normal" in contrast to individuals with disabilities whose illnesses he can use to explain and develop his theory.
3. David Morris argues that "*[s]ens* is not a meaning abstracted from the world, it is meaning directed toward and fit with the world. It has this character precisely because it is in movement; and sens could not have . . . lability . . . if it were not in movement" (*The Sense of Space*, 82). Lability is the "proneness to lapse, instability of form or nature" (*Oxford English Dictionary*).
4. "And You Know" was included in *Some Trees* (Yale University Press, 1956), Ashbery's first volume of poetry, which was awarded the Yale Series of Younger Poets in 1955. It first appeared in *Poetry* 87, no. 3 (December 1955): 149–51.
5. "The Skaters" was included in *Rivers and Mountains*. According to Mark Ford's chronology, Ashbery started work on this poem in 1963 (*CP*, 998). For a complete digital edition of this poem, see Text/works, http://www.text-works.org/Texts/Ashbery/JA-Sk_data/JA-Sk_EdN.html.
6. Macann, *Four Phenomenological Philosophers*, 174.
7. Low, *Merleau-Ponty's Last Vision*, 71.
8. Note here a clear link to Ashbery's collage based on the Parmigianino self-portrait (see fig. 5.2 in the previous chapter).
9. Diffen, "Centrifugal Force vs. Centripetal Force."
10. *Oxford English Dictionary*, 2nd ed., s.v. "stereotype." "Method or process of printing in which a solid plate or type-metal, cast from a papier-mâché or plaster mold taken from the surface of a form of type, is used for printing from instead of the form itself."
11. *Oxford English Dictionary*, 2nd ed., s.v. "cliché." "To click, applied by die sinkers to the striking of melted lead in order to obtain a proof or cast."
12. Hargraves, "How to Revive the Worn Out Cliche."
13. R. Porter, "From Clichés to Slogans," 233.
14. Deleuze and Guattari, *A Thousand Plateaus*, 76.
15. R. Porter, "From Clichés to Slogans," 239; and Lecercle, *Deleuze and Language*, 169.
16. Deleuze and Guattari, *A Thousand Plateaus*, 79–80; and R. Porter, "From Clichés to Slogans," 236. Jean-Jacques Lecercle suggests that there is "no such thing as an individual speaker (a subject) or an individual utterance: the utterance is always secondary, always already indirect, because it is the output of a collective assemblage" (*Deleuze and Language*, 171).
17. Deleuze and Guattari, *A Thousand Plateaus*, 89.
18. Robert Porter says, "By intervening directly in the production of meaning or sign-value, we could say that language or the statement/slogan has a certain ideological power or capacity to produce meaning" ("From Clichés to Slogans," 241).
19. Ibid., 240.
20. Ibid., 243.

21. "Variations, Calypso and Fugue on a Theme of Ella Wheeler Wilcox" was included in *The Double Dream of Spring*, having originally appeared in Bill Berkson, ed., *Best & Company* (New York: Chapel Press, 1969), 169–73. Mark Silverberg describes Wilcox (1850–1916) as the "most famous 'bad' poet of the past [nineteenth] century" ("Laughter and Uncertainty," 299).
22. Wilcox, *Every-Day Thoughts*, 292.
23. Altieri, "John Ashbery and the Challenge of Postmodernism," 817.
24. See the notion of "stuplimity" discussed above in chapter 1 (Ngai, *Ugly Feelings*).
25. Jackson, *Acts of Mind*, 72.
26. "Wishing"

    Do you wish the world were better?
        Let me tell you what to do.
    Set a watch upon your actions,
        Keep them always straight and true.
    Rid your mind of selfish motives,
        Let your thoughts be clean and high.
    You can make a little Eden
        Of the sphere you occupy.

    Do you wish the world were wiser?
        Well, suppose you make a start,
    By accumulating wisdom
        In the scrapbook of your heart;
    Do not waste one page on folly;
        Live to learn, and learn to live.
    If you want to give men knowledge
        You must get it, ere you give.

    Do you wish the world were happy?
        Then remember day by day
    Just to scatter seeds of kindness
        As you pass along the way,
    For the pleasures of the many
        May be ofttimes traced to one,
    As the hand that plants an acorn
        Shelters armies from the sun. (Wilcox, *Poems of Power*, 18–19)

27. The focus here, as with "And You Know," is on travel, as if he had taken these trips and "met many prominent literary men" "at the age of ten" (*CP*, 190).
28. The cliché is, of course, modified here to talk about art rather than the heart or love/intuition.
29. See Cao and Zhang, "The Fractal Structure," for more details about the Great Wall of China.

Chapter 6

1. Merleau-Ponty, *Phenomenology of Perception* (2012), 141.
2. In this quotation and in others, Merleau-Ponty describes people as "normal" in contrast to individuals with disabilities whose illnesses he can use to explain and develop his theory.
3. David Morris argues that "*[s]ens* is not a meaning abstracted from the world, it is meaning directed toward and fit with the world. It has this character precisely because it is in movement; and sens could not have . . . lability . . . if it were not in movement" (*The Sense of Space*, 82). Lability is the "proneness to lapse, instability of form or nature" (*Oxford English Dictionary*).
4. "And You Know" was included in *Some Trees* (Yale University Press, 1956), Ashbery's first volume of poetry, which was awarded the Yale Series of Younger Poets in 1955. It first appeared in *Poetry* 87, no. 3 (December 1955): 149–51.
5. "The Skaters" was included in *Rivers and Mountains*. According to Mark Ford's chronology, Ashbery started work on this poem in 1963 (CP, 998). For a complete digital edition of this poem, see Text/works, http://www.text-works.org/Texts/Ashbery/JA-Sk_data/JA-Sk_EdN.html.
6. Macann, *Four Phenomenological Philosophers*, 174.
7. Low, *Merleau-Ponty's Last Vision*, 71.
8. Note here a clear link to Ashbery's collage based on the Parmigianino self-portrait (see fig. 5.2 in the previous chapter).
9. Diffen, "Centrifugal Force vs. Centripetal Force."
10. *Oxford English Dictionary*, 2nd ed., s.v. "stereotype." "Method or process of printing in which a solid plate or type-metal, cast from a papier-mâché or plaster mold taken from the surface of a form of type, is used for printing from instead of the form itself."
11. *Oxford English Dictionary*, 2nd ed., s.v. "cliché." "To click, applied by die sinkers to the striking of melted lead in order to obtain a proof or cast."
12. Hargraves, "How to Revive the Worn Out Cliche."
13. R. Porter, "From Clichés to Slogans," 233.
14. Deleuze and Guattari, *A Thousand Plateaus*, 76.
15. R. Porter, "From Clichés to Slogans," 239; and Lecercle, *Deleuze and Language*, 169.
16. Deleuze and Guattari, *A Thousand Plateaus*, 79–80; and R. Porter, "From Clichés to Slogans," 236. Jean-Jacques Lecercle suggests that there is "no such thing as an individual speaker (a subject) or an individual utterance: the utterance is always secondary, always already indirect, because it is the output of a collective assemblage" (*Deleuze and Language*, 171).
17. Deleuze and Guattari, *A Thousand Plateaus*, 89.
18. Robert Porter says, "By intervening directly in the production of meaning or sign-value, we could say that language or the statement/slogan has a certain ideological power or capacity to produce meaning" ("From Clichés to Slogans," 241).
19. Ibid., 240.
20. Ibid., 243.

21. "Variations, Calypso and Fugue on a Theme of Ella Wheeler Wilcox" was included in *The Double Dream of Spring*, having originally appeared in Bill Berkson, ed., *Best & Company* (New York: Chapel Press, 1969), 169–73. Mark Silverberg describes Wilcox (1850–1916) as the "most famous 'bad' poet of the past [nineteenth] century" ("Laughter and Uncertainty," 299).
22. Wilcox, *Every-Day Thoughts*, 292.
23. Altieri, "John Ashbery and the Challenge of Postmodernism," 817.
24. See the notion of "stuplimity" discussed above in chapter 1 (Ngai, *Ugly Feelings*).
25. Jackson, *Acts of Mind*, 72.
26. "Wishing"

    Do you wish the world were better?
     Let me tell you what to do.
    Set a watch upon your actions,
     Keep them always straight and true.
    Rid your mind of selfish motives,
     Let your thoughts be clean and high.
    You can make a little Eden
     Of the sphere you occupy.

    Do you wish the world were wiser?
     Well, suppose you make a start,
    By accumulating wisdom
     In the scrapbook of your heart;
    Do not waste one page on folly;
     Live to learn, and learn to live.
    If you want to give men knowledge
     You must get it, ere you give.

    Do you wish the world were happy?
     Then remember day by day
    Just to scatter seeds of kindness
     As you pass along the way,
    For the pleasures of the many
     May be ofttimes traced to one,
    As the hand that plants an acorn
     Shelters armies from the sun. (Wilcox, *Poems of Power*, 18–19)

27. The focus here, as with "And You Know," is on travel, as if he had taken these trips and "met many prominent literary men" "at the age of ten" (*CP*, 190).
28. The cliché is, of course, modified here to talk about art rather than the heart or love/intuition.
29. See Cao and Zhang, "The Fractal Structure," for more details about the Great Wall of China.

30. Temple, *The Life of Pill Garlick*, 249.
31. Ellis-Reifsnider, *Unforgiven*, 265.
32. Beattie, *The Minstrel*, 216.
33. *Oxford English Dictionary*, 2nd ed., s.v. "fugue." "Related to 'flee' and 'flight.' Psychiatry: a flight from one's own identity often involving travel to some unconsciously desired locality."
34. Spiegel, "Dissociative Fugue."
35. Tim Ingold describes this repetitive yet slightly different movement as a component of the "taskscape," where activity occurs ("The Temporality of the Landscape," 152–74).

Chapter 7

1. Merleau-Ponty, *The Visible and the Invisible*, 155.
2. Ashbery, *Collected Poems, 1956–1987*, 74. "Measles" was included in *The Tennis Court Oath*.
3. In "What Are Poets For?," Heidegger writes: "The poet things his way into the locality defined by that lightness of Being.... The locality ... is a manifestness of Being, a manifestness which itself belongs to the destiny of Being and which, out of that destiny, is intended for the poet" (Heidegger, *Poetry, Language, Thought*, 95).
4. For analysis on Merleau-Ponty's approach see, among others Ahmed, *Queer Phenomenology*, 27–29; McCosh, "The Sublime," 136; and Diprose, *Corporeal Generosity*, 100.
5. It is apparent in *A Poetics* that Charles Bernstein is reading Merleau-Ponty, but rather than using the visible/invisible analogy, he turns to sight/insight. He says: "Phenomena ... do not approximate a displaced 'physical reality.' They are the products of mediation by the membrane of consciousness, which is language, and hence actualizations of such a reality" (*A Poetics*, 123–24); "By 'sight' I mean something more limited than that word might otherwise permit; I'm referring to the object-focused, extra temporal, singled perspective that is, in actuality, a static idealization of the experience of looking" (137); "Correlative to 'sight' is 'insight,' as the one assumes a world of constituted objects, the other assumes a constituted self (bringing again to mind Piaget's observation that perception of an object in a unity space and the perception of a subject as a unitary self are constructed simultaneously)" (139); and "[V]ision [is] a process of constituting and reconstituting the world" (141).
6. "For John Clare" appeared in *Poetry* 114, no. 1 (April 1969): 5–6 and was included in *The Double Dream of Spring*.
7. Weiner, *Clare's Lyric*, 162.
8. In *Corporeal Generosity*, Rosalyn Diprose argues that "[e]very situation is open,

and meaning is indeterminate. Meaning is indeterminate for Merleau-Ponty, partly because ... he claims meaning arises in the interval between terms, and partly because ... existence is indeterminate or ambiguously 'between' bodies" (104).

9. Merleau-Ponty left *The Visible and the Invisible* unfinished at his death. Claude Lefort edited the manuscript that is now available to us, much of which Merleau-Ponty left in relatively complete form. Lefort gathered together Merleau-Ponty's remaining notes and included them in a final section of this volume. This quotation comes from this "Working Notes" section of this book.
10. Merleau-Ponty writes that "[what] is irreplaceable in the work of art ... is that it contains, better than ideas, *matrices of ideas*," a comparable conception with the frame-worked "filigree" (*PW*, 90, emphasis in the original).
11. Ashbery, interview with Peter Stitt, 44–45.
12. Ben Lerner concurs with this approach, saying, "In Ashbery's poems, meaning might not be fully present; but we have a graceful kind of non-absence: each moment feels authorized by a truth that has yet to arrive, and if it never arrives, if there is 'no luck,' we then read the poem as referring to the evanescence of reference as it evanesces" ("The Future Continuous," 206).
13. Ashbery, "Respect for Things As They Are," 13. For more analysis of Ashbery's essay on Porter, but also for greater assessment of meaning and experience, see Richard Deming, *Art of the Ordinary*.
14. Wittgenstein, *Philosophical Investigations*, I.98.
15. F. Porter, "Letter: To Claire Nicholas White," 296.
16. Ashbery, "Respect for Things As They Are," 13.
17. Wittgenstein, *Philosophical Investigations*, I.97–98, I.106. Note in particular the quotation marks surrounding "is in order as it is."
18. To add to this, in *Tractatus Logico-Philosophicus*, Wittgenstein says, "In fact, all the propositions of our everyday language, just as they stand, are in perfect logical order.—That utterly simple thing, which we have to formulate here, is not a likeness of the truth, but the truth itself in its entirety" (*Tractatus Logico-Philosophicus*, 5.5563).
19. "Dreams of Adulthood" appeared in *Sulfur* 7, no. 1 (Spring 1987): 70–71 and was included in *April Galleons*.
20. Wittgenstein, *Philosophical Investigations*, II.xi.197.
21. "On Autumn Lake" appeared in *Crazy Horse* 15 (Fall 1974) and was included in *Self-Portrait in a Convex Mirror*.
22. "Down by the Station, Early in the Morning" appeared in the *New Yorker*, February 20, 1984, and was included in *A Wave*.
23. "Finnish Rhapsody" appeared in *Conjunctions* 10 (Spring 1987): 91–92 and was included in *April Galleons*.
24. Peirce, "On a New List of Categories," §5, 25.
25. Ashbery, "Respect for Things As They Are," 9, 13.

26. Wittgenstein, *Philosophical Investigations*, II.xi.215.
27. Moran, *Introduction to Phenomenology*, 17.
28. Ashbery's poetry has often been connected to phenomenology. James McCorkle, for example, argues that "Ashbery's poetry finds in the tracing of thoughts voicings of a phenomenology that necessitates and inscribes a social world" ("Nimbus of Sensations," 123). And, in the essay "Poetical Space," Ashbery himself refers, if not to his own poetry, to poetry in general as "a kind of phenomenology" (*Selected Prose*, 210).
29. "Rivers and Mountains" was included in the volume of the same name.
30. "Disguised Zenith" appeared in *Poetry Review* 75, no. 2 (1985): 26 and was included in *April Galleons*.
31. "October at the Window" also appeared in *Poetry Review* 75, no. 2 (1985): 26–27 and was also included in *April Galleons*.
32. "By the Flooded Canal" appeared in the *Times Literary Supplement*, April 27, 1984, 456 and was included in *April Galleons*.
33. For more focus on this topic, see Hugh Silverman's essay on Merleau-Ponty ("Art and Aesthetics").
34. Ibid., 101.
35. In her introduction to *The Tribe of John: Ashbery and Contemporary Poetry*, Susan Schultz writes that "Ashbery's real importance may lie in the fact that we cannot separate his work from the language we use each time we think about the world" (9–10).
36. In his interview with Bloom and Losada, Ashbery says, "My poetry is often criticized for a failure to communicate, but I take issue with this; my intention is to communicate and my feeling is that a poem that communicates something that's already known by the reader is not really communicating anything to him and in fact shows a lack of respect for him" (Ashbery, interview with Janet Bloom and Robert Losada, 112). I would suggest that this "modulation" is a reappraisal of experience, too, that is new to its audience.
37. "Idaho" appeared in *Locus Solus* 1 (Winter 1961): 55–60 and was included in *The Tennis Court Oath*.
38. In his essay "Typical John," Jonathan Morse writes, "Ashbery sublimates all that is nonverbal of his life onto the page, becoming . . . himself a true poem" (18). John Gery describes his "voice [as] consisting of multiple, 'decentered' layers" ("Ashbery's Menagerie," 129). Ashbery himself describes his move toward soundings when he explains in his Robert Frost Medal Address, "I wanted to stretch the bond between language and communication but not to sever it" (*Selected Prose*, 251).
39. Merleau-Ponty describes both this perceptual connection with the world and the importance of being able to articulate it in *Phenomenology of Perception*, too: "What I discover and recognize is the profound movement of transcendence that is my very being, the simultaneous contact with my being and with

the being of the world.... When it is said that thought is spontaneous, this does not mean that it coincides with itself; rather, it means that thought transcends itself, and speech is precisely the act by which it in fact becomes eternal" (*PP*, 408).

40. In reinforcing the essential role of vision in perception and in transcendence, Merleau-Ponty also writes in *Signs*: "But are the visible things of the visible world constructed any differently? They are always behind what I see of them, as horizons, and what we call visibility is this very transcendence. No thing, no side of a thing, shows itself except by actively hiding the others, denouncing them in the act of concealing them. To see is a matter of principle to see further than one sees, to reach a latent existence. The invisible is the outline and the depth of the visible" (*S*, 20).

41. Both Richard Deming and Karin Roffman confirm this link between everyday language and experience and transcendence. Deming argues that "a poem reimagines ordinary language" and provides a greater "fullness of meaning" (*Art of the Ordinary*, 79). Roffman talks about the "combination of experience and transcendence" that was a goal of Ashbery's (*The Songs We Know Best*, 171).

42. "Soonest Mended" appeared in *Paris Review* 12 (Summer 1969): 14–16 and was included in *The Double Dream of Spring*.

43. Critical attention to "Soonest Mended" includes that of David Herd, who argues that it is a poem about the poet and poetry (*John Ashbery and American Poetry*, 119–21); Andrew Epstein, who describes it as "power inherent in remaining self-reliant, noncommitted, and evasive" and considers the avant-garde as nonconformists (*Beautiful Enemies*, 158–59); and Stephen Paul Miller, who argues that it is about the 1960s and alienation ("Periodizing Ashbery," 150–52).

44. There is an interesting pronoun reference slippage here, where the "they" could possibly refer to the hazards, since "the course *was* hazards and nothing else." Also, it would be too tangential to take up here, but an analysis of Wittgenstein's consideration of rules and private language would be a very interesting approach.

Works Cited

Adams, Harry. "Expression." In *Merleau-Ponty: Key Concepts*, edited by Rosalyn Diprose and Jack Reynolds, 152–93. Abingdon, Oxon., England: Routledge, 2014.
Ahmed, Sara. *Queer Phenomenology: Orientations, Objects, Others*. Durham, NC: Duke University Press, 2006.
Altieri, Charles. "John Ashbery and the Challenge of Postmodernism in the Visual Arts." *Critical Inquiry* 14, no. 4 (Summer 1988): 805–30.
———. *Wallace Stevens and the Demands of Modernity: Toward a Phenomenology of Value*. Ithaca, NY: Cornell University Press, 2013.
Ashbery, John. "Artist's Statement." In *Joe Brainard's Art*, edited by Yasmine Shamma, 32–33. Edinburgh: Edinburgh University Press, 2019.
———. *Collected Poems, 1956–1987*. New York: Library of America, 2008.
———. *Collected Poems, 1991–2000*. New York: Library of America, 2017.
———. Interview with Alfred A. Poulin Jr. "The Experience of Experience: A Conversation with John Ashbery." *Michigan Quarterly Review* 20, no. 3 (1981): 242–55.
———. Interview with Brett Lauer. PennSound, May 27, 1973. http://writing.upenn.edu/pennsound/x/Ashbery.php.
———. Interview with Charles Bernstein. "John Ashbery in Conversation." *Close Listening*, Clocktower Radio, March 18, 2016. https://jacket2.org/commentary/john-ashbery-close-listening.
———. Interview with Janet Bloom and Robert Losada. "Craft Interview with John Ashbery." In *The Craft of Poetry: Interviews from "The New York Quarterly,"* edited by William Packard, 112–32. New York: Doubleday, 1974.
———. Interview with Louis Osti. "The Craft of John Ashbery." *Confrontation*, no. 9 (Fall 1974): 84–96.
———. Interview with Michael Silverblatt. "Bookworm: John Ashbery." KCRW, May 21, 2009. https://www.kcrw.com/culture/shows/bookworm/john-ashbery-1.
———. Interview with Peter Stitt. "The Art of Poetry no. 33." *Paris Review*, no. 90 (Winter 1983): 35–59.
———. Interview with Rich Kelley. "Remembering John Ashbery: LOA's 2008 Interview." Library of America, October 2, 2008. https://www.loa.org/news-and-views/1312-remembering-john-ashbery-loas-2008-interview.
———. Interview with Ron Padgett. "Oral History Initiative: On Frank O'Hara." PennSound, April 5, 2011. http://writing.upenn.edu/pennsound/x/Ashbery.php.

———. Interview with Ross Labrie. "An Interview (of John Ashbery)." *American Poetry Review* 13, no. 3 (May–June 1984): 29–33.

———. Interview with Tom Smith. "Reading and Interview on *The Book Show*." PennSound, 1992. http://writing.upenn.edu/pennsound/x/Ashbery.php.

———. "John Ashbery: By the Book." *New York Times*, May 7, 2015.

———. "A Place for Everything." *ArtNews* 69, no. 1 (March 1970): 32, 73–75.

———. *Planisphere*. New York: Ecco Press, 2009.

———. *Reported Sightings: Art Chronicles, 1957–1987*. Edited by David Bergman. New York: Alfred A. Knopf, 1989.

———. "Respect for Things As They Are." In *Fairfield Porter: Realist Painter in an Age of Abstraction*, edited by John Ashbery and Kenworth Moffett, 7–13. Boston: Museum of Fine Arts, 1982.

———. "Second Presentation of Elizabeth Bishop." *World Literature Today* 51, no. 1 (Winter 1977): 8–11.

———. *Selected Prose*. Edited by Eugene Richie. Ann Arbor: University of Michigan Press, 2004.

———. "Throughout Is This Quality of Thingness: Elizabeth Bishop." *New York Times Book Review*, June 1, 1969.

———. *A Worldly Country*. New York: Ecco Press, 2008.

Ashbery, John, and Alex Katz. *Fragment*. Los Angeles: Black Sparrow Press, 1969.

Baker, Peter. *Obdurate Brilliance: Exteriority and the Modern Long Poem*. Gainesville: University Press of Florida, 1991.

Barbaras, Renaud. "Perception and Movement: The End of the Metaphysical Approach." In *Chiasms: Merleau-Ponty's Notion of Flesh*, edited by Fred Evans and Leonard Lawlor, 77–87. Albany: State University of New York Press, 2000.

Beattie, James. *The Minstrel, in Two Books*. London: Parsons and Galignani, 1804.

Berg, Stephen, ed. *My Business Is Circumference: Poets on Influence and Mastery*. Philadelphia: Paul Dry Books, 2001.

Bergman, David. Introduction to *Reported Sightings: Art Chronicles, 1957–1987*, by John Ashbery, edited by David Bergman. New York: Alfred A. Knopf, 1989.

Bernstein, Charles. *A Poetics*. Cambridge, MA: Harvard University Press, 1992.

Bessa, Antonio Sergio. *John Ashbery: The Construction of Fiction*. Brooklyn: Pratt Institute of Art, 2018.

Cameron, Sharon. *Lyric Time: Dickinson and the Limits of Genre*. Baltimore: Johns Hopkins University Press, 1979.

Cao, Yingchun, and Yukun Zhang. "The Fractal Structure of the Ming Great Wall Military Defense System: A Revised Horizon over the Relationship between the Great Wall and the Military Defense Settlements." *Journal of Cultural Heritage* 33 (April 2018): 159–69.

Carbery, Matthew. *Phenomenology and the Late Twentieth-Century American Long Poem*. Cham, Switzerland: Palgrave Macmillan, 2019.

Carman, Taylor. "Between Empiricism and Intellectualism." In *Merleau-Ponty: Key*

Concepts, edited by Rosalyn Diprose and Jack Reynolds, 44–56. Abingdon, Oxon., England: Routledge, 2014.

Carman, Taylor and Mark B. N. Hansen. Introduction to *The Cambridge Companion to Merleau-Ponty*, edited by Taylor Carman and Mark B. N. Hansen, 1–25. Cambridge: Cambridge University Press, 2005.

Cerbone, David R. "Perception." In *Merleau-Ponty: Key Concepts*, edited by Rosalyn Diprose and Jack Reynolds, 121–30. Abingdon, Oxon., England: Routledge, 2014.

Costello, Bonnie. "John Ashbery and the Idea of the Reader." *Contemporary Literature* 23, no. 4 (Autumn 1982): 493–514.

Cotkin, George. *Existential America*. Baltimore: Johns Hopkins University Press, 2003.

Cotton, Jess. "Joe Brainard's Still-Life Poetics." In *Joe Brainard's Art*, edited by Yasmine Shamma, 80–102. Edinburgh: Edinburgh University Press, 2019.

Cran, Rona. "'Men with a Pair of Scissors': Joe Brainard and John Ashbery's Aestheticism." In *Joe Brainard's Art*, edited by Yasmine Shamma, 103–26. Edinburgh: Edinburgh University Press, 2019.

Crossley, Nick. "Phenomenology, Structuralism and History: Merleau-Ponty's Social Theory." *Theoria*, no. 103 (April 2004): 88–121.

Culler, Jonathan. *Theory of the Lyric*. Cambridge, MA: Harvard University Press, 2015.

Dastur, Françoise. "World, Flesh, Vision." In *Chiasms: Merleau-Ponty's Notion of Flesh*, edited by Fred Evans and Leonard Lawlor, 23–50. Albany: State University of New York Press, 2000.

Davis, Duane H. "Reversible Subjectivity: The Problem of Transcendence and Language." In *Merleau-Ponty Vivant*, edited by Martin C. Dillon, 31–46. Albany: State University of New York Press, 1991.

Deleuze, Gilles, and Félix Guattari. *A Thousand Plateaus: Capitalism and Schizophrenia*. Translated by Brian Massumi. London: Athlone Press, 1988.

Deming, John. "Ashbery, Proust and Time." *Coldfront*, 2009. http://coldfrontmag.com/ashbery-proust-and-time/.

Deming, Richard. *Art of the Ordinary: The Everyday Domain of Art, Film, Philosophy, and Poetry*. Ithaca, NY: Cornell University Press, 2018.

Derrida, Jacques. *Speech and Phenomena and Other Essays on Husserl's Theory of Signs*. Translated by David Allison. Evanston, IL: Northwestern University Press, 1973.

Dick, David. "'A Serpentine | Gesture': The Synthetic Reconstruction of Ashbery's Poetic Voice." *Cordite Poetry Review*, August 1, 2017. http://cordite.org.au/scholarly/a-serpentine-gesture/.

Diffen. "Centrifugal Force vs. Centripetal Force." https://www.diffen.com/difference/Centrifugal_Force_vs_Centripetal_Force.

Diprose, Rosalyn. *Corporeal Generosity: On Giving with Nietzsche, Merleau-Ponty, and Levinas*. Albany: State University of New York Press, 2002.

Ellis-Reifsnider, Anna C. *Unforgiven*. St. Louis: Anna C. Reifsnider Book Company, 1893.

Epstein, Andrew. *Attention Equals Life: The Pursuit of the Everyday in Contemporary Poetry and Culture*. Oxford: Oxford University Press, 2016.

———. *Beautiful Enemies: Friendship and Postwar American Poetry*. Oxford: Oxford University Press, 2006.

Ernest, John. "Fossilized Fish and the World of Unknowing: John Ashbery and William Bronk." In *The Tribe of John: Ashbery and Contemporary Poetry*, edited by Susan M. Schultz, 168–89. Tuscaloosa: University of Alabama Press, 1995.

Fite, David. "John Ashbery: The Effort to Make Sense." *Missouri Review* 2, nos. 2–3 (Spring 1979): 123–30.

———. "On the Virtues of Modesty: John Ashbery's Tactics against Transcendence." *Modern Language Quarterly* 42, no. 1 (March 1981): 65–84.

Fredman, Stephen. *Contextual Practice: Assemblage and the Erotic in Postwar Poetry and Art*. Stanford, CA: Stanford University Press, 2010.

Friedman, Norman. "John Ashbery." In *Contemporary Poets*, 2nd ed., edited by James Vinson, 35–37. New York: St. Martin's Press, 1975.

Gery, John. "Ashbery's Menagerie and the Anxiety of Influence." In *The Tribe of John: Ashbery and Contemporary Poetry*, edited by Susan M. Schultz, 126–45. Tuscaloosa: University of Alabama Press, 1995.

Gilson, Annette. "Disseminating 'Circumference': The Diachronic Presence of Dickinson in John Ashbery's 'Clepsydra.'" *Twentieth Century Literature* 44, no. 4 (Winter 1998): 484–505.

Hargraves, Orin. "How to Revive the Worn Out Cliche." Interview with Rachel Martin. *Weekend Edition Sunday*, National Public Radio, January 11, 2015. https://www.npr.org/2015/01/11/376496372/how-to-revive-the-worn-out-cliche.

Harman, Graham. "Time, Space, Essence, and Eidos: A New Theory of Causation." *Cosmos and History* 6, no. 1 (2010): 1–17.

Hass, Lawrence. *Merleau-Ponty's Philosophy*. Bloomington: Indiana University Press, 2008.

Heidegger, Martin. *Being and Time*. Translated by John Macquarrie and Edward Robinson. Oxford: Blackwell, 1962.

———. *On the Way to Language*. Translated by Peter D. Hertz. New York: Harper and Row, 1971.

———. *Poetry, Language, Thought*. Translated by Albert Hofstadter. New York: Harper and Row, 1971.

Herd, David. *John Ashbery and American Poetry*. Manchester: Manchester University Press, 2009.

Hickman, Ben. *John Ashbery and English Poetry*. Edinburgh: Edinburgh University Press, 2012.

Howard, Richard. "John Ashbery." In *John Ashbery: Modern Critical Views*, edited by Harold Bloom, 17–48. New York: Chelsea House, 1985.

Hulse, Michael. "John Ashbery." *PN Review* 99 21, no. 1 (September–October 1994): 58–59. https://www.pnreview.co.uk/cgi-bin/scribe?toc=1;volume=21.
Hunt, David. "The Association of the Lady and the Unicorn, and the Hunting Mythology of the Caucasus." *Folklore* 114, no. 1 (April 2003): 75–90.
Ingold, Tim. "The Temporality of the Landscape." *World Archaeology* 25, no. 2 (October 1993): 152–74.
Jackson, Richard. *Acts of Mind: Conversations with Contemporary Poets*. Tuscaloosa: University of Alabama Press, 1983.
Joyce, Elisabeth W. *Cultural Critique and Abstraction: Marianne Moore and the Avant-Garde*. Lewisburg, PA: Bucknell University Press, 1998.
Keller, Lynn. *Forms of Expansion: Recent Long Poems by Women*. Chicago: University of Chicago Press, 1997.
———. "'Thinkers without Final Thoughts': John Ashbery's Evolving Debt to Wallace Stevens." *ELH* 49, no. 1 (Spring 1982): 235–61.
Kelly, Michael R. "The Subject as Time: Merleau-Ponty's Transition from Phenomenology to Ontology." In *Time, Memory, and Institution: Merleau-Ponty's New Ontology of Self*, edited by David Morris and Kym Maclaren, 199–216. Athens: Ohio University Press, 2015.
Kernan, Nathan. "Joe Brainard: The Madonna of the Future." In *Joe Brainard's Art*, edited by Yasmine Shamma, 41–68. Edinburgh: Edinburgh University Press, 2019.
Kitses, Jasmine. "'Round / Shiny Fixed / Alternatives': Tracing the Colon in Pound and Oppen." *Modern Philology* 113, no. 2 (November 2015): 267–93.
Koethe, John, and John Ashbery. "An Interview with John Ashbery." *SubStance* 11–12 (1982–1983): 178–86.
Kostelanetz, Richard. "How to Be a Difficult Poet." *New York Times Magazine*, May 23, 1976, 18–33.
Krauss, Rosalind. "In the Name of Picasso." *October* 16 (Spring 1981): 5–22.
Krell, David Farrell. *Lunar Voices: Of Tragedy, Poetry, Fiction, and Thought*. Chicago: University of Chicago Press, 1995.
Lecercle, Jean-Jacques. *Deleuze and Language*. Basingstoke, Hants., England: Palgrave Macmillan, 2002.
Le Queux, William. *Beryl of the Biplane: Being the Romance of an Air-Woman of Today*. London: C. Arthur Pearson, 1917.
Lerner, Ben. "The Future Continuous: Ashbery's Lyric Mediacy." *boundary 2* 37, no. 1 (Spring 2010): 201–13.
Levertov, Denise. "Some Notes on Organic Form." In *New and Selected Essays*, 67–73. New York: New Directions, 1992.
Levy, Ellen. *Criminal Ingenuity: Moore, Cornell, Ashbery, and the Struggle between the Arts*. New York: Oxford University Press, 2011.
Lewallen, Constance M. *Joe Brainard: A Retrospective*. New York: Granary Books, 2001.

Lieberman, Laurence. *Unassigned Frequencies: American Poetry in Review, 1964–1977*. Urbana: University of Illinois Press, 1977.

Longenbach, James. "Ashbery and the Individual Talent." *American Literary History* 9, no. 1 (Spring 1997): 103–27.

———. *Modern Poetry after Modernism*. Oxford: Oxford University Press, 1997.

Love, Heather. *Feeling Backward: Loss and the Politics of Queer History*. Cambridge, MA: Harvard University Press, 2007.

Low, Douglas. *Merleau-Ponty's Last Vision: A Proposal for the Completion of "The Visible and the Invisible."* Evanston, IL: Northwestern University Press, 2000.

Macann, Christopher. *Four Phenomenological Philosophers: Husserl, Heidegger, Sartre, Merleau-Ponty*. London: Routledge, 2005.

Madison, Gary Brent. *Phenomenology of Merleau-Ponty: A Search for the Limits of Consciousness*. Athens: Ohio University Press, 1981.

Maldiney, Henri. "Flesh and Verb in the Philosophy of Merleau-Ponty." In *Chiasms: Merleau-Ponty's Notion of Flesh*, edited by Fred Evans and Leonard Lawlor, 51–76. Albany: State University of New York Press, 2000.

Mallin, Samuel B. *Merleau-Ponty's Philosophy*. New Haven, CT: Yale University Press, 1979.

McCorkle, James. "Nimbus of Sensations: Eros and Reverie in the Poetry of John Ashbery and Ann Lauterbach." In *The Tribe of John: Ashbery and Contemporary Poetry*, edited by Susan M. Schultz, 101–25. Tuscaloosa: University of Alabama Press, 1995.

McCosh, Lisa. "The Sublime: Process and Mediation." In *Carnal Knowledge: Towards a "New Materialism" through the Arts*, edited by Estelle Barrett and Barbara Bolt, 127–38. London: I. B. Tauris, 2013.

McGuinness, Patrick. "Ashbery." *PN Review* 99 21, no. 1 (September–October 1994): 64–66. https://www.pnreview.co.uk/cgi-bin/scribe?toc=1;volume=21.

McHale, Brian G. *The Obligation toward the Difficult Whole: Postmodernist Long Poems*. Tuscaloosa: University of Alabama Press, 2004.

Merleau-Ponty, Maurice. *Phénoménologie de la perception*. Paris: Éditions Gallimard, 1945.

———. *Phenomenology of Perception*. Translated by Colin Smith. London: Routledge and Kegan Paul, 1962.

———. *Phenomenology of Perception*. Translated by Donald A. Landes. Abingdon, Oxon., England: Routledge, 2012.

———. *The Prose of the World*. Edited by Claude Lefort. Translated by John O'Neill. Evanston, IL: Northwestern University Press, 1973.

———. "The Sensible World and the World of Expression." In *Themes from the Lectures at the Collège de France, 1952–1960*, translated by John O'Neill, 3–11. Evanston, IL: Northwestern University Press, 1970.

———. *Signs*. Translated by Richard C. McCleary. Evanston, IL: Northwestern University Press, 1964.

———. *The Structure of Behavior*. Translated by Alden L. Fisher. Pittsburgh: Duquesne University Press, 1983. Originally published as *La structure du comportement*, Paris: Presses Universitaires de France, 1942.

———. *The Visible and the Invisible*. Edited by Claude Lefort. Translated by Alphonso Lingis. Evanston, IL: Northwestern University Press, 1968. Originally published as *Le visible et l'invisible, suivi de notes de travail*, Paris: Éditions Gallimard, 1964.

———. *The World of Perception*. Translated by Oliver Davis. Abingdon, Oxon., England: Routledge, 2004.

Mildenberg, Ariane. "Through the Wrong End of the Telescope: Thresholds of Perception in Joseph Cornell, John Ashbery and Maurice Merleau-Ponty." In *Joseph Cornell: Opening the Box*, edited by Jason Edwards and Stephanie L. Taylor, 137–58. New York: Peter Lang, 2007.

Miller, Stephen Paul. "Periodizing Ashbery and His Influence." In *The Tribe of John: Ashbery and Contemporary Poetry*, edited by Susan M. Schultz, 146–67. Tuscaloosa: University of Alabama Press, 1995.

Moramarco, Fred. "Coming Full Circle: John Ashbery's Later Poetry." In *The Tribe of John: Ashbery and Contemporary Poetry*, edited by Susan M. Schultz, 38–59. Tuscaloosa: University of Alabama Press, 1995.

Moran, Dermot. *Introduction to Phenomenology*. Abingdon, Oxon., England: Routledge, 2000.

Morris, David. *The Sense of Space*. Albany: State University of New York Press, 2013.

Morris, David, and Kym Maclaren. Introduction to *Time, Memory, and Institution: Merleau-Ponty's New Ontology of Self*, edited by David Morris and Kym Maclaren, 1–15. Athens: Ohio University Press, 2015.

Morse, Jonathan. "Typical John." In *The Tribe of John: Ashbery and Contemporary Poetry*, edited by Susan M. Schultz, 15–25. Tuscaloosa: University of Alabama Press, 1995.

Mulhauser, Ruth. *Maurice Scève*. Boston: Twayne Publishers, 1977.

Ngai, Sianne. *Ugly Feelings*. Cambridge, MA: Harvard University Press, 2005.

Norton, Jody. "'Whispers out of Time': The Syntax of Being in the Poetry of John Ashbery." *Twentieth Century Literature* 41, no. 3 (Autumn 1995): 281–305.

Olson, Charles. *Selected Writings*. Edited by Robert Creeley. New York: New Directions, 1966.

Peirce, Charles Sanders. "On a New List of Categories." In *Peirce on Signs: Writings on Semiotic by Charles Sanders Peirce*, edited by James Hoopes, 23–33. Chapel Hill: University of North Carolina Press, 1991.

Pietersma, Henry. *Phenomenological Epistemology*. Oxford: Oxford University Press, 2000.

Pollio, R. Howard, Tracy B. Henley and J. Craig Thompson, eds. *The Phenomenology of Everyday Life: Empirical Investigations of Human Experience*. Cambridge: Cambridge University Press, 2006.

Porter, Fairfield. "Letter: To Claire Nicholas White." In *Material Witness: The Selected Letters of Fairfield Porter*, edited by Ted Leigh, 294–96. Ann Arbor: University of Michigan Press, 2005.

Porter, Robert. "From Clichés to Slogans: Towards a Deleuze-Guattarian Critique of Ideology." *Social Semiotics* 20, no. 3 (2010): 233–45.

Poulet, Georges. *Proustian Space*. Translated by Elliott Coleman. Baltimore: Johns Hopkins University Press, 1977.

Priest, Stephen. *Merleau-Ponty*. London: Routledge, 1998.

Proust, Marcel. *Swann's Way*. Vol. 1 of *Remembrance of Things Past*. Translated by C. K. Scott Moncrieff. New York: Henry Holt, 1922.

Ricoeur, Paul. *Husserl: An Analysis of His Phenomenology*. Evanston, IL: Northwestern University Press, 2007.

Riukas, Stanley. "The Problem of the Transcendental Ego in Husserl." In *Life: Scientific Philosophy, Phenomenology of Life, and the Sciences of Life*, edited by Anna-Teresa Tymieniecka, 501–10. Dordrecht: Springer, 1999.

Roberts, Teresa Noelle. "The Unicorn: Creature of Love." *Mythlore* 8, no. 4 (Winter 1982): 39–41.

Roffman, Karin. *The Songs We Know Best: John Ashbery's Early Life*. New York: Farrar, Straus and Giroux, 2017.

Romdenh-Romluc, Komarine. "Maurice Merleau-Ponty." In *The Routledge Companion to Phenomenology*, edited by Sebastian Luft and Søren Overgaard, 103–12. Abingdon, Oxon., England: Routledge, 2012.

Ronell, Avital. *The Telephone Book: Technology, Schizophrenia, Electric Speech*. Lincoln: University of Nebraska Press, 1989.

Rosenbaum, Susan. "Mixed Feelings: Ashbery, Duchamp, Roussel, and the Animation of Cliché." *Genre* 45, no. 1 (Spring 2012): 87–119.

———. "'Permeation, Ventilation, Occlusion': Reading John Ashbery and Joe Brainard's *The Vermont Notebook* in the Tradition of Surrealist Collaboration." In *New York School Collaborations: The Color of Vowels*, edited by Mark Silverberg, 59–89. New York: Palgrave Macmillan, 2013.

Ross, Stephen J. *Invisible Terrain: John Ashbery and the Aesthetics of Nature*. Oxford: Oxford University Press, 2017.

Schneiderman, Josh. "Whispers out of Time: John Ashbery's Collages." *Art in America*, October 10, 2018. https://www.artinamericamagazine.com/news-features/news/whispers-time-john-ashberys-collages/.

Schultz, Susan M. Introduction to *The Tribe of John: Ashbery and Contemporary Poetry*, edited by Susan M. Schultz, 1–14. Tuscaloosa: University of Alabama Press, 1995.

Shamma, Yasmine. Introduction to *Joe Brainard's Art*, edited by Yasmine Shamma, 1–18. Edinburgh: Edinburgh University Press, 2019.

Shoptaw, John. "The Music of Construction: Measure and Polyphony in Ashbery and Bernstein." In *The Tribe of John: Ashbery and Contemporary Poetry*, edited by Susan M. Schultz, 211–57. Tuscaloosa: University of Alabama Press, 1995.

———. *On the Outside Looking Out: John Ashbery's Poetry*. Cambridge, MA: Harvard University Press, 1995.

Silverberg, Mark. "Laughter and Uncertainty: John Ashbery's Low-Key Camp." *Contemporary Literature* 43, no. 2 (Summer 2002): 285–316.

Silverman, Hugh J. "Art and Aesthetics." In *Merleau-Ponty: Key Concepts*, edited by Rosalyn Diprose and Jack Reynolds, 95–108. Abingdon, Oxon., England: Routledge, 2014.

Spiegel, David. "Dissociative Fugue." Last modified March 2021. *Merck Manual, Consumer Version*. https://www.merckmanuals.com/home/mental-health-disorders/dissociative-disorders/dissociative-fugue.

Spittle, David Graham Parnel. "John Ashbery and Surrealism." PhD thesis, Newcastle University, 2016.

Stewart, Jon. *The Debate between Sartre and Merleau-Ponty*. Evanston, IL: Northwestern University Press, 1998.

Strogatz, Steven. "Why Pi Matters." *New Yorker*, March 13, 2015.

Strum, Nick. "'Fuck Work': The Reciprocity of Labor and Pleasure in Joe Brainard's Writing." In *Joe Brainard's Art*, edited by Yasmine Shamma, 183–99. Edinburgh: Edinburgh University Press, 2019.

Sweet, David LeHardy. *Savage Sight/Constructed Noise: Poetic Adaptations of Painterly Techniques in the French and American Avant-Gardes*. Chapel Hill: University of North Carolina Press, 2003.

Switzer, Robert. "Tactile Cogito: Horizons of Corporeity, Animality, and Affect in Merleau-Ponty." In *Merleau-Ponty and the Art of Perception*, edited by Duane H. Davis and William S. Hamrick, 259–78. Albany: State University of New York Press, 2016.

Temple, Edmond. *The Life of Pill Garlick; Rather a Whimsical Sort of Fellow*. Dublin: John Miller, 1815.

Toadvine, Ted. "Phenomenology and 'Hyper-Reflection.'" In *Merleau-Ponty: Key Concepts*, edited by Rosalyn Diprose and Jack Reynolds, 17–29. Abingdon, Oxon., England: Routledge, 2014.

Tranter, John. "John Ashbery in Conversation with John Tranter." *Jacket 2*, no. 2 (April 20, 1985). http://jacketmagazine.com/02/jaiv1985.html.

Vendler, Helen. *Invisible Listeners: Lyric Intimacy in Herbert, Whitman, and Ashbery*. Princeton, NJ: Princeton University Press, 2005.

Von Hallberg, Robert. *Lyric Powers*. Chicago: University of Chicago Press, 2008.

Waldenfels, Bernhard. "Coming and Going of Time." In *Time, Memory, and Institution: Merleau-Ponty's New Ontology of Self*, edited by David Morris and Kym Maclaren, 217–37. Athens: Ohio University Press, 2015.

———. "The Paradox of Expression." In *Chiasms: Merleau-Ponty's Notion of Flesh*, edited by Fred Evans and Leonard Lawlor, 89–102. Albany: State University of New York Press, 2000.

Weiner, Stephanie Kuduk. *Clare's Lyric: John Clare and Three Modern Poets*. Oxford: Oxford University Press, 2014.

Wilcox, Ella Wheeler. *Every-Day Thoughts in Prose and Verse.* Chicago: W. B. Conkey, 1901.

———. *Poems of Power.* Chicago: W. B. Conkey, 1902.

Willis, Elizabeth. "The Arena in the Garden: Some Thoughts on the Late Lyric." In *Telling It Slant: Avant-Garde Poetics of the 1990s,* edited by Mark Wallace and Steven Marks, 225–35. Tuscaloosa: University of Alabama Press, 2002.

Wittgenstein, Ludwig. *Philosophical Investigations.* Translated by G. E. M. Anscombe. 3rd ed. New York: Macmillan, 1958.

———. *Tractatus Logico-Philosophicus.* Translated by David Francis Pears and Brian McGuinness. London: Routledge, 2001.

Wolf, Werner. "The Lyric: Problems of Definition and a Proposal for Reconceptualization." In *Theory into Poetry: New Approaches to the Lyric,* edited by Eva Müller-Zettelmann and Margarete Rubik, 21–56. Amsterdam: Rodopi, 2005.

Ziarek, Krzysztof. *Language after Heidegger.* Bloomington: Indiana University Press, 2013.

Credits

Grateful acknowledgment is made for permission to reprint excerpts from the following copyrighted works:

Excerpts from John Ashbery's published texts quoted herein © 1956–2017. All rights reserved. Used by arrangement with Georges Borchardt, Inc., for the estate.

Excerpts from John Ashbery's unpublished correspondence, interviews, and other archival material quoted herein © 2022 by JA Projects, Inc. All rights reserved. Used by arrangement with Georges Borchardt, Inc., for the estate, and MS AM 3189, Houghton Library, Harvard University.

Reproduction of John Ashbery's collages are courtesy of the Estate of John Ashbery and the Tibor de Nagy Gallery. © 2022 by JA Projects, Inc. All rights reserved. Used by arrangement with Georges Borchardt, Inc., for the estate.

Excerpts Reprinted

By John Ashbery, from "Clepsydra" from *Rivers and Mountains* © 1966 Estate of John Ashbery. All rights reserved. Used by arrangement with Georges Borchardt, Inc.

By John Ashbery, from *Fragment*, "Definition of Blue" and "Soonest Mended" from *The Double Dream of Spring* © 1970 Estate of John Ashbery. All rights reserved. Used by arrangement with Georges Borchardt, Inc.

By John Ashbery, from "The New Spirit," "The Recital" and "The System" from *Three Poems* © 1972 Estate of John Ashbery. All rights reserved. Used by arrangement with Georges Borchardt, Inc.

By John Ashbery, from "Self-Portrait in a Convex Mirror" from *Self-Portrait in a Convex Mirror* © 1975 Estate of John Ashbery. All rights reserved. Used by arrangement with Georges Borchardt, Inc. Reprinted by permission of Penguin Random House.

By John Ashbery, from *Litany* from *As We Know* © 1979 Estate of John Ashbery. All rights reserved. Used by arrangement with Georges Borchardt, Inc.

By John Ashbery, from "A Wave" from *A Wave* © 1984 Estate of John Ashbery. All rights reserved. Used by arrangement with Georges Borchardt, Inc.

By Maurice Merleau-Ponty, reproduced from *The Phenomenology of Perception*—Landes NIP, 1st Edition. Originally published in French under the title *Phénoménology de la perception*. © 1945 by Éditions Gallimard, Paris. English translation © 2009 Routledge. Reproduced by arrangement with Taylor & Francis Group.

By Maurice Merleau-Ponty, from *The Visible and the Invisible*. Originally published in French under the title *Le visible et l'invisible*. © 1964 by Éditions Gallimard, Paris. English translation © 1968 by Northwestern University Press. First printing 1968. All rights reserved.

By Samuel B. Mallin, from *Merleau-Ponty's Philosophy* © 1979. Reprinted with permission from Yale University Press.

By Gary Brent Madison, from *Phenomenology of Merleau-Ponty* © 1981. Reprinted with permission from Ohio University Press.

By Lawrence Hass, from *Merleau-Ponty's Philosophy* © 2008. Reprinted with permission from Indiana University Press.

Images Reprinted

John Ashbery, *Uncle Wiggily*, 2008. Collage. 16 x 15.875 in. Reprinted by permission of the Estate of John Ashbery and the Tibor de Nagy Gallery. All rights reserved. Used by arrangement with Georges Borchardt, Inc.

John Ashbery, *Chutes and Ladders III* (for David Kermani), 2008. Collage, 18.5 × 18.375 in. Reprinted by permission of the Estate of John Ashbery and the Tibor de Nagy Gallery. All rights reserved. Used by arrangement with Georges Borchardt, Inc.

John Ashbery, *Corona*, 2011. Collage, digitized print, 16.5 × 16.5 in. Reprinted by permission of the Estate of John Ashbery and the Tibor de Nagy Gallery. All rights reserved. Used by arrangement with Georges Borchardt, Inc.

John Ashbery, *Bingo Beethoven*, 2014. Collage on vintage Bingo board, 8.25 × 7.5 in. Reprinted by permission of the Estate of John Ashbery and the Tibor de Nagy Gallery. All rights reserved. Used by arrangement with Georges Borchardt, Inc.

John Ashbery, *Still Life*, 2016. Collage, 11 × 8.5 in. Reprinted by permission of the Estate of John Ashbery and the Tibor de Nagy Gallery. All rights reserved. Used by arrangement with Georges Borchardt, Inc.

Alex Katz, images from *Fragment*. Art © Alex Katz / VAGA at Artists Rights Society (ARS), NY.

Joe Brainard, images from *The Vermont Notebook* reprinted with the very kind permission of Ron Padgett for the estate of Joe Brainard.

Maurice Scève, image from *Délie: Object de plus haulte vertu*. Gordon 1564 .S47. Special Collections, University of Virginia, Charlottesville, VA.

Maurice Scève, image from *Délie: Object de plus haulte vertu*. 1544. © Bodleian Library, University of Oxford. 2005. Douce S 35. P.7

Parmigianino, *Self-Portrait in a Convex Mirror*, 1524. Kunsthistorisches Museum, Wien.

Index

Page numbers in italic text indicate illustrations.

abstract expressionism, 26
Adams, Harry, 190n33
Adams, R. Joseph, 1
"Album Leaf" (Ashbery), 129
Altieri, Charles, 1, 162
"And You Know," (Ashbery), 7, 156–60; immobility and perception, 158; movement, 158; and perception, 157–59; travel, 157, 217n27
"Are You Ticklish?" (Ashbery), 30
ARTnews, 26, 39
"As We Know" (Ashbery), 196n139
articulation, 7, 15, 42–43; and Being, 22, 24, 191n59; and chiasms, 42; and creativity, 16–18, 163; and excess, 21–22; and experience, 42, 154, 198n19; and meaning, 16; and order, 178; and poetry, 2, 4–5, 19, 53, 146; and perception, 15, 42; and thoughts, 15; and time, 21; and transcendence, 16, 24. *See also* Merleau-Ponty, Maurice; individual poems
Ashbery, John: banality, 32, 161; Being, 41; biography, 24–27; clichés, 163; and experience, 2, 4, 20, 24, 142, 176; and emblems, 114; and flux, 30, 32–33, 67; and fragments, 114; and gesture, 72; and language, 20, 163, 219n35, 219–20n38; and memory, 7, 20, 31, 126, 137–54, 167; and perception, 35, 91; order, 39–40;

and perception, 154; phenomenology, 170, 185, 194n112, 197n5, 198n18, 219n28; poetic collage, 132–36; and revelation, 32; and time, 29; and the visual arts, 39–40. *See also* individual poems
—collage, 126–32, 152–53, 208–9nn37–40; and bingo, 129–31; and experience, 126; poetic, 209–10n50; and time, 127. *See also* Brainard, Joe
—poetry, 28, 31, 38–39, 197n5, 197–98n12; as experience, 28–31, 38–39; and phenomena, 67; and thought, 195n128
—reflection, 142–46; and distortion, 154
Auden, W. H., 25–26

Bachelard, Gaston, 26
Baker, Peter, 196n149
Bakhtin, Mikhail, 90
Barbaras, Renaud, 16, 22
Bearden, Romare, 125
Beattie, James, 166
Beauvoir, Simone de, 2
Berg, Stephen, 1
Bergman, David, 26
Bergson, Henri, 3
Being, 4, 17, 19, 21; and ambiguity, 23; and articulation, 22, 24; and *ekstase*, 23; and field of presence, 110; and flux, 23; and history, 21; and language, 23–34; and

Being (*continued*)
  meaning, 2, 40–41, 117; and the past, 103; and presence of absence, 24; and order, 22; and the other, 21–22; and poetry, 19, 44–45; and perception, 21, 89; phenomenology of, 3, 9; and spatial orientation, 22; and time, 23; and transcendence, 21; and the visible, 23–24. *See also* Heidegger, Martin; Merleau-Ponty, Maurice
Berman, Marshall, 214n36
Bernstein, Charles, 27, 37, 41, 198n19, 214n38; and articulation, 198n19; and collage, 134, 209n38; and experience, 198n19; and perception, 217–18n5; and phenomenology, 217n5; and reflection, 142; and weaving, 43
Bessa, Antonio Sergio, 126
Bingo Beethoven (Ashbery), 131
"Bird's Eye View of the Tool and Die Co." (Ashbery), 140–41
Bishop, Elizabeth, 40–41, 197n12
Black Mountain poets, 199n26
Black Sparrow Press (Los Angeles), 114, 207n14
Bloom, Janet: and experience, 28; and *Fragment*, 110, 116; and reflection, 142, 214n35, 291n36; and sense-making, 39
"Blue Sonata" (Ashbery), 143–44, and reflection, 143–44; and space, 144; and time, 143
Bly, Robert, 25
body: and change, 190n25; and experience, 9, 19; and expression, 24; and gesture, 65; and movement, 7, 156–57; presence vs. absence of, 24; and transcendental ego, 3; vs. the flesh, 23, 193n77
Bonnard, Pierre, 197n12, 211n6, 214n37

Booth, Philip, 31
Borges, Jorg Luis, 32
Bourdieu, Pierre, 4
Bowering, George, 1
Brainard, Joe: and *The Vermont Notebook*, 6, 119, 120, 121, 122, 123, 124, 207n28, 208n33, 208n36; and collage, 126, 209n46
"Bungalows, The" (Ashbery), 29, 41
"By the Flooded Canal" (Ashbery), 179

Cage, John, 28
Cameron, Sharon, 86–87, 89
Carbery, Matthew, 33–34, 194n109, 196n149
Carman, Taylor, 2, 3, 11, 188n6
Carter, Elliott, 94–95
Cartesian dualism, 4, 10; refuting of 68, 202n13
Cerbone, David R., 188n5, 189n12
Cézanne, Paul, 18–19
chiasm, 42
Chutes and Ladders III (for David Kermani) (Ashbery), 128
circularity, 7, 11, 68, 90; of time, 33, 90; and transcendence, 189n20
Clare, John, 171–72
clearing, 10–12, 14, 22–23, 33, 188n9, 192n61; spatial, 109–10
"Clepsydra" (Ashbery), 2, 6, 64–85; as argument, 2, 6, 64, 68, 79, 202n10, 205n58; and articulation, 66, 71–72, 75; and Being, 81; and the body, 85; and circularity, 33, 68, 70, 148, 213n29; and the clock, (water) 6, (water) 64, 79, 202n16, 206n64; and the colon, 79–80, 202–3n17–n18, 203n20; and disorganized space, 82; and experience, 6, 64–68, 79, 202n10; and field of perception, 75; and gesture, 65–66, 71–72; and the horizon, 73–74; and

Index 237

inarticulation, 71–72, 202n10; and incompleteness of perception, 74, 81, 202n10; and the invisible, 78, 83; and language, 71, 80; and light vs. dark, 68, 83–84; and meaning, 64, 66, 69, 71, 78; and memory, 82; and metaphor, 204n45; and movement, 78, 202n10; and no meaning, 72, 75, 79, 84–85; and order, 64, 67, 81–83; and perception, 64–70, 72–78, 80–81, 83–85, 202n15; and Parmigianino self-portrait, 215n8; and the past, 82–83; and phenomenology, 64, 66–67, 69; and reflection, 213n29; and scale, 73–74; and space, 73, 78; and time, 64–85, 201–2n10, 202–3n17; and the visible, 74, the visible vs. the invisible, 68–69, 71, 83–84; water motif, 68–69
cliché, 7, 215n11, 215n16; and meaning, 161–162; and loss of meaning, 161; and movement, 155, 160–68; as readymade, 134
"Clouds" (Ashbery), 41
collage, 6, 108, 110, 125–136; and experience, 126, 136; and memory, 125; and nostalgia, 125, 131–32; and poetry, 28; and readymades, 134; and space, 108; and time, 127. *See also* Cornell, Joseph
Collège de France, the, 2
colon, 79–80, 100, 181; definition, 203n18; and Heidegger, 203n23; and materiality, 202–3n17, 203n24; and sentence structure, 203n20; and time, 202–3n17, 203n23–n24. *See also* "Clepsydra"
Columbia University, 25
Cornell, Joseph, 108, 194n112
Corona (Ashbery), 130
Costello, Bonnie, 212n24

Cotkin, George, 26
Cotton, Jess, 119, 208n34
Cran, Rona, 208n35, 208–9n37, 209n40, 209n46
Creeley, Robert, 25, 214n36
Cubism, 26
Culler, Jonathan, 85, 89

"Daffy Duck in Hollywood" (Ashbery), 173; and allegory, 173
Darger, Henry, 209–10n50
Dastur, Françoise, 11
Davis, Duane H., 14
De Chirico, Giorgio, 26
"Decoy" (Ashbery), 7
"Definition of Blue" (Ashbery), 92–94; and experience, 93; and field of presence, 93–94; and meaning, 93; and perception, 92–94; and space, 93; and thrust of time, 92; and time, 93
"Disguised Zenith" (Ashbery), 179
De Kooning, Willem, 174
Deerfield Academy, 24
Deleuze, Gilles, 4, 160–62
Deming, Richard, 220n41
Derrida, Jacques: phenomenology and, 3, 27; reflection and, 139, 198n18, 106n63, 213n28
Descartes, René, 10
Dewey, John, 26
Dick, David, 33, 202n10, 202–3n17
Dickinson, Emily, 86, 150
Diprose, Rosalyn, 213n27, 213n31, 218n8
Double Dream of Spring, The (Ashbery), 172
"Down by the Station, Early in the Morning" (Ashbery), 154, 176
"Dreams of Adulthood" (Ashbery), 175
Duchamp, Marcel, 134
Duncan, Robert, 27, 194n109
DuPlessis, Rachel Blau, 33

238   Inedx

École Normale Supérieure, Paris, 2
Ellis-Reifsnider, Anna C., 166
Elmslie, Kenward, 207n28, 208n36
emblem book, 6, 108, 110–25, 136; *Délie*, 110–14, 116, 120
emblems, 206n2
Emerson, Ralph Waldo, 26; Emersonian self-reliance, 26; transcendentalism, 31, 54
Epstein, Andrew, 214n35, 220n43; and Abstract Expressionism, 26; and the everyday, 27–28, 31, 194n112, 194n117, 195n121; and pragmatism, 34
Ernest, John, 199n28
"Europe" (Ashbery), 6, 126, 135–36, 208, 210n53; and collage, 6, 132, 134; and *Beryl of the Biplane*, 132–133; and experience, 210n53; and fragments, 135; and meaning, 133; and movement, 135
existentialism, 3–4, 9, 26
experience, 2, 5; and art, 199n23; and articulation, 191n54; and the body, 189n12; everyday, 8, 194n117; field, 19, 41, 195n119; flow, 37–38; flux, 37, 40, 91; intertwining of, 4; and language, 19; lived, 19–20, 34; and meaning, 174, 191n53, 218n13; and order, 19, 177; and perception, 12, 38, 188n5; and phenomenology, 9, 40, 68; and poetry, 4, 7, 20, 168, 171, 176, 194n117, 195n121; and pragmatism, 34; and reversibility, 13, 189n18; and transcendence, 8, 14–15, 19, 190n30, 220n41; and the visual arts, 177

field, 10, 33, 91; of excess, 14; of existence, 12; of experience, 11, 19, 36, 40–41; of immersion, 45; interior vs. exterior, 69; and language, 17; of perception, 11–12, 38, 52, 56; of presence, 38, 69, 92, 136; of the present, 67. *See also* Merleau-Ponty, Maurice
"Finnish Rhapsody" (Ashbery), 177
Fite, David, 31, 194n117, 196n139
flesh, 10, 43. *See also* Bernstein, Charles; Merleau-Ponty, Maurice
Flow Chart (Ashbery), 129–30
Ford, Mark, 215n5
"For John Clare" (Ashbery), 171–72; and articulation, 172; and perception, 172; and the visible, 172
Foucault, Michel, 3, 25, 27
Fragment (Ashbery), 6, 29, 114–19, 207n14; and experience, 118, 207n15; and field of presence, 110, 115, 118–19; and meaning, 117; and memory, 118–19; and movement, 117; and music composition, 207n15; and perception, 117–19; and time, 117–18
France, 25–27, 34, 64, 201n1, 205n56, 209n38
Fredman, Stephen, 209n39
"French Poems" (Ashbery), 32, 37–38, 42–43; and light, 43; and movement, 37
Fulbright scholarship, 25

Gery, John, 199n28, 219n38
Gestalt psychology, 3–4, 157
gesture, 65–66, 72, 151, 181–82; and meaning, 66; and movement, 7; and poetry, 66
Gilson, Annette, 33
Girls on the Run (Ashbery), 209–10n50
Gizzi, Peter, 64
"Grand Galop" (Ashbery), 29, 154
Great Wall of China, the, 165
Guattari, Félix, 160–162

Gurevitch, Zali, 201n6

Hansen, Mark B. N., 2, 3, 188n6
Hargraves, Orin, 160
Harman, Graham, 152
Harvard University, 24–25
Hass, Lawrence: and the body, 190n25; and *écart*, 12, 189n15; and experience, 19; and expression, 190n42; and flesh, 193n77; and the invisible, 25; and language, 16, 17, 24; and nondualism, 202n13; and perception, 10, 11; and reversibility, 13; and transcendence, 14
Hawkes, John, 25
Heath-Stubbs, John, 134
Hegel, Georg, 3
Heidegger, Martin, 4, 89, 173; and the colon, 80, 203n23; and *ecstasis*, 192n73; and phenomenology, 2–3, 169; and poetry, 89, 217n3
Herd, David, 34, 129, 202n10, 220n43
hermeneutical, 9
Hickman, Ben, 202n10, 210n53, 213n29, 214n36
horizon, horizontal, 12, 19, 72, 109
horizon, vertical, 13, 19, 72–73, 109, 189n20
Howard, Richard, 33
Howe, Susan, 85
Hudson River school of painting, 31
Hulse, Michael, 28
Husserl, Edmund, 2–3, 76 169, 173
hyper-reflection, 8, 182, 185

"Idaho" (Ashbery), 181–82; influences, 25–26
indeterminacy, 12
Ingold, Tim, 217n35
interspace, 89
invisible, 7, 173–174. *See also* Merleau-Ponty, Maurice; the visible

Jackson, Richard, 27–30, 32, 94, 163, 195n128
James, William, 26
Jefferson, Thomas, 166
"Joseph Cornell" (Ashbery), 108, 194n112

Katz, Alex, 6, 114–15, *115*, *116*, *117*, 207n14
Keller, Lynn, 85, 202n10, 203n26
Kelley, Rich, 94, 134, 202n16, 212n25
Kelly, Michael, 86, 89
Kelly, Robert, 33
Kermani, David, 126, 199n25, 211n12
Kernan, Nathan, 208n36
Kitses, Jasmine, 80, 203n17, 203n24
Koch, Kenneth, 25
Koethe, John, 204n49, 207n14
Kostelanetz, Richard, 67, 201n8
Krauss, Rosalind, 126
Krell, David Farrell, 80

Labrie, Ross, 140, 208n32, 210n53
Lacan, Jacques, 4, 27
Landes, Donald A., 189n19, 193n75
language: artistic, 18; and breath, 52–53, 199n26; everyday, 7–8, 180, 185, 218n18, 220n41; and experience, 44, 46, 198n19; and gesture, 66; and link between body and sociocultural structure, 24; materiality, 79, 202–3n17, 203n24; meaning, 180, 190n29, 216n18; membrane of consciousness, 214n38; 217n5; order, 174; poetic, 18, 41–42, 44, 181; and presence, 213n33; and reflection, 191n53; and reversibility, 24, 31; sequential, 177; and silence, 18, 42, 190n29; as social institution, 4, 180–82; and subjectivity, 213n32; and transcendence, 7–8, 16, 18, 183, 190n30, 220n41
"Last World, A" (Ashbery), 7

Lauer, Brett, 25–26, 30–31
LDA analysis, 203–204n26
"Leaving the Atocha Station" (Ashbery), 197n5
Lecercle, Jean-Jacques, 160, 215n16
Lefort, Claude, 218n9
Léger, Fernand, 26
"Le livre est sur la table" (Ashbery), 27
Leopardi, Giacomo, 134
Le Queux, William, 132–33, 135
Lerner, Ben, 142, 203n20, 213n33, 218n12
Levinas, Emmanuel, 196n149
Lévi-Strauss, Claude, 2
Lichtenstein, Roy, 122
Lieberman, Laurence, 31, 114, 207n15
light, 70; of comprehension, 107, 137; as consciousness, 174, 177; as idea, 174, 177; as meaning, 198n15; as perceived, 198; and reflection, 125, 137; refraction of, 101, 175; transmission of, 175
Litany (Ashbery), 94–107; and articulation, 96–98, 106–7, 134, 177; and the body, 101, 103; and chants, 96; and circularity, 97–99, 205n59; and collage, 134; and experience, 97–98, 100–107, 185; and gesture, 102, 182; and invisibility, 104–5; and lists, 95–97; and meaning, 96–98, 100, 102, 104–6; and memory, 100–106; and motifs, 95–96; and movement, 95–96, 98–99, 103; and order, 102, 105–6; and perception, 96–98, 99–105, 107; and reflection, 105; and sedimentation, 102; and senses, 97–98; and space, 96; and time, 96–97, 99–102, 105, 205n61; and thickness of time, 6, 64, 94; and transcendence, 31–32; and visibility, 103–4
"Lithuanian Dance Band" (Ashbery), 147; meaning, 41, 173–74, 218n12

Longenbach, James, 201n10, 210n53
Losada, Robert, 209n42; and experience, 28; and sense-making, 39; and *Fragment*, 110, 116; and reflection, 142, 214n35, 219n36
Love, Heather, 125
Low, Douglas, 157
Lyotard, Jean-François, 4
lyric, 6, 64, 162, 85–94; and experience, 64, 89; process of thinking, 204n33; and time, 6, 64, 86–87, 91

Macann, Christopher, 156
Maclaren, Kym, 90
Madison, Gary Brent, 19–24, 190n37; and articulation, 15; and Being, 191–92n59; and expression, 17; and language, 16, 190n29–n30, 191n53; and nondualism, 10; and poetry, 191n44; and transcendence, 13, 189n20, 189–190n22; and truth, 191n51
Maldiney, Henri: and clearing 11; and horizons 12, 15, and reversibility 13, 189n18
Mallin, Samuel B., 188; articulation, 15; and artistic expression, 17–19; and Being, 21–22, 191–92n59, 192n61; and clearing, 10, 188n9; and dialectic, 68; and *ekstase*, 23, 192–93n74; and horizon, 12; and nondualism 202n13
Martory, Pierre, 25, 27
Matthiessen, F. O., 25–26
McCorkle, James, 142, 219n28
McGuinness, Patrick, 194–95n119
McHale, Brian G., 85
McManus, James L., 206n4
McNeil, Helen, 134
meaning, 7, 10; and articulation, 16, 64; and experience, 2, 171, 191n53; gaps, proliferation of, 90; and

gesture, 65–66; and lyric, 85–86; and order, 7, 33, 64, 174; and perception, 173; and phenomenology, 9; and poetry, 18, 40, 220n41; and recursion, 168; and sedimentation, 16, 17–18, 190n33; and silence, 190n29; and space, 7; and invisible, 7, 172, 174

memory, 31, 137–54; and experience, 154; and Proust, 139–41, 211n6; and repositories, 5, 46; and reflection, 6, 142, 146, 149

"Measles" (Ashbery), 169

Merleau-Ponty, Maurice: biography, 2–3; and *écart*, 12; and emblems, 206n2; and incoherence, 81; and indeterminacy of experience, 12; and intermersion, 68; and light, 70; and metaphor, 178; and painting, 18–19; and poetry, 20, 180–81; and reversibility, 13, 14; situations, 158, 161, 171, 178, 202n13; tangibility, 170; transcendental field, 6, 109–10, 182; and weaving, 42. *See also* Duncan, Robert; Olson, Charles; *specific works*

—Being, 2, 9, 15; and the body, 24; and change, 17; and clearings, 188, 192n61; and *ekstase*, 192–93n74; and experience, 38, 40, 43–44, 90; and field of presence, 99; and meaning, 40, 89; and order, 22; and poetry, 44; and reflection, 138; and transcendence, 88; and the visible, 43

—body, 3, 38, 189n12; and chiasm, 178; and gesture, 65–66; and lack of movement, 158–59; light, 69; and meaning, 157; and movement, 158, 161; and perception, 68, 76, 109; and the other, 213; and poetry, 44–45; and space and time, 155; and the visible, 69–70, 171

—experience, 4–5, 35, 38, 42, 90; and aesthetic space, 109–10, 180; and articulation, 178; and the body, 157; definitions of, 191–92n59; and gesture, 151–52; and movement, 168; and past, 101; and reflection, 182; and time and space, 90; and transcendence, 183

—field, 10, 11; of action, 202n13; of Being, 192n61; of experience, 36, 148; of perception, 109–10, 163; of the phenomenal field, 6, 188n6; of presence, 86–87; transcendent, 6, 76, 138, 182; of truths, 201n5

—flesh, 23, 33, 87–88, 193n77; and memory, 150; perception, 108–9; and the present, 149–50

—gesture, 65–66, 70–71, 151–52, 181–82; linguistic, 201n5; and meaning, 66; and transcendence, 16

—horizon, horizontal, 72; and articulation, 72

—horizon, vertical, 13, 19, 72–73, 109; and meaning, 72; and transcendence, 189n20

—hyper-reflection, 182, 185; and transcendence, 8

—invisible, 171, 174; inner world, 69, 71; and language, 180; and latent existence, 220n40; and light, 198n15; and meaning, 69, 171–72; and memory, 88–89, 149–50; and perception, 43, 69; truth, 171; vertical axis of, 109; and the visible, 24, 68, 71, 73, 83, 173

—language, 76, 178; acquired, 17; of art, 19; barrier from things and the past, 214n42; and Being, 23–24; and body, 24; and culture, 24, 76; everyday, 183; experience, 19, 44; expression, 20, 71, 81; and gesture,

Merleau-Ponty, Maurice (*continued*)
66, 71, 182; institutional, 180–81; literary, 180; muted, 181–82; perception, 53; and poetry, 20, 44–45; and readymade, 28; spoken, 180; and transcendence, 183; and visible and invisible, 69–70

—meaning, 90, 161–63; and art, 19; and articulation, 15–16; and Being, 22; indeterminate, 218n8; and intersubjectivity, 76; and invisibility, 69, 198n15; and language, 178, 181–82, 216n18; and literary language, 180; making, 69; and perception, 11; and poetry, 20; and surroundings, 163

—memory, 7, 58, 137–39, 149–50; fragmentation of, 138; and invisible, 88, 150; and language, 21n42; and perception, 36–37; and reflection, 137–39; and series of presents, 87–88

—movement, 7, 155–60, 164; abstract, 151–52; 155, 159–60, 168; concrete, 159; conscious movement, 159; lack thereof, 158–59; and meaning, 157; motricity, 166; and perception, 155–56; potential for, 157; shift of state, 157; and spatial orientation, 161; and time, 164; and time and space, 90–91, 109; and transcendence, 39, 220; virtual, 157–58

—order, 50, 178; and coherence, 81; and invisible, 69; and language, 69–70, 178; and unity of object, 83; word, 86

—perception, 4, 27, 35–39, 109; and articulation, 23, 70, 102, 110, 182; and creativity, 165; and *écart*, 12–13; and experience, 38, 198n19; and failure to, 43–44; and field, 33, 188n6; and field of presence, 86–87; Gestalt psychology, 4; and hyper-reflection, 182; and immobility, 158; incompleteness of, 213n30; intermeshing, 36; and the invisible, 173; and meaning, 84, 155; and movement, 155–56, 164, 166; and net analogy, 197n8; and the past, 213n34; and reflection, 137–38; and senses, 109; and sight, 169–70, 220n40; and space, 109; and spatial orientation, 21, 188n5; and time, 23, 87–88; and transcendence, 170–71, 182; and the visible, 23–24, 183; and visible vs. invisible, 24, 109, 149–50

—phenomenology, 2–3, 5; and existentialism, 3; and meaning, 90; and nondualism, 202n13; and partial access to memory, 138; and reflection, 137; and time, 87; and transcendence, 138, 220n39; and the visible, 170

—poetic language, 18, 41, 44, 66, 178, 180–81; gesture of meaning, 71

—reflection, 6, 15, 33, 137–39, 182; and abstract movement, 159; and articulation, 139; of the body, 70; and creativity, 138; and hyper-reflection, 182; and language, 191n53; and memory, 137; partial, 138; and the past, 213n34; and perception, 84, 86, 137–39; and phenomenology, 137; and self-reflection, 213n31; and transcendence, 191n53; and truth, 191

—space, 90, 108–109; abstract movement, 159–60; aesthetic, 110; and the body, 155; and experience, 38, 90; human, 159; and interaction, 76; and the mirror, 213n27; and movement, 162; and perception, 109, 171, 188n5, 195–96n135; spatial

orientation, 161; and time, 38, 87, 90, 108–89; and transcendence, 109–10
—time, 87; and Being, 21; circular, 33; and excess, 21; and experience, 38, 90; as field, 6; flux of, 33; and language, 214n42; and perception, 23; presence, 6; the present, 87–89; present and past, 137; simultaneity, 90–91; and space, 87, 90, 108, 155; thickness of, 88; thrust, 87, 90–91; transcendence, 14, 170
—transcendence, 169–85, 189–90n22; and the aesthetic world, 109–10; and Being, 21–22; and circularity, 189n20; and *ekstase*, 192–93n74; and expression, 190n30; and gesture, 65; and immanence, 13–14, 189n21; and language, 16, 183, 191n53, 220n39; and meaning, 73; and perception, 170, 182–83; and phenomenology, 13, 88; and poetry, 19–21; and reflection, 191n53; and verticality, 289n20; and visibility, 72–73, 170; and vision, 220n40
—visible, 170–71; and articulation, 24; and Being, 21–22, 43–44, 69; 192n61; and the body, 69; and experience, 69, 171; and horizons, 72–73, 220n40; invisible, 43, 69–70, 73, 172–73, 217n5; and light, 198n15; and meaning, 69; and perception, 23–24, 43–44, 69, 103, 171; poetry, 171; and the tangible, 170; and transcendence, 170–71, 220n40; vertical axis of, 109
metaphor, 41, 47, 50–52, 68, 70, 73, 162–65; clearing, 109–10; clock, 75, 79; cultivation, 185; and *ekstase*, 192–93; field, 109–10; map, 178–79; memory, 150; sail, 172; sphere, 147–48; visible and invisible, 83, 170; weaving, 43, 56, 106
Mildenberg, Ariane, 194n112
Miller, Stephen Paul, 220n43
Montpellier, France, 25
Moore, Marianne, 26
Moran, Dermot, 178
Morris, David, 90, 215n3
Morse, Jonathan, 45, 219n38
movement, 155–68; auto-, 11; and cliché, 160–62; and emblem books, 110, 113; and gesture, 7, 65; motility, 156; motricity, 156; retrograde, 70, 191n51; and *sens*, 215n3; and spatial orientation, 7; and taskscape, 217n35; and transcendence, 189–90n22, 190n30; vertical, 13
Mulhauser, Ruth, 206n7

nature, 14, 34, 195n123; and the external world, 37; *See also* James Schuyler
New Spirit, The (Ashbery), 48–54; and articulation, 52–53; and the body, 49, 53; and breath, 52–53; and everyday language, 53–54, 59; and everyday phenomena, 51, 53; and experience, 48, 50; and the invisible, 51; and light, 51–52; and movement, 50; and new language, 61; and order, 50, 52–53; and others, 49; and perception, 49–54; and phenomenology, 48; and quest for truth, 53–54; and reflection, 53–54; and relationships, 48; and sensory input, 48–49; and space, 51–52; and time, 50, 54; and transcendence, 54
New York University, 25
Ngai, Sianne, 31, 216n24
"Night" (Ashbery), 91
Norton, Jody, 142, 213n32

Nye, Robert, 210n50

"October at the Window" (Ashbery), 179
O'Hara, Frank, 25–26
Olson, Charles, 27, 194n109, 198n19
"On Autumn Lake" (Ashbery), 176; order, 174–77
ontological, 9, 22
Oppen, George, 203n24
order, 7; and artistic effort, 171, 174; and perception, 59–60, 105; and π, 74; and poetry, 7, 19; random, 133; spherical, 74; word, 160, 162, 177
Origo, Iris, 134
Osti, Louis, 33, 210n53
"Our Youth" (Ashbery), 7, 143

Padgett, Ron, 208n36
"Paradoxes and Oxymorons" (Ashbery), 85
Paris, 2, 25–26, 134
Paris Herald Tribune, 26
Parmigianino (painter), 7, 146–47, 147, 195n119, 213n27; and Ashbery's collage, 152, 215n8; and source for *Self-Portrait in a Convex Mirror*, 212n25
Peirce, Charles Sanders, 177
perception, 2, 10–24, 35–39, 64–107; and absence and presence, 24; and American poetry, 34; and articulation, 15–16, 18, 21; and Being, 21; and collaboration, 114; and creativity, 16–18; definition of, 10–11, 16, 35; and circularity, 11; embodiment, 3; excess of, 14, 190n25; and experience, 2; and field, 11, 136; and horizon, 12, 28–29; and incompleteness, 89; intermingling, 5; intertwining, 11; and flux, 12; and language, 5; and maps, 179; and meaning, 7, 10, 30–31; and memory, 7, 36–37, 143; and movement, 7, 155–68; objects of, 10; and order, 7, 52, 176; and the past, 179; and phenomenology, 5, 10, 35; and poetry, 4, 18–20, 28, 39–41, 89, 163; and reflection, 6; and senses, 30; as spatial, 11, 22, 195–96n135; and time, 11, 30, 89; and transcendence, 2, 8–9, 14, 32; and the visible, 21; and the visible and the invisible, 7; and weaving, 42
phenomenology: and Being, 3, 89; and between space, 89; and circularity, 11; and consciousness, 3; definition of, 9; existential, 3; and experience, 9; and gesture, 65; and hermeneutics, 9; and human exchange, 76; and intermersion, 68; and memory, 154; metaphysical, 9; and movement, 7, 155–56; ontological, 9; and order vs. randomness, 74; and perception, 5, 10–12, 35; and reflection, 6; and rejection of dualism, 68; and space, 108–9; and time, 108; and transcendence, 6, 13, 18, 170. *See also* Heidegger, Martin; Stevens, Wallace
—poetry, 27, 33–34, 37, 41; and ethics, 196
Phenomenology of Perception (Merleau-Ponty), 3
"Picture of Little J. A. in a Prospect of Flowers, The" (Ashbery), 143
Pietersma, Henry, 11
poetry: and chiasm, 178; and experience, 20, 43; and gesture, 71; and meaning, 20, 71; and painting, 18–19
—expression: power of, 44; new mode

of, 44, 181–82. *See also* Ashbery, John; Merleau-Ponty, Maurice
"Polite Distortions" (Ashbery), 154
Pollock, Jackson, 174
Porter, Fairfield, 27, 174, 177
Porter, Robert, 160–61, 216n18
Poulet, Georges, 139–40
Poulin, Alfred A., Jr., 197n5
pragmatism, 26, 34, 196n141; and phenomenology, 34
Priest, Stephen, 3, 24
Prince, F. T., 26
"Prophet Bird" (Ashbery), 29
The Prose of the World (Merleau-Ponty), 180
Proust, Marcel, 25, 139–41, 204n49, 211n6, 211nn11–12
"Proust's Questionnaire" (Ashbery), 141, 211n12; and experience, 141; and memory, 141; and time, 141. *See also* Proust, Marcel

Queneau, Raymond, 26

"Rain" (Ashbery), 143
Rauschenberg, Robert, 133
"Rivers and Mountains" (Ashbery), 178–79
Recital, The (Ashbery), 45–48; and articulation, 45–47; and cliché, 163; and experience, 45–48; and memory, 46; and movement, 47; and not making sense, 47; and order, 46–47; and perception, 45, 50–51, 56; and time, 46
readymades, 6, 133–34, 209n40; and experience, 134
reflection, 6–7, 142; chaotic, 149; and distortion, 146, 150–51; and experience, 28, 142; and hyper-reflection, 8; and mirroring, 6, 146; and the past, 149; and poetry, 39, 45, 142–43, 243n32, 214n35; and reflection of, 148; and remembering, 6. *See also* Derrida, Jacques
Rennes, France, 25
reversibility: articulation, 70; *écart*, 13; experience, 189n18; flesh, 193n77; intertwining, 13, 24; seeing and the visible, 70; and transcendence, 13–14; visible and invisible, 24
Rochester, NY, 24, 125
Roffman, Karin, 34, 209n42, 220n41
Romdenh-Romluc, Komarine, 187n8
Ronell, Avital, 203n23
Rosenbaum, Susan, 134, 20n14
Ross, Stephen J., 31, 33–34, 195n123, 201n1
Roussel, Raymond, 25, 134, 213n29
Ryan, Anne, 39

Sartre, Jean-Paul, 2–4
Saussure, Ferdinand de, 3–4
"Saying It to Keep It from Happening" (Ashbery), 202n16
Scève, Maurice, 110–11, *112*, *113*, 113–114, 116, 206n4, 206n7
Scheler, Max, 191n44
Schneiderman, Josh, 208n32
Schultz, Susan M., 219n35
Schuyler, James, 27, 33
Schwitters, Kurt, 125
"Self-Portrait in a Convex Mirror" (Ashbery), 7, 146–53; and articulation, 151; and experience, 147–50, 152, 212n24, 213n32; and field of experience, 194–95n119; and gesture, 151; and lyric, 194n119; and memory, 7, 149–50; and metaphor, 214n36; and movement, 151; and order, 148; and past, 149; and perception, 148–50, 152; and present, 149; and reflection, 150–54; and the sphere, 148–49; and silence,

"Self-Portrait in a Convex Mirror"
    (*continued*)
    28; and space, 148; and time, 148–
    49; transcendental, 194–95n119
Shoptaw, John, 34, 110, 197n5, 198n21; on
    the System, 199n28; on "Clepsy-
    dra," 64, 201n1–n2, 202n11, 213n29
Signs (Merleau-Ponty), 42, 44
Silverberg, Mark, 216n21
Silverblatt, Michael, 25–26
Silverman, Hugh J., 180
situation, 17, 21, 35, 55, 61, and cliché,
    160–61; and collage, 132; definition
    of, 11; and dialectic, 68; and lan-
    guage, 71; and lyric, 204n33; and
    meaning, 72, 102, 181; and mem-
    ory, 101; and movement, 156; and
    perception, 189n18; and time-
    space gap, 90; and vision, 84
"Skaters, The" (Ashbery), 156, 203–4n26
Smith, Colin, 189n19, 193n75
Smith, Tom, 28
"Soonest Mended" (Ashbery), 29, 183–
    85, 196n139, 220n43; and articula-
    tion, 184; and experience, 183–85;
    and hyper-reflection, 185; and
    meaning, 183, 185; and memory,
    184; and nonconformity, 183; and
    order, 185; and perception, 183–85;
    and phenomenology, 183; and
    time, 184; and transcendence,
    196n139; and the visible, 185
Sorbonne, the, 2
space, 108–36; and articulation, 16; and
    collage, 6, 126; and field, 11; and
    memory, 140; and movement, 117,
    156; and perception, 10–11, 89;
    phenomenological, 6, 125; poetic,
    27, 91; social, 4; and time, 9, 110,
    114–15, 136, 164. *See also* Proust,
    Marcel
spatial orientation, 7, 15, 22, 29, 78, 117;

    and Being, 22; and compass, 126;
    and movement, 156
Spittle, David Graham Parnel, 199n22
Stein, Gertrude, 30, 197n5
Stevens, Wallace, 198n18, 212n24; influ-
    ence on Ashbery, 26–27, 206n66;
    and lyric, 204n33; and order, 174;
    203–204n26
Still Life (Ashbery), 153
Stitt, Peter, 38, 140, 173
Strogatz, Stephen, 74
structuralism, 4
Structure of Behavior, The (Merleau-
    Ponty), 3
Strum, Nick, 208n36
"Sunrise in Suburbia" (Ashbery), 91–92;
    and experience, 92; and time, 92
surrealism, 26, 203–4n26
Sweet, David LeHardy, 133
Switzer, Robert, 18
"Syringa," (Ashbery), 143
System, The (Ashbery), 29–30, 48, 55–63,
    64, 199n28; and articulation, 55,
    58–59; and experience, 55–56; and
    gesture, 200n30; and the horizon,
    56–57; and the light of nature, 47;
    and logic, 55; and the lyric, 62; and
    memory, 58, 62–63; and move-
    ment, 57, 199–200n28–n29; no-
    space, 57; no-time, 57–58; and
    order, 59–63, 200n32; and the past,
    62; and perception, 55–60, 62–63,
    199–200n28; and phenomenology,
    45, 59, 199–200n28; and reflection,
    61; and sensory data, 55; and
    silence, 58; and time, 55, 57–59,
    199–200n28–n31; and the under-
    standing of existence, 62–63

Tanguy, Yves, 211n6
"Tapestry" (Ashbery), 32–33; and order,
    33; and perception, 33

Temple, Edmond, 166
temporal fusion, 87
"This Room" (Ashbery), 85; time, 28–30
Three Poems (Ashbery), 2, 28–29, 35, 45–63; and experience, 2, 5, 35; and perception, 5, 45–63; and phenomenology, 45, 55, 199n22
time, 5–6, 9, 64–107, 155; chiasm of, 89; and collage, 136, 209n39; and cubism, 30, 173; and dihesence, 89–90; and *ekstase*, 23; and emblem books, 113–14, 136; and the flux of, 29–30, 65, 67; materiality, 79; moment of, 28, 85–86, 89; and movement, 164; orientation in, 140; passing, 68, 75; and the past, 87; and perception, 11, 75, 89, 117; and phenomenology, 9, 64, 67; and Poetry, 195n121; and presence, 91; and the present, 86–87; and the situation, 11; and space, 6, 9, 87, 108–10, 155; thickness of, 6, 64, 87–88, 91; and time-space gap, 90; and transcendence, 23, 90. *See also* "Clepsydra" (Ashbery); Merleau-Ponty, Maurice; Proust, Marcel
"To the Same Degree" (Ashbery), 94, 177; transcendence, 31–32; travel, 156
Toadvine, Ted, 13–14, 189n21
transcendence, 2, 5, 9, 31, 169–85; and language, 7, 32, 220n41; and experience, 19, 183, 220n41; and perception, 8–9, 170; and poetry, 18, 28, 31–32; and Romanticism, 31; and time, 88, 90; and space, 88
transcendental ego, 3
transcendental field, 6–7
transcendentalists, 54, 189n20
transcendental phenomenology, 6

Tranter, John, 210n54

Uncle Wiggily (Ashbery), 127
Université de Lyons, 2

"Variations, Calypso and Fugue on a Theme of Ella Wheeler Wilcox" (Ashbery), 7, 162–68; and cliché, 7, 165–66; and fugue, 167; and meaning, 162–63, 165–66; and memory, 167; and metaphor, 163–65; and perceptual field, 164; and recursion, 167–68; and space, 164–65
Vaughan, Henry, 195n123
Vendler, Helen, 85, 91
Vermont Notebook, The (Ashbery), 6, 119–25, 207n28, 208n32, 208n36; and collage, 208n35; and everyday experience, 120; and time, 208n36
Vincent, John Emil, 34
visible, 7, 21, 50–52, 69–70; and experience, 171; flesh, 43; and meaning, 78; and perception, 11, 78; and transcendence, 72–73; and writing, 41–43. *See also* the invisible
Visible and the Invisible, The (Merleau-Ponty), 3, 23–24, 40, 69, 88, 108, 170, 173
Von Hallberg, Robert, 90
Vuillard, Jean-Édouard, 211n6

Waldenfels, Bernhard, 16–17, 21, 23, 88–89, 191n54
"Wave, A" (Ashbery), 143–46; and experience, 144–45; and memory, 144–46; and reflection, 144–45; and space, 146
weaving, 33, 42–43, 56, 68, 103; and fabric, 102–3, 206n64
Weiner, Stephanie Kuduk, 172
Whitehead, Alfred North, 26, 166
Wilcox, Ella Wheeler, 162–63, 216n21

Williams, William Carlos, 26
Willis, Elizabeth, 85, 89
Wittgenstein, Ludwig, 27, 142; and articulation, 178; and experience, 174–57; and field of the present, 175; and language, 174–75; and metaphors, 175; and order, 174–78, 218n17–18; and perception, 176, 178; phenomenologist, 3; on private language, 220n44; on rules, 220n44
Wolf, Werner, 90

Ziarek, Krzysztof, 80

www.ingramcontent.com/pod-product-compliance
Lightning Source LLC
Chambersburg PA
CBHW020757230426
43666CB00007B/736